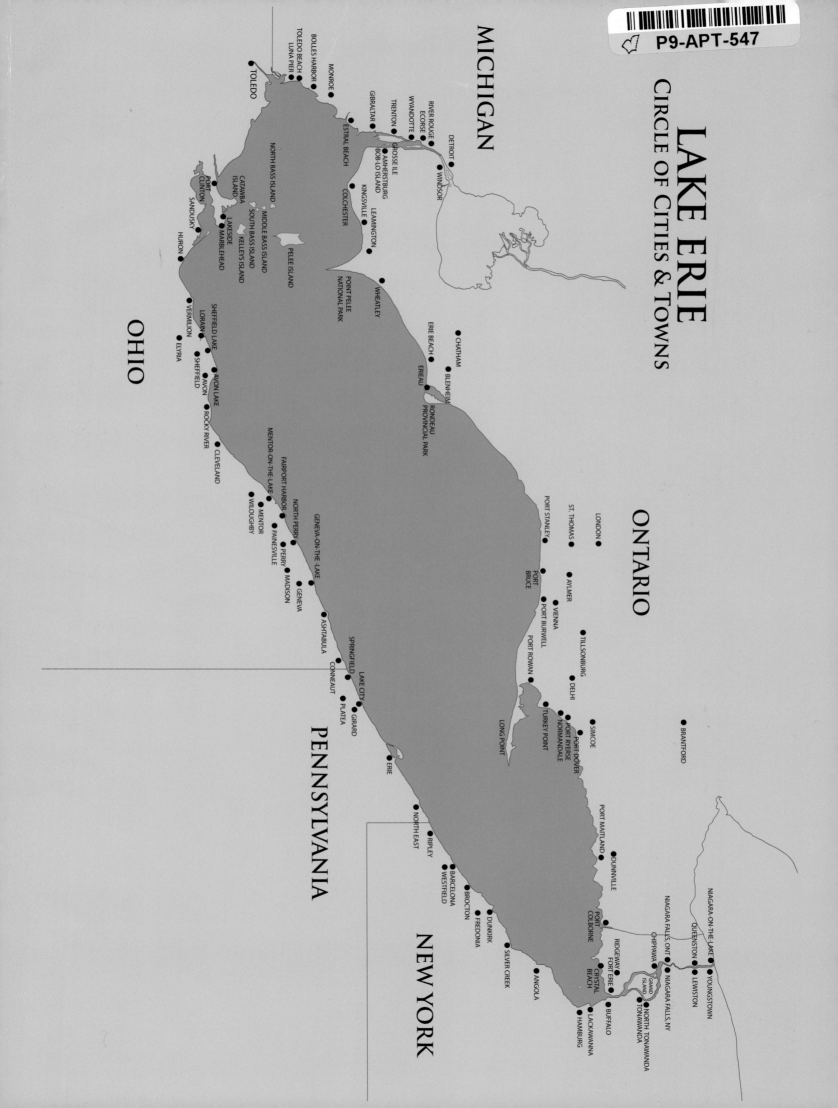

Lake Erie: History and Views

Author
Tom Langmyer

DESIGN/LAYOUT: GARRY MCMICHAEL, DIGITAL IMAGING AND DESIGN, LLC

PUBLISHER: THE BLUE WATER GROUP, LLC

Library of Congress Cataloging-in-Publication Data

Langmyer, Tom, 1961-
        Lake Erie: History and Views
1st Edition
312 pages
Includes bibliographical references and index.
Summary: A chronological depiction of the history of the Lake Erie region. Chapters cover
the physical aspects of Lake Erie, geology, discovery and early inhabitants, its role in wars, early
settlement, transportation, histories of each of the cities and towns surrounding the lake and a
glimpse at life aboard a lakeboat.

Library of Congress Catalog Card Number: 2009911463
ISBN: 978-0-692-00637-5
1. Erie, Lake, Region—History. 2. Erie, Lake—History. 3. Erie, Lake History, Region—History—Pictorial works. I. Langmyer, Tom II. Title.

First Published in the United States of America in 2009 by
The Blue Water Group, LLC
St. Louis, Missouri

© 2009 Tom Langmyer

Website: http://www.LakeErieHistory.com

Contact: information@LakeErieHistory.com

Although the publisher has made a diligent effort to insure accuracy in a project of this scope,
inaccuracies are inevitable. The publisher and the author accept no responsibility for any loss or
inconvenience attributed to the information in this book. The public is encouraged to submit
corrections, additions and materials for use in subsequent editions.

Printed in the U.S.A. by
Evangel Press
Nappanee, Indiana

BOARD WALK AND ROLLER COASTER, PORT STANLEY, ONT.

Fishermen's Nets on Lake Erie at Barcelona, Westfield, N. Y.

Scene on the Maumee, Toledo, Ohio.

TABLE OF CONTENTS

PREFACE

From the time I was a small boy, the Great Lakes have been a passion. Their waters provided my first drink, first bath, first swim and the lake-effect snow to build my first snowman and make my first ski down its ancient shoreline. The lakes kept the area in which I grew up cooler in the summer and warmer in the fall and early winter. They have helped shape my most profound feelings that include a passion for history and a fear and love of nature.

Many of our family's roots were planted along the shores of Lake Erie during the 19th and early 20th centuries. On my father's side, two generations of immigrants worked near Lake Erie in factories and machine shops. My mother's side of the family owned and operated hotels and livery stables in harbor towns along this southernmost Great Lake. Both parents received higher education in institutions with Lake Erie as a backdrop. One of my mother's first teaching experiences was in the Cleveland Public Schools, educating the children of steelworkers.

My parents cultivated my mind through travel around the region and considerable storytelling. This exposure included picnics while watching giant iron-ore laden boats lock through the Welland Canal; seeing Niagara Falls from every angle; and picking apples, cherries and peaches along the agricultural belt. We also watched as the finishing touches were being put on a huge new hydroelectric power project along the Niagara River.

I covered the Love Canal saga as a young radio reporter and interviewed a grown-up Roger Woodward on the 20th anniversary of his plunge over Niagara Falls wearing nothing but a bathing suit and life jacket. One winter, I worked in the vineyards on Lake Erie's southern shore, pruning and tying vines that produced grapes for the National Grape Cooperative and Welch's.

My sister's interests in the natural aspects of the lakes helped to move her to an advanced degree in geology. My wife's life has similarly been shaped by the Great Lakes. Her father fished Lake Erie and the Niagara River on Saturday mornings in search of perch, walleye and the elusive muskie. My wife, children and I still enjoy time during the summer at "The Peninsula" (Presque Isle) at Erie, Pennsylvania. Our best times together as a whole family are when we are drawn together in the comfort of the view of one the lakes.

When I was a child, radio stations far from our home in Buffalo fueled my interest in the cities around the Great Lakes. I was transported from my bedroom nightly as I tuned in stations from Chicago, Detroit, Cleveland and Toronto. These stations delivered the feel and distinct personalities of each of these important lake cities. The sounds of hosts, newsmakers and callers reflected the unique dialects and colloquialisms of the areas they served.

WGN Radio conveyed the feel of a town built as the major connecting point to the great agricultural Midwest. Unique farm reports mixed with the business news of a big city. The station's polite personalities discussed cultural events and covered the cult following of Cubs baseball, painting a picture of Chicago. WJR, the "Great Voice of the Great Lakes," reported on the woes of Detroit's striking and unemployed auto workers and provided relief from the news of the day with the "Afternoon Music Hall." The gritty blue-collar spirit of Cleveland could be heard over the airwaves of WWWE (WTAM), where Pete Franklin would squabble nightly with gravel-voiced sports nuts calling from bars around the steel mills about the Browns, Cavs and Indians. Sixty miles to the north from my home, yet a world away, Gordon Sinclair and Betty Kennedy were broadcasting to the Dominion in British-influenced Canadian tones. CFRB projected a Toronto that was a more sophisticated metropolis than its counterparts on the U.S. side.

One of my favorite views has always been along Interstate 90 between the New York State line and Erie, Pennsylvania. This stretch of highway traverses the beds of Erie's predecessor lakes, Warren and Whittlesey. As the road climbs the ancient shoreline of Lake Whittlesey, the panoramic view of Lake Erie is at its best. On a clear day, I could see across the lake to Long Point, Ontario and beyond, nearly 60 miles, to the stacks of the coal-fired power plant at Nanticoke. In between, spaced neatly on the bright blue water, were silhouettes of the unmistakable lakeboats with their plumes of black smoke.

The lakes were a constant influence on our lives. Lake-effect snows drifted to the second story of our home in 1977 as we bonded with neighbors, sharing shoveling duties and hot chocolate. Winter's bone-chilling winds, blowing unbroken for 241 miles from Toledo, chapped the faces of my father and me, along with 16,000 other hockey fans, as we marched across open parking lots to the back steps of Buffalo's Memorial Auditorium. There we entered the smoke-filled, beer-drenched hall to watch the NHL's Sabres do battle on a manmade slab of ice, just feet from the head of the vast frozen Lake Erie.

In my twenties, I scoped out traffic conditions from an airplane for several years, reporting for WGR radio in Buffalo to thousands of Western New Yorkers on the frequent closings of N.Y. Route 5, because of ice-cold waves crashing across the roadways; motorists stranded on the Buffalo Skyway; and about the rescues of trapped ice fisherman. A few years later I mourned the death of a mentor, friend and co-worker who lost his life in a helicopter crash into the Niagara River in January of 1993, while he performed my former duties.

My favorite literature has always centered on the Great Lakes region. In the back of my mind are Holling Clancy Holling's fictional *Paddle-to-the-Sea*; detailed descriptions penned by the unnamed authors of the W.P.A. Federal Writers' Project of the Depression era; histories about the lake cities; and volumes on industry, sociology, geography, geology, archaeology, plants and wildlife.

Growing up along the Great Lakes in the Buffalo, New York area meant that Lake Erie and Lake Ontario were especially close at hand. Just a few miles from our home was the mighty Niagara River, more of a strait with no major tributaries, between two vast inland seas.

Niagara Falls is where I have often stood in wonder over my 40-plus years. It is the focal point where my thoughts begin to shift from day-to-day concerns to how this part of the earth has shaped who we are today. As the water passes by, I think about how this region must have looked before man walked the earth, how early humans must have reacted when they first gazed upon the immense bodies of water and heard the deafening roar of the cataract, back before the days when so much water was diverted to generate power, move ships and support industry. Back to a time when the faint smell of wood burning from a distant village along one of the lakes' shores meant an Indian hunter aboard a dug-out canoe was getting close to home. The lakes' natural beauty and allure must have been incredibly moving for the first European explorers, perhaps of greater significance for their time than the current generation's knowledge of the first astronauts landing on the moon in 1969.

My thoughts move forward in time to the Great Lakes' beginning as a route for early commerce, the setting for several bloody wars, and the end of a journey to freedom for slaves as a young nation struggled to understand the meaning of the words "Land of the Free." I consider the building of the many Great Lakes cities and towns possible through the vision and sweat of hundreds of thousands of immigrants who came to this land and region for opportunity or out of necessity.

Along the shores of these bodies of water, thousands of men and women labored for countless hours in great factories to support the efforts of the United States, Canada and other nations in global wars. I also sadly recall how man turned his back on the lakes, partly out of greed and ignorance and later because of an economy that lessened the importance of heavy industry in the region. I think of what was left in the shadows of the 1960s and 1970s as the desire to be near the lakes diminished. Access to many areas along the lakeshores was lost for years, blocked by rusting fences, shuttered mills and polluted beaches.

Happily I shift to the past 35 years as people have worked more closely with nature, and I am amazed at how the Great Lakes show their resilience!

I have visited countless museums and libraries; driven around each of the lakes; flown over them; pored over books, maps, nautical charts, the Internet and information from historical societies; and had the rare privilege, inaccessible to the public, of traveling up the Great Lakes aboard a 1,000-foot lakeboat.

This book explores the formation of Lake Erie, its discovery and settlement, and the history of the towns and cities that encircle it. I also take you on a trip to the upper Great Lakes aboard the *M/V Walter J. McCarthy Jr*. I hope you will enjoy this book and use it to learn more about the great Lake Erie and the region that forms the backbone of two great nations. And I hope that it will help to encourage you to explore your roots and to continue to grow roots in the place *you* live!

Tom Langmyer

INTRODUCTION

Many business travelers experience the view of Lake Erie from a commercial jetliner flying from Chicago to New York at 30,000 feet. The southern shore of the lake lies under one of North America's major air routes.

Flying out of Chicago's O'Hare International Airport, the traveler doesn't see much. It's an overcast day and clouds obscure the view of Lake Michigan. But as the plane continues east, the cloud cover gives way to a clear view of the ground. From the left side of the plane, passengers can see the flat land of western Ohio, supporting a neatly laid-out patchwork quilt of farms. As the Maumee River comes into view, America's Heartland is about to give way to Lake Erie.

The lake is now in sight and the highways and buildings of Toledo are right below. Looking up the western lakeshore to the north, one sees Detroit and Windsor split by the Detroit River, which provides Lake Erie with most of its water. Past Toledo, Point Pelee on the Canadian side looks like an arrow in the water, pointing directly south at the plane.

Within a few moments passengers are looking down at Lake Erie's western islands. A large monument dedicated to Oliver Hazard Perry and the Battle of Lake Erie is spotted on South Bass Island. The tiny specks in the water are actually pleasure boats dotting the lake around the islands.

Soon the southern shoreline slips beneath the plane as the aircraft begins to fly directly over the water. One sees the wake of a lake freighter headed for Cleveland, creating a huge "V" in what seem to be tiny ripples on the lake's surface. Passengers on the right side of the plane look down upon sprawling Cleveland and, further along the lakeshore, see a plume of steam from the power plant at North Perry, Ohio. On the left, the Canadian shoreline looks isolated and peaceful.

As the southern shoreline comes back into view for those on the left side of the plane, two arms can be seen gesturing toward the eastern end of the lake. The sandy Presque Isle peninsula at Erie, Pennsylvania, is in the foreground, and across the lake, the larger arm of Long Point, Ontario.

The view of the lake shifts further off to the left as the plane heads over the Allegheny Plateau and the hills of western New York. The sight is dramatic before the lake ends abruptly at Buffalo. On the Canadian side, a straight ribbon of water, the Welland Ship Canal, joins Lake Erie with the distant blue of Lake Ontario. North of Buffalo, the Niagara River also winds its way to Lake Ontario, carrying the bulk of Erie's waters. What looks like a puffy white cotton ball, midway between the lakes along the river, is the mist from Niagara Falls.

Within moments, Lake Erie's panoramic view disappears, ending the passengers' moments of interest, reflection and wonder. After this half-hour portion of the flight, they return to their newspapers or take a snooze before the plane lands at LaGuardia.

A RICH PAST AND FUTURE

Lake Erie, the second smallest of the five Great Lakes, is rich in geologic and human history. Carved by glaciers, and preceded by other lakes, Lake Erie is named for the Eriez Indians who lived in the region. *Eriez* is believed to mean "wildcat" or "people of the panther." French explorers referred to the lake as *Lac du Chat* (Lake of the Cat).

Control of the lake was highly contested because it provided a route for transportation and trade. The region's rich agricultural land and natural resources were also sought-after. Eventually, Canada and the United States shared the lake.

Settlements grew into cities as canals to the interior and routes to the sea connected the lake with the world. Iron ore from Minnesota was shipped down to the growing lake cities as Pennsylvania and West Virginia coal was brought northward by the trainload to make steel. Lake Erie steel was used to build cars that poured off assembly lines. Within a relatively short time, the lake became overburdened and polluted and the great fishing and recreation industries were nearly destroyed.

Environmental legislation and activity to reduce pollution has helped to clean the lake during the past 35 years. Lake Erie once again supports fishing, recreation and a booming tourist industry. While the work is far from over, the odds are now in Erie's favor.

LAKE ERIE: HISTORY AND VIEWS

The purpose of this book is to take the reader on a journey back in time to understand how the lake came to be, become familiar with its physical characteristics, and learn about the people who settled here and their communities. The book also looks at the present through text and photos. By no means is this considered to contain comprehensive information on the lake or surrounding communities. Other fine books go into great detail on a variety of subjects related to Lake Erie. This book is also not intended to be a tourist guide with lists of attractions, amusements, dining spots and lodging. Many guidebooks exist for that purpose.

It is hoped that the text, numerous illustrations, graphics, historic postcards and photos will catch the eye and help fuel interest in the lake and region. Younger generations will be able to see now desolate retail and industrial cores of many lake towns and learn of the bustling activity of years past, before these centers of activity were left behind by suburban sprawl, subdivisions and strip malls. Perhaps this book may bring back some forgotten memories and its views from all angles might inspire more interest in this Great Lake. So please sit back, relax and enjoy the story of Lake Erie.

CLOCKWISE FROM TOP RIGHT: Fishing boats at Port Stanley, Ontario. The Terminal Tower building, Cleveland. The south shore of Kelleys Island, Ohio. Detroit's 47-story Penobscot building, completed in 1928.

CLOCKWISE FROM TOP RIGHT: Niagara's Horseshoe Falls. Buffalo's skyline from the Erie Basin Marina. A peaceful view of vineyards and land along Lake Erie at Ripley, New York. Downtown Erie, Pennsylvania, from the Bicentennial Tower. The breakwater and lighthouse at Port Dover, Ontario.

1 Description

Lake Erie's shoreline begins where the Detroit River empties the waters of the three upper lakes. The lake's northern shoreline, dotted by only a few small towns, belongs to Canada. This shoreline is punctuated by Point Pelee and Rondeau Peninsula in the west and Long Point to the east. Between these points of land are small fishing villages, marshes, beaches, resorts and parks. A few small creeks wind their way to the lake through ravines along Ontario's portion of the lake. A larger river, the Grand, enters the lake at Port Maitland, and a few miles further to the east, the Welland Canal slices through the Niagara Peninsula en route to Lake Ontario. This is agricultural country with fruits, vegetables and tobacco grown in abundance within a few miles of the moderating effects of this southernmost Great Lake.

ABOVE: Niagara Falls delivers the outflow of Lakes Superior, Michigan, Huron and Erie to Lake Ontario.

PAGE 3: The Detroit River Light was completed in 1885 by the U.S. Army Corps of Engineers. Located in Lake Erie just south of the mouth of the Detroit River, this is the place where upbound vessels make the turn into the Detroit River. (Dave Wobster)

In contrast, the names of the cities along the southern shore read like a *Who's Who* of places with foundations built during America's Industrial Revolution. Detroit, Toledo, Sandusky, Huron, Lorain, Cleveland, Fairport Harbor, Ashtabula, Conneaut, Erie, Dunkirk and Buffalo are spread along the U.S. side. Still, the moderating effects of this Great Lake have helped leave much of this region for farming and recreation. In addition to vegetable farming, the region is famous for the production of fruit, most notably grapes.

Both the Canadian and U.S. shorelines converge to the east at Buffalo, New York and Fort Erie, Ontario, where most of Lake Erie's water empties into the 35-mile-long Niagara River. From there, the water rushes downstream before plunging over one of the world's natural wonders, Niagara Falls. In all, Lake Erie's water drops 326 feet along the course of the Niagara River before reaching Lake Ontario, the last of the five Great Lakes. Some of the water reaches Lake Ontario by other means: diverted around the falls for the production of hydroelectric power, used for industry and municipal water supplies; feeding the New York State Barge Canal (Erie Canal); or passing through the 27-mile-long Welland Canal. The Welland Canal lifts and lowers ocean-going freighters and lake boats around the falls. From Lake Ontario, the water eventually heads through the St. Lawrence River on its journey to the Atlantic Ocean.

Lake Erie is the 12th largest lake in the world (surface area) and the fourth largest of the five Great Lakes, covering an area larger than the state of Vermont. By volume, Lake Erie is the smallest of the Great Lakes. Lake Erie is bordered by the states of New York, Pennsylvania, Ohio and Michigan and by the Canadian province of Ontario. It is the shallowest and warmest of the Great Lakes. Lake Erie is 241 miles long, 57 miles wide and has 871 miles of shoreline. The lake is 210 feet deep at its deepest point with an average depth of 62 feet.

GREAT LAKES AND FACTS AND FIGURES

		Superior	Michigan	Huron	ERIE	Ontario	Totals
Elevation[a]	(feet)**	602	579	579	571	245	
	(meters)	183	176	176	173	74	
Length	(miles)*	350	307	206	241	193	
	(kilometers)	563	494	332	388	311	
Breadth	(miles)*	160	118	183	57	53	
	(kilometers)	257	190	245	92	85	
Average Depth[a]	(feet)**	483	279	195	62	283	
	(meters)	147	85	59	19	86	
Maximum Depth[a]	(feet)*	1,332	925	750	210	802	
	(meters)	406	282	229	64	244	
Volume[a]	(cu. miles)*	2,900	1,180	850	116	393	5,439
	(km3)	12,100	4,920	3,540	484	1,640	22,684
Water Area	(sq. mi.)*	31,700	22,300	23,000	9,910	7,340	94,250
	(km2)	82,100	57,800	59,600	25,700	18,960	244,160
Land Drainage Area[b]	(sq. mi.)*	49,300	45,600	51,700	30,140	24,720	201,460
	(km2)	127,700	118,000	134,100	78,000	64,030	21,830
Total Area	(sq. mi.)*	81,000	67,900	74,700	40,050	2,060	295,710
	(km2)	209,800	175,800	193,700	103,700	82,990	765,990
Shoreline Length[c]	(miles)*	2,726	1,638	3,827	871	712	10,210[d]
	(kilometers)	4,385	2,633	6,157	1,402	1,146	17,017[d]
Retention Time	(years)**	191	99	22	2.6	6	
Outlet		St. Mary's River	Straits of Mackinac	St. Clair River	Niagara River/ Welland Canal	St. Lawrence River	

Notes:
[a] Measured at Low Water Datum.
[b] Land Drainage Area for Lake Huron includes St. Mary's River.
   Lake Erie includes the St. Clair-Detroit system.
   Lake Ontario includes the Niagara River.
[c] Including islands.
[d] These totals are greater than the sum of the shoreline length for the lakes because they include the connecting channels (excluding the St. Lawrence River).

Sources:
* Coordinating Committee on Great Lakes Basic Hydraulic and Hydrologic Data, Coordinated Great Lakes Physical Data. May, 1992
** Extension Bulletins E-1866-70, Michigan Sea Grant College Program, Cooperative Extension Service, Michigan State University, E. Lansing, Michigan, 1985

The lake has three basins. The eastern basin is the deepest with an average depth of 80 feet and extends from Buffalo to Long Point on the Canadian side and to Erie, Pennsylvania, on the U.S. shoreline. Lake Erie's islands mark the western end of the central basin, with an average depth of 60 feet. The western basin, extending to the mouths of the Detroit and Maumee rivers, is much shallower, with an average depth of just 24 feet.

THE GREAT LAKE'S PERSPECTIVE

One fifth of the world's supply of fresh surface water (six quadrillion gallons) is contained in the Great Lakes. If their volume were spread evenly over the continental United States, it would submerge the entire country in more than nine feet of water. The total area of the Great Lakes is over 94,000 square miles, an area larger than the combined area of the states of New York, New Jersey, Connecticut, Rhode Island, Massachusetts, Vermont and New Hampshire. This also amounts to nearly one-quarter of the square mileage of the province of Ontario. The total watershed of the Great Lakes is nearly 296,000 square miles. The Great Lakes' coastline, including the mainland, connecting channels and islands, is 10,210 miles in length.

LAKE ERIE'S EFFECT

Most of Lake Erie's water comes from the Detroit River, which carries the flow of Lake St. Clair and the three upper Great Lakes. The Detroit River makes up more than 90 percent of Lake Erie's inflow. The remainder of Lake Erie's water comes from other rivers such as the Maumee, smaller tributaries, precipitation and runoff. About 36 inches of rain fall directly on the lake annually, and roughly 24 inches evaporate from the lake surface every year. The combination of evaporation and the lake's water temperature can have acute effects on weather conditions in the region. From keeping winters a few degrees higher and summers cooler, to dumping several feet of snow along its legendary snow belt, Lake Erie's effect on the weather is felt by the millions of people who live within a few miles of its shoreline.

ABOVE: A peaceful view of the Detroit River from Amherstburg, Ontario, at dusk. The smokestacks of Detroit Edison's Trenton Channel Power Plant are on the horizon.

RIGHT: A resident of suburban Buffalo, New York, shovels snow from the roof of his home after a lake-effect storm hit the area.

Because Lake Erie is the shallowest of the Great Lakes and it sits in line with the prevailing winds from the southwest, it is susceptible to fluctuating water levels. Winds blowing from one end of the lake to the other can set up significant short-term differences in water levels. Variances of over 16 feet between the eastern and western ends of the lake have been recorded, caused by wind "set-up." Because of the lake's shallowness and alignment, Lake Erie is notorious for how wind can quickly whip up waves of terrifying size.

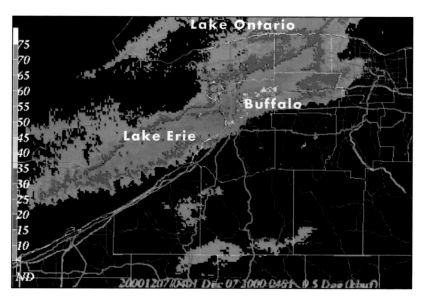

Lake Erie's water supports navigation, commerce, manufacturing, power production and industry. Additionally, because the lake moderates the temperatures in the region, it supports a longer recreational and agricultural growing season.

Much of the ice that is formed in the winter is pushed to the eastern end of Lake Erie by the prevailing winds. Ice can form to a thickness of more than 12 feet in this part of the lake, and winter winds can force this ice out of the lake and into the Niagara River, where it flows downstream. The ice can do heavy damage to property along the river and block the water intakes for the hydroelectric power plants on the river. To reduce this threat, an ice boom has been installed at the eastern end of Lake Erie every winter since 1964.

The Lake Erie-Niagara River Ice Boom is put in place at the entrance to the Niagara River, between Buffalo, New York and Fort Erie, Ontario. The boom uses 242 steel pontoons, divided into sections linked together by steel cables. The pontoons are 2.5 feet in diameter and 30 feet long.

The ice boom is put in when Lake Erie's water temperature drops to 39 degrees. It is removed by April 1 every year, unless a significant amount of ice remains at the eastern end of the lake.

ABOVE: This radar image shows bands of lake-effect snow falling on Buffalo and northern Erie County, and in portions of Niagara, Genesee and Orleans counties. The snow is represented in green and blue. Winds from the southwest pick up moisture from Lake Erie and dump it in the form of snow on Buffalo, which is at the center of the image. (NOAA)

BOTTOM: An aerial view of the ice boom at the entrance to the Niagara River. The boom prevents ice from clogging power plant and municipal water intakes, and damaging the shoreline. The downtown portion of the city of Buffalo, New York, is at the upper right. Fort Erie, Ontario, is on the left. (New York Power Authority)

2 Geology

The only thing that is constant is change. No different is the geologic history of Lake Erie, a story of constant evolution. From winds building sand dunes to waves cutting into the cliffs and swallowing houses, to ice sheets that carve rock and great "moving" waterfalls, nature continues to shape and reshape Lake Erie.

Lake Erie was the last of the Great Lakes to be discovered, yet the first to be formed. Once, a great river flowed here. Then the great hand of a glacier pushed southward over the land to scoop out a place for the lake.

Eons of carving, grinding, digging and leaving piles of earth in terminal moraines began nature's construction of the lake. Before Lake Erie came to be, several other lakes of various shapes and sizes covered this area, the ancestors of today's lake.

Lake Erie is quite young in geological terms, and its glacial predecessors date back only 14,000 years. The lake in its present form is less than 4,000 years old. From the time of the lake's ancestors, to the modern-day Lake Erie, water levels have varied greatly. The various lake stages may have been as much as 230 feet higher and more than 100 feet lower than to-day's Lake Erie. These changing levels shaped the land around the lake, playing a key role in how the area was eventually settled and developed. Higher and varying lake levels left several beach ridges, which later served as trails for Indians, pioneers and early settlers on both sides of the lake. More recently, these beach ridges have served as beds for railroads and roadbeds for today's interstate highways. Fertile lake sediments were also deposited over the area before the water level dropped, creating some of the richest agricultural land in the United States.

PAGE 8: The American falls at Niagara were dewatered in 1969 to study their geology and determine if measures could be taken to change their appearance, by removing rock at the base of the cataract. It was determined that nature should be allowed to take its course. (Local History Department, Niagara Falls, New York Public Library)

PAGE 9: Much of the geological story of the Great Lakes region is exposed where Niagara Falls has sliced through ancient rock. The Niagara River carries the outflow of Lake Erie's waters. The falls mark the halfway point along the journey from Lake Erie to Lake Ontario.

BOTTOM: A view of the cliffs at Port Bruce, Ontario.

BEFORE THE LAKES

Well before Lake Erie or its predecessors existed, a vast shallow and warm saltwater sea covered much of North America. The oldest rocks, into which the Lake Erie basin was carved, are about 400 million years old and were formed in a tropical ocean reef environment. When this sea drained and evaporated, it exposed much of the land from the Great Lakes region to Great Plains. Part of this area was the basin in which the present Lake Erie was formed.

More than 2 million years ago, a large river flowed eastward through a valley where Lake Erie now sits. The ancient Erigan River flowed through a valley 200 feet or more in depth. From the Erie Basin, the Erigan River turned north through a channel about 40 miles west of the Niagara River, which did not exist at the time. The river then passed down the Dundas Valley into the head of the Ontario basin near present day Hamilton, Ontario. The river had no great waterfalls, although rapids may have existed.

The advances of several glaciers wiped out this drainage system and deepened the basin. The western portion of Lake Erie's basin was underlain by resistant rock, while the central and eastern portion had a less resistant shale foundation. As a result, glaciers were able to dig deeper into the rock in the central and eastern basins. The western part of the lake sits on harder limestone and dolomite and averages only 24 feet in depth, while the eastern basin, with its softer shale, boasts the lake's deepest point at 210 feet.

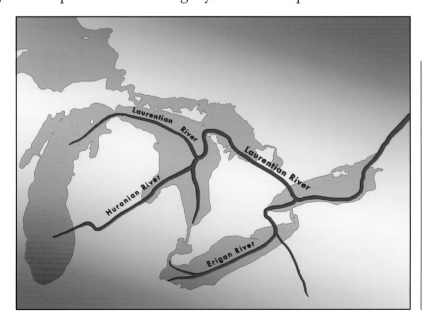

PANORAMA: Rock is exposed in this view of the Niagara River rapids from the Three Sisters Islands.

MAP: A prehistoric river, known as the Erigan, flowed where Lake Erie is now located. This river system also included a tributary, which extended into what is now Pennsylvania. The Allegheny River now flows in the opposite direction toward the Ohio River system, through the valley that was created by that ancient river. Other rivers drained the areas, which are now occupied by the other Great Lakes.

LAKE ERIE'S GLACIAL ANCESTORS

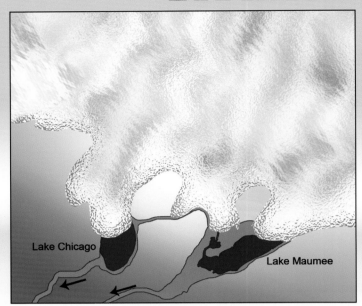

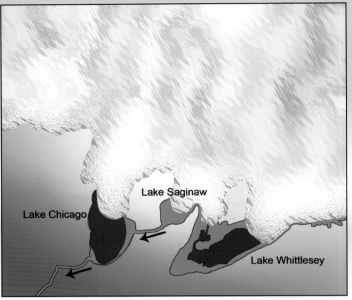

Lake Maumee - Existing between 13,600 and 14,000 years ago, this lake initially drained westward at Fort Wayne, Indiana. As the ice margin retreated, a new outlet was created across Michigan. Lake levels were between 760 and 800 feet. The water levels then dropped further as Lake Arkona (not shown) was created.

Lake Whittlesey - The glacier readvanced 13,000 years ago, bringing water levels up again to 740 feet. Lake Whittlesey drained into Lake Saginaw through a spillway at Ubly, Michigan.

LAKE ERIE'S PREDECESSORS

Lake Erie's ancestor lakes were built as water levels changed in the basin when glaciers advanced and then retreated to the north. Several related factors created various lakes and stages. Ice dams prevented drainage in some places while several outlets drained the basin in other locations. Additionally, the earth's land surface actually rose (isostatic rebound) after it was relieved of the immense weight of the glacial ice, which had actually depressed the land.

Lake Maumee was the first lake in the Erie basin, forming about 14,000 years ago. At its highest level, the lake drained over what is now Toledo, Ohio. The water continued through an outlet at a low point of the glacial moraine near present-day Fort Wayne, Indiana. From there, the water flowed down the Wabash River into the Mississippi River drainage system. As the glaciers retreated further, the dropping lake found a different outlet channel, flowing through Michigan via the Grand River, to Lake Chicago (Lake Michigan's predecessor) and down the Mississippi drainage system.

Lake Arkona (not shown) resulted from the continuing northward retreat of the ice and the downcutting of the Grand River in Michigan. This lake reached its lowest stage about 13,600 years ago.

Lake Whittlesey was the next major lake in the area, existing 13,000 years ago. It was named for Charles Whittlesey, a geologist and topographer who worked as a geological surveyor in Ohio in 1837-1838. The lake was created when the Wisconsinan glacier advanced and blocked part of the Grand River drainage outlet, raising lake levels once again. The new outlet, the Ubly channel, sent drainage to the Grand River along a different route through central Michigan. Lake Whittlesey's beach ridges, along the south shore of Lake Erie, are quite visible today. Another significant retreat of the glacier marked the end of Lake Whittlesey. Drainage then occurred through the Niagara Gorge area (St. David's Gorge).

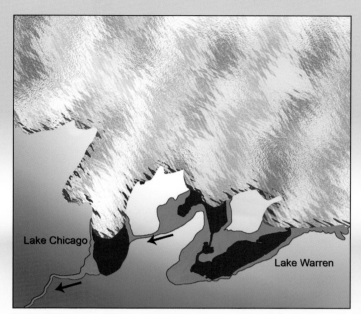

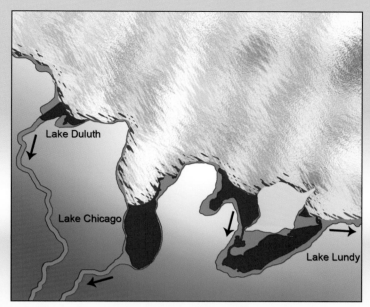

Lake Warren - The ice margin retreated and Lake Warren and intermediate Lake Wayne were present between 12,000 and 13,000 years ago. These bodies of water, with levels between 660 and 685 feet, also drained to the west through Michigan to Lake Chicago.

Lake Lundy - The last of the predecessor lakes in the Erie basin was Lake Lundy. It is believed this lake drained through the Mohawk River Valley in New York, but there may have been a western outlet. Several substage lakes had levels varying between 590 and 640 feet.

It is believed the lake level actually dropped well below present Lake Erie levels because the land in the St. David's Gorge area was still depressed, slowly rebounding from the recent retreat of the glacier.

Lake Warren came into existence when the ice readvanced, raising water levels to approximately 685 feet. Lake Wayne existed as an intermediate lake as well, with water draining through the Mohawk River Valley in New York State. These lakes existed between 12,000 and 13,000 years ago.

Lake Lundy was formed when the Wisconsinan glacier made its final retreat. This lake may have had two outlets, one in Michigan and the other through the Mohawk River Valley in New York State. This lake was similar in shape to the present-day Lake Erie.

LEFT: The southernmost tip of Canada's mainland is at Point Pelee, where the land slips under Lake Erie's waters.

13

PRESENT-DAY LAKE ERIE

Lake Erie, as we know it today, was created after the land in the region began to rebound after the glacier had retreated for the last time. The Niagara River area was still depressed and therefore it (and other outlets in New York State) had initially drained the lake to a point well below present-day levels. Some 4,000 years ago, the land in this area rebounded and the lake became deeper once again. But the rebound was fairly slow, and as a result, the lake was still about 30 feet below present-day levels. About 2,600 years ago, lake levels rose nearly 20 feet when the upper Great Lakes began to drain into Lake Erie (the upper lakes had previously drained through other outlets). The land, continuing to rise as a result of glacial rebounding, has finally brought Lake Erie to its current level of 571 feet above sea level.

Remnants of glacial activity may still be seen in a number of places in the Great Lakes region. In Ohio, Glacial Grooves State Park on Kelleys Island preserves a section of limestone carved by glacial activity. The ancient St. David's Gorge, on the Niagara River, was the outlet of a predecessor of Lake Erie and can be viewed at Niagara's Whirlpool. The Illinois River formerly drained the Great Lakes into the Mississippi River system. North of St. Louis, Missouri, evidence of this can be seen along the Illinois River Valley, where rock was carved by the river, near its confluence with the Mississippi.

The region encompassing the Lake Erie basin is rich in natural resources. From the largest sandstone quarry in the world near Lorain, to limestone quarries operating on Lake Erie's western islands and along the nearby shore, the mining of rock continues. Salt deposits extending under Lake Erie, remnants of the vast ancient inland sea, are mined under the lake at Cleveland and Fairport Harbor, Ohio. Sand, gravel and gypsum used for construction are also plentiful. More than three trillion cubic feet of natural gas is located under Lake Erie. The United States does not operate wells because of environmental concerns. Canada currently operates 500 natural gas wells, producing 55 percent of Ontario's natural gas.

ABOVE: Limestone is exposed along Lake Erie's shoreline at Marblehead, Ohio.

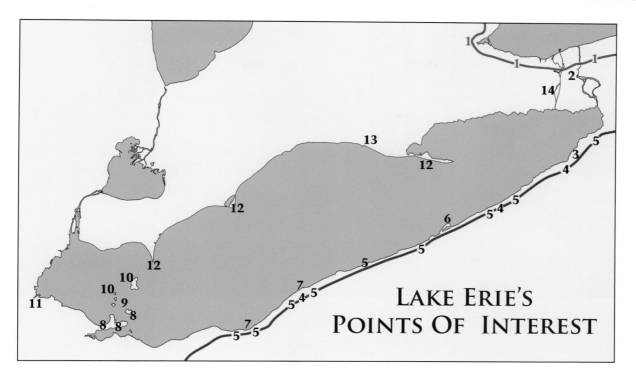

GEOLOGICAL POINTS OF INTEREST

The **Niagara Escarpment (1)** is a long ridge, over which Lake Erie's waters drop, creating Niagara Falls. The escarpment's origins date back 450 million years ago, when a warm shallow sea covered the area. The sea filled a depression centered by what is now Michigan. The outer rim of this saucer-shaped feature is the Niagara Escarpment. The escarpment can be traced from east of Rochester, New York, running south of Lake Ontario to Hamilton, Ontario. From there, it runs north as the backbone of the Bruce Peninsula on Lake Huron. It then rounds northern Michigan and down the western side of Lake Michigan into Wisconsin. The escarpment can be seen where it is sliced by the Niagara River Gorge between Lewiston, New York and Queenston, Ontario. For navigation, the **Welland Canal (14)** and its Flight Locks at Thorold, Ontario, negotiate its heights.

Niagara Falls (2) handles much of the 326-foot drop between lakes Erie and Ontario. The falls along the 35-mile-long Niagara River have moved seven miles upstream from their original location (at Lewiston, New York and Queenston, Ontario) during the last 12,000 years.

Cattaraugus Creek (3) is a 68-mile-long stream winding down to Lake Erie from the Allegheny Plateau. Indians named the creek *Cattaraugus*, meaning "foul-smelling riverbank," for the natural gas that bubbles from

the river mud. Its deep valley is geologically significant, as it once was the course for the preglacial ancestor of the Allegheny River, which drained into the Lake Erie basin. The Allegheny River's water flow later reversed becoming part of the Ohio River system.

The **Lake Warren/Whittlesey Shorelines (4)** can be clearly seen to the south of Lake Erie. Natives used the beach ridges of these ancestor lakes as trails, and the ridges were later used as beds for highways. In many places in New York, Pennsylvania and Ohio, roads along these ancient shorelines are often named "Ridge Road," "Center Ridge Road" or "Upper Ridge Road."

Deep Cut Gorges (5) were created by rivers and streams making their way to Lake Erie.

MAP: The Lake Erie basin holds the answers to many questions about the formation of Great Lakes. See map (above) for the corresponding locations where the geologic story may be interpreted.

DIAGRAM: Niagara's falls have migrated seven miles upstream from where they were formed 12,000 years ago. The falling water continues to erode the rock at the base of the falls. The cap rock collapses once it loses its support from the softer rock below. This action causes the falls to recede up the Niagara River toward Lake Erie.

A few notable examples include Eighteen-Mile Creek and Chautauqua Creek in New York; Twenty-Mile Creek, Four-Mile Creek and Elk Creek in Pennsylvania; and the Ashtabula River, Grand River, Chagrin River, Cuyahoga River and Rocky River in Ohio.

Presque Isle (6) was created 14,000 years ago when the Lake Erie region was covered by a glacier. As the glacier retreated, a moraine was created. Later as the waves of Lake Erie deposited sand on the moraine, Presque Isle was created. The peninsula has migrated nearly three miles to the east since its formation.

Salt Mines (7) operate below the floor of Lake Erie at Fairport Harbor and Cleveland, Ohio. Salt deposits were formed here over 400 million years ago, when a warm, saltwater sea covered the area. As the sea evaporated, it left behind salt deposits up to 50 feet thick. Nearly 2,000 feet below the surface, these mining operations extend two miles out under Lake Erie. The Cleveland mine is nearly three square miles in size. Salt from these mines is primarily used to control ice on streets and highways.

Limestone Quarries (8) continue to operate near Lake Erie in northern Ohio. A 150-year-old quarry covers much of the interior of the Marblehead Peninsula. Limestone is also quarried on Kelleys Island. This harder bedrock prevented glaciers from carving the western basin of Lake Erie to greater depths. Underlain by softer shale, the eastern basin of Lake Erie is much deeper.

Glacial Grooves (9) on the north side of Kelleys Island were scoured into solid limestone bedrock about 12,000 years ago by the great ice sheet, which covered this part of North America. Much of the evidence of this carving has disappeared because of quarrying, but a section of the grooves remains protected in a park on the island.

Lake Erie's Western Islands (10) are part of a pre-glacial reef system, which was created when a shallow tropical sea covered the area. The islands mark the eastern side of the western basin of Lake Erie. The three Bass Islands, along with Kelleys and Pelee, are the largest of these islands.

ABOVE: The Morton Salt mine at Fairport Harbor, Ohio extends two miles under Lake Erie to extract salt for road de-icing. In 1959, the company developed what was the world's deepest salt mine. (Morton International, Inc.)

RIGHT: Sandy cliffs line Lake Erie's central basin along the Canadian shoreline.

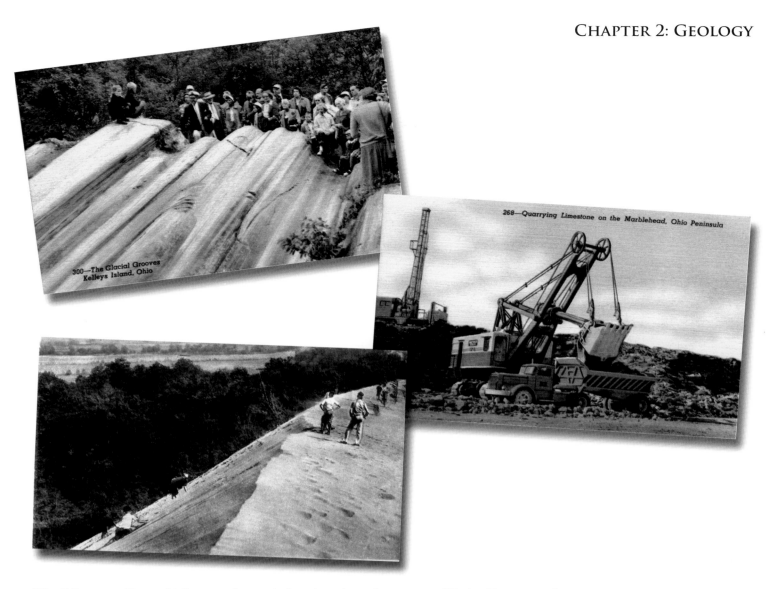

300—The Glacial Grooves Kelleys Island, Ohio

268—Quarrying Limestone on the Marblehead, Ohio Peninsula

The **Maumee River (11)** once drained the glacial predecessors of Lake Erie into the Mississippi River system. Its wide river valley extends into Indiana. After the glaciers retreated, the river reversed direction and began flowing into Lake Erie. The Maumee River empties into Lake Erie at Toledo, Ohio.

Canadian Sandspits (12) include Point Pelee, Rondeau Peninsula and Long Point. Point Pelee was created 10,000 years ago as glaciers retreated and formed by shifting sands moved by water currents and winds. Its base is limestone bedrock with overlying layers of glacial till and clays. The tip may have once been two or three miles longer than it is today. The Rondeau Peninsula was formed when melting glacial ice caused water levels to rise, eroding cliffs in the area. The erosion and deposition of sand created sandbars and, as water levels dropped, the sandbars were exposed to form the peninsula. Long Point was formed 7,600 years ago at the location of a cross-lake glacial moraine. The materials deposited at Long Point were transported from the clay and sand bluffs along the Lake Erie shoreline, extending 60 miles west of the point.

The **Houghton Sand Hills (13)**, eight miles east of Port Burwell, tower 450 feet above Lake Erie. The sands in the region were deposited, creating a delta in glacial Lake Warren. As the glacier retreated, the sand deposits were eroded. The hills continue to be shaped by wind.

The **Welland Canal (14)** routes lakeboats and recreational craft around Niagara Falls, traversing the Niagara Peninsula and the **Niagara Escarpment (1)**, a few miles west of the Niagara River. The canal mediates the 326-foot difference between Lakes Erie and Ontario. There are several places to view the locks and shipping along the 27-mile-long canal.

TOP: Carved into the limestone approximately 12,000 years ago by the Wisconsinan glacier, the grooves on Kelleys Island are exposed at Glacial Grooves State Park.

MIDDLE: Over the years, limestone from the quarries at Marblehead, Ohio has been used to build the locks at Sault Ste. Marie, the Henry Ford Estate near Detroit and buildings in Cleveland and in other Great Lakes cities.

BOTTOM: The sand dunes and cliffs rise 450 feet above the surface of Lake Erie at Sand Hill Park near Port Burwell, Ontario.

17

3 Discovery

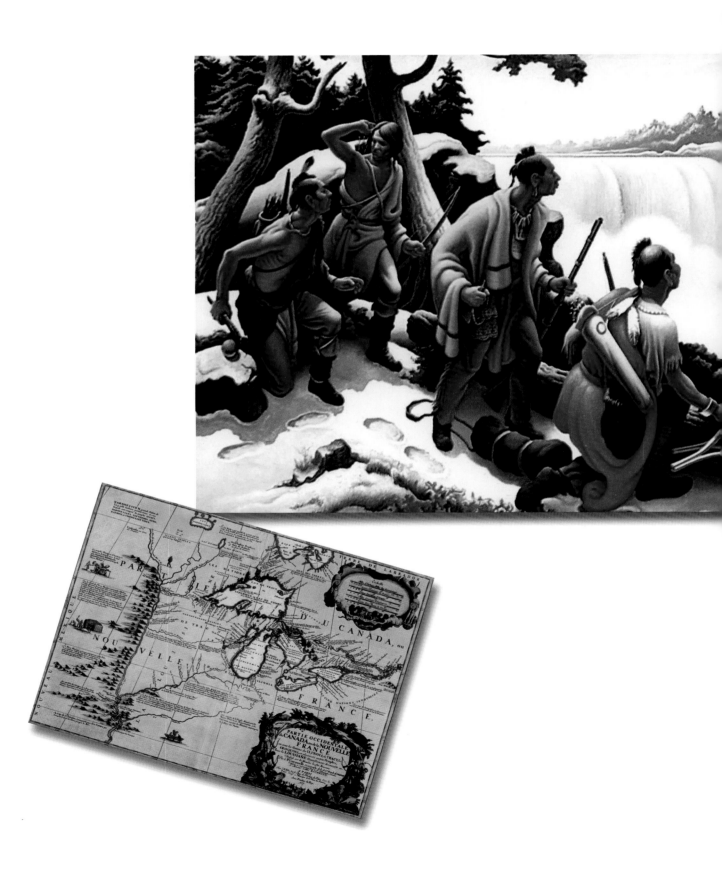

The Great Lakes region has attracted people for thousands of years. From the first humans migrating from Asia to European explorers, the area has been a geographical magnet. Early human history has close ties to modern settlement around Lake Erie.

THE FIRST HUMANS

It is believed that the first humans made their way to North America across a land bridge from Asia. Between 10,000 and 12,000 years ago during the Paleo-Indian Period, these nomadic hunters arrived in the Great Lakes region. The area around Lake Erie looked much different from today, as the land was rebounding from the retreating glaciers and covered in tundra and spruce forests. These early hunters camped along the Lake Erie shoreline seeking moose, elk, caribou and mastodons.

During the Archaic Period from 3,000 to 9,000 years ago, hunter-gatherers lived on a diet of plants, deer, moose and fish all found near the lake. The forest was deciduous by this time, and larger groups of people set up camps along the lakeshore at the mouths of creeks and rivers.

From 300 to 3,000 years ago, during the Woodland Period, the primary sources of food were cultivated. As agriculture became the way of life, corn, beans and squash became the basic diet. This period also marked the peak of the Iroquois culture. The population grew with a political system based on extended families and alliances between villages.

The Iroquois Confederacy comprised five tribes generally living near Lake Ontario in New York State. The Mohawk, Oneida, Onondaga, Cayuga and Seneca tribes made up the Iroquois Nation. Between 1642 and 1653, the Iroquois, intent upon expanding their territory along both sides of Lake Erie, were at war with the Eriez, Hurons, Neutrals and other tribes. The Neutrals living north of Lake Erie, and the Eriez tribe, who lived on south side of the lake, were completely destroyed. This occurred before any European exploration of Lake Erie.

EUROPEAN DISCOVERY OF LAKE ERIE

ABOVE: Samuel de Champlain (1567-1635), a French explorer, mapped much of northeastern America and began a settlement in Quebec. (Library of Congress, Prints & Photographs Division LC-USZ62-97748)

BOTTOM: French Explorer Jacques Cartier (1491-1557) ascending the St. Lawrence River. (Library of Congress, Prints & Photographs Division LC-USZ62-3018)

PREVIOUS PAGES: Artist Thomas Hart Benton was commissioned to paint this mural in 1961 for the Niagara Power Project. The work depicts Father Louis Hennepin and a group of Native Americans viewing Niagara Falls during Hennepin's 1678 expedition to the New World. (New York Power Authority)

INSET: Vincenzo Coronelli, cartographer to King Louis XIV, created this map of Western New France in 1688. It was the first printed map to show the Great Lakes in their entirety. (Library and Archives Canada-6411)

Lake Erie was the last of the five Great Lakes to be discovered by Europeans. The French, who discovered Lakes Ontario, Huron, Michigan and Superior, also were the first to see Lake Erie.

While it may seem surprising today, Lake Erie was the last of these inland seas to be discovered for two key reasons. First, Indians who the French met at Montreal had already been using a northern route up the Ottawa River and across a portage to the upper Great Lakes. Second, the highly organized Iroquois controlled both Lake Erie and Lake Ontario along with the portages between both lakes. The Europeans avoided the Iroquois because they were known to be hostile.

The discovery of the Great Lakes by the French took years and several expeditions. In 1535, Jacques Cartier made his way up the St. Lawrence River only as far as Montreal before returning to France. In 1615, Samuel de Champlain made his way to the upper lakes via the northern route, which reached the lakes by way of the Ottawa River and portages. Récollet (reformed Franciscan) friars and Jesuit missionaries later used this same northern route, a fur-trading avenue for the Indians, as their road for ceremony and discovery.

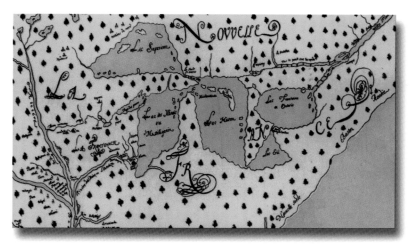

After seeing the upper lakes, Champlain took a different route on his return trip, traveling from Lake Huron's Georgian Bay across land, lakes and rivers to Lake Ontario, never seeing Lake Erie or Niagara Falls. This left Lake Erie to be discovered by other Frenchmen.

Late in the summer of 1669, a young Louis Joliet cast his eyes upon Lake Erie. Joliet had been sent along the northern route, up the Ottawa River and directly across to Lake Superior in search of a copper mine that the Indians had talked about. He never found the mine, but on the return trip, discovered Lake Erie. Joliet's Iroquois guide took him on a southern route for the return. They made their way down the St. Clair River, across Lake St. Clair and down the Detroit River to Lake Erie. Fear of hostile Indians along the Niagara portage route forced Joliet and his guide to turn north and head across the land of Ontario's Niagara Peninsula to Lake Ontario near present-day Hamilton, Ontario.

Within a few weeks, others also found Lake Erie. René Robert Cavalier Sieur de La Salle left Montreal in the summer of 1669 with several friendly Senecas and two Sulpician priests, François Dollier de Casson and René de Brehaut de Galinée. They followed the south shore of Lake Ontario, at this point a less risky route than previously. The risk was reduced because a large force of French had recently passed through the area, routing Indian warriors, burning villages and imposing conditions on the Iroquois. Before reaching the western end of Lake Ontario, La Salle's party passed the mouth of the Niagara River, hearing but not seeing the mighty cataract. La Salle, who had become ill, separated from the priests and did not continue toward Lake Erie. Dollier and Galinée, who remarkably had met Joliet on his return from seeing Lake Erie, followed Joliet's directions to the lake. The priests made their way to present-day Port Dover in early October, setting up camp and remaining in this "earthly paradise of Canada" for more than five months. When spring arrived, Dollier and Galineé headed westward along Lake Erie's northern shoreline, eventually making their way up to Sault Ste. Marie.

History didn't leave La Salle on the shores of Lake Ontario. Once his illness had subsided, it is believed that he and a few other men from his party traveled east along the shoreline of Lake Ontario to central New York, then headed south through the interior, eventually making their way west and down the Ohio River system to Louisville. By 1670, accounts indicate that La Salle

ABOVE: Louis Joliet (1645-1700), a French Canadian, played a key role in the exploration of North America. He was the first European to discover Lake Erie. This bronze statue stands in front of the public library in Joliet, Illinois.

MAP: This 1674 map of New France (North America) has been attributed to Louis Joliet. (*The Jesuit Relations and Allied Documents, vol. 59. Bibliothéque et Archives nationales du Québec*)

LEFT: René Robert Cavalier Sieur de La Salle (1643-1687) built the first sailing vessel to ply the Great Lakes as he attempted to set up a chain of trading posts through the region and down the Mississippi River. (Local History Department, Niagara Falls, New York Public Library)

BOTTOM: Samuel de Champlain exploring the Canadian Wilderness. (Library of Congress, Prints & Photographs Division LC-USZ62-3019)

may have returned from his tour through the interior via Lake Erie and the Detroit River. Regardless of the route, this significant journey inspired more exploration.

On December 8, 1678, La Salle and his group saw Niagara Falls for the fist time. A priest in the group, Father Louis Hennepin, made the first known sketch of the falls. Twenty years later, this drawing appeared in the book *New Discovery of a Vast Country in America.*

In 1679, La Salle built the first ship to sail on Lake Erie. The *Griffin*, built on the Niagara River, set sail from present-day Buffalo, traveling the length of Lake Erie and up the Detroit River and Lake Huron to Green Bay on Lake Michigan. After reaching Green Bay, La Salle sent the *Griffin* back to deliver furs to creditors in Montreal. La Salle pushed forward across a portage and on to the Mississippi River. He reached the Gulf of Mexico in the spring of 1682, planting a cross and claiming the middle of the North American continent for France. Meanwhile, the *Griffin* and her crew were not so fortunate. On the return voyage, the ship sank somewhere on the upper Great Lakes, losing all hands.

ABOVE: Father Louis Hennepin (1626-1705) was born in Belgium. He arrived in Quebec in 1675 and explored the Great Lakes region and the upper Mississippi River with La Salle. Hennepin died in Holland. (Minnesota Historical Society)

MIDDLE: Father Louis Hennepin was among the first Europeans to see the falls in 1678. This rendering appeared 20 years later in Hennepin's book *New Discovery of a Vast Country in America.* (Local History Department, Niagara Falls, New York Public Library)

BOTTOM: The *Griffin* was built between 1678 and 1679 along the Niagara River. Once completed, the ship was towed to present-day Buffalo, where she set sail on Lake Erie. (Library of Congress, Prints & Photographs Division LC-USZ62-90556)

TOP: French explorer René Robert Cavalier Sieur de La Salle's *Griffin* was the first European ship to sail the upper Great Lakes. She sank on her maiden voyage in 1769. (Library of Congress, Rare Books and Special Collections Division LC-USZ62-3283)

MAP: An early French map of the Great Lakes region. (Library of Congress, Geography and Map Division)

23

4 Battles

For centuries, people have recognized the value of the Great Lakes and fought to maintain access to them. Early humans were drawn to the lakes for food and fresh water. Indian tribes, who lived along the lakes' shorelines, fished their waters and used them for transportation and trade.

Europeans saw the Great Lakes as a possible route to the Far East before appreciating them for their valuable location near America's most fertile lands and the continent's vast natural resources. When the Europeans saw the densely wooded forests, fur trading possibilities, lands and resources, they became intent upon claiming the New World for their mother countries.

Control of the Great Lakes was of major importance to warring tribes in the region and to nations located thousands of miles away.

THE FRENCH AND INDIAN WAR

During the 17th and 18th centuries, several European countries attempted to annex North America. Britain and France were of greatest note.

The British had initially controlled the Eastern Seaboard, but for generations did not have much interest in what was behind it or the expense of defending an area that far west. They also had more pressing issues in other parts of the world. Behind the British-controlled East was the huge wall of the Appalachian Mountains, stretching from the St. Lawrence region, north of Vermont and New Hampshire, all the way to Georgia.

In the meantime, France's entry into the North American "real-estate market" opened through the St. Lawrence River. Ultimately, this passage routed the French around the British and through the Great Lakes region. Through more exploration and a few short portages to the Mississippi River system, France secured control of the middle of the North American continent. Save for a few skirmishes with Indians in the region, Britain and France initially went about their business in North America with few problems with one another.

The peace between the British and French ended when both countries became more interested in fur trading and expanding their empires. The Appalachians were not as impermeable as once thought. The Mohawk Valley of New York provided an easy route between both territories through the Appalachians. The tension between the British, French and Indians began to heighten.

Trouble was brewing between Britain and France overseas as well. The French were pitted against the Austrians and Spanish for control of other areas around the globe.

Back in North America, between 1754 and 1763, the British battled the French and Indians in skirmishes from the Ohio Valley to Quebec. In September of 1759, the British attacked Quebec, and after five days of fighting, captured the city. This ended France's control of Canada. In February 1763, the Treaty of Paris was signed, ceding all French territory east of the Mississippi to Britain.

THE AMERICAN REVOLUTIONARY WAR

BOTTOM: The Boston Tea Party was a protest by the Sons of Liberty against the British East India Company. Colonists were angered by the British decision to tax the colonies with no representation in the Westminster Parliament. The protesters destroyed 342 crates of tea from three ships in Boston Harbor. The incident was pivotal in sparking the American Revolution. (Library of Congress, Prints & Photographs Division LC-USZC4-523)

PAGE 25: Commodore Oliver Hazard Perry is depicted heading to the flagship *Niagara* in this painting by William H. Powell. The painting hangs in the U.S. Capitol Building in Washington D.C. The Battle of Lake Erie took place on September 10, 1813 between nine U.S. Navy vessels and six British ships. (Library of Congress/Picture History)

Many scholars believe the French and Indian War was a significant catalyst for the American Revolutionary War. Resentment in the colonies was building over taxes the British had levied to pay for the war effort. The British began taxing cargo shipped into ports, leading to protests from the colonists. In Boston in 1774, men dressed as Indians, dumped crates of tea into the harbor to protest a tax the British had levied against imported tea. The Boston Tea Party symbolized the start of the American Revolution. Many of those who supported this revolution joined the colonial army. Those remaining loyal to Britain were known as Loyalists, who often joined the British army.

Most of the battles of the Revolutionary War were waged far from Lake Erie, but the repercussions were felt along its shores. Much of the area along the southern shore of Lake Ontario and around Lake Erie was Indian land, and the Indians were loyal to the British. Additionally, not all colonists

were united in rebellion against their mother country.

The Revolutionary War officially ended in September of 1783 with the Second Treaty of Paris. This agreement split the border between the United States and British Canada down the middle of Lake Erie.

After the war, many colonial Loyalists lost their property and could not return to their homes. There were also people on the Canadian side of the border who were sympathetic to the Americans against the British. As a result, the colonial Loyalists were awarded land on the north shore of Lake Erie and those Canadians, who had supported the rebellious Americans, were awarded land east of Columbus, Ohio.

Despite these reparations, more trouble developed at the western end of Lake Erie. The fur trade was very lucrative for the British, who were not about to give up control of the fort at Detroit. Tensions were compounded as the Indians were being forced further west along Lake Erie's shores as settlers pushed their way into Ohio.

In 1792, George Washington placed General "Mad" Anthony Wayne in command of the U.S. Army and made him responsible for fighting the Indian wars. As several attempts to negotiate failed, numerous battles broke out in western Ohio. The British, though not forceful, supported the Indians in their fight against the American settlers.

Indian occupation and its British support ended in 1794 at the Battle of Fallen Timbers. This bloody confrontation (near present-day Toledo) took place in an area where trees had fallen in a tornado. General Wayne's troops defeated the Indians in this battle, virtually ending all Indian wars in the Lake Erie region. In 1796, the British surrendered Detroit without bloodshed and Loyalists abandoned the city, settling in Ontario. Soon however, the region would be the stage of yet more conflict.

THE WAR OF 1812

The American Revolutionary War and the British-supported battles with the Indians in the region may have been over, but neither side forgot them. Thousands of miles from Lake Erie, the British were still at war with France. While Britain resented the Americans for their aid to Napoleon, the Americans resented the British for their naval blockades. The Americans also took exception when the British boarded American ships either jailing their seamen or impressing them into service for the British Royal Navy. It is also believed there was concern the Americans were taking advantage of Britain's struggle with Napoleon. Britain had its sights set on seizing a large portion of Canada, including the St. Lawrence region and land on the north sides of lakes Erie and Ontario.

War was finally declared on June 18, 1812. The Americans and the British tangled on the Atlantic as the British sealed American ports. While demonstrating their naval prowess on the salt water, there were initially fewer British troops guarding the Canadian border along

ABOVE: General "Mad" Anthony Wayne (1745-1796) led an American Army to defeat the Indians at the Battle of Fallen Timbers near present-day Toledo, Ohio. The next year, he negotiated the Treaty of Greenville, opening the Northwest Territory to white settlement. (Library of Congress, Prints & Photographs Division LC-USZ61-333)

TOP LEFT: This memorial, near where the Battle of Fallen Timbers was fought, commemorates the signing of the Treaty of Greenville in 1795.

Lake Erie and Lake Ontario. However, it was not long before a number of key battles were fought in the Lake Erie region.

THE BATTLE OF DETROIT

On July 12, Brigadier-General William Hull entered Canada from Detroit, leading a force of more than 2,000 American troops. The Americans occupied the town of Sandwich (now part of Windsor, Ontario) in the first American invasion of Canada.

When word of Major-General Sir Isaac Brock's advancing British army reached Hull, he took his forces back across the river to Detroit. After an attack on Detroit, Brock's forces marched toward the American fort. Hull surrendered to Brock at Detroit on Aug. 16.

THE BATTLE OF QUEENSTON HEIGHTS

The Battle of Queenston Heights was fought on October 13, 1812. American Major-General Stephen Van Rensselaer and 4,000 troops took control of Queenston Heights by

crossing the Niagara River into Canada from Lewiston, New York. British Major-General Sir Isaac Brock arrived from downriver Fort George to attempt to regain control of Queenston Heights.

The sound of cannons rumbled through the Niagara River gorge and shots were exchanged between the opposing forts Niagara and George. Brock was killed on the ridge during the battle, but his replacement, Major-General Roger Hale Sheaffe, with help from Indians, recaptured Queenston Heights.

THE BATTLE OF RIVER RAISIN

At the western end of Lake Erie, the Battle of River Raisin (Frenchtown) took place in January of 1813 (near what is now Monroe, Michigan). Major-General William Henry Harrison, who was victorious at Tippecanoe, and General James Winchester, led the Americans. Harrison hoped to recapture Detroit, which had fallen to the British a few months earlier. Retaking Detroit would allow the American forces to invade Upper Canada.

American forces numbering more than 6,000 marched north along Lake Erie's western shore toward Detroit. General Winchester traveled ahead of the main force with an advance guard. The Americans easily took Frenchtown on the River Raisin, but were not prepared for a counter-attack.

British Colonel Henry Procter staged an early morning attack on the Americans with more than 500 troops and 600 Indians. Approximately 500 Americans, including General Winchester, were captured, and nearly 400 were killed. Because the Americans were unprepared and suffered such heavy losses, the battle is also known as the "River Raisin Massacre."

General Harrison retreated and oversaw the construction of Fort Meigs, a few miles up the Maumee River from present-day Toledo.

TOP: General William Hull (1753-1825) was a veteran of the American Revolution. He is shown surrendering Fort Detroit to British Major-General Sir Isaac Brock in 1812. (Library and Archives Canada, C-134303)

LEFT: Major-General Sir Isaac Brock (1769-1812) was known as the "Hero of Upper Canada" during the War of 1812. He was killed in the Battle of Queenston Heights along the Niagara River. (Government of Ontario Art Collection, Toronto)

"We have met the enemy and they are ours."
Commodore Oliver Hazard Perry

THE BATTLE OF LAKE ERIE

After several bloody battles left the Americans the worse for wear, the sound of gunfire rumbled at the western end of Lake Erie. On September 10, 1813, Commodore Oliver Hazard Perry won a decisive battle over the British fleet in the Battle of Lake Erie. Perry and his squadron hid amongst Lake Erie's western islands waiting for six British ships to arrive and engage in battle.

The British did heavy damage to Perry's flagship. Most of the crew of the *Lawrence* were either killed or seriously wounded. Amidst the shelling and gunfire, Perry made a dramatic half-mile dash to another warship, the *Niagara*, which had been lagging behind. Upon taking control of the *Niagara*, Perry was able to soundly defeat the British fleet by immobilizing the *Detroit*, a British ship.

Perry wrote a note on the back of an envelope to Major-General William Henry Harrison with his assessment of the situation: "We have met the enemy and they are ours." This battle secured control of Lake Erie for the United States.

TOP LEFT: The Battle of Lake Erie took place on September 10, 1813 between nine U.S. Navy vessels and six British ships.

TOP RIGHT: Commodore Oliver Hazard Perry (1785-1819) led the Americans in the Battle of Lake Erie in 1813. (U.S. Navy)

BOTTOM: The British ships had taken heavy cannon fire and were unable to effectively fight the *Niagara*. By nightfall, the British had lowered their flag and surrendered to Perry.

BATTLE OF THE THAMES

The Battle of Lake Erie paved the way for Major-General William Henry Harrison to invade the western portion of Upper Canada.

Harrison's army forced British Colonel Henry Procter back to Detroit and to Fort Malden. Procter then decided to retreat further toward Lake Ontario. Shawnee Chief Tecumseh disagreed with Procter's plan of withdrawal, knowing retreat would mean the Indians who fought alongside the British would be abadoned.

General Harrison's forces caught up with the demoralized British troops as they slowly retreated to the east. The battle took place along the Thames River near Moraviantown on October 5, 1813. The exhausted British troops surrendered after the first American charge. Eight hundred Indian warriors continued to fight, retreating after their leader Tecumseh was killed in the battle.

The American General Harrison returned to Detroit. Procter, the British Colonel, was court martialed for his conduct at the Battle of the Thames.

MORE BATTLES ALONG THE NIAGARA RIVER

In December of 1813, Fort George on the Niagara River was evacuated and the Americans burned the British town of Newark (now Niagara-on-the-Lake, Ontario). The burning of the town left residents and soldiers without shelter.

Angered by this attack, more than 500 British soldiers crossed the Niagara River on the night of December 18, 1813, taking control of Fort Niagara. The British then marched up the Niagara River to Lewiston, burning the American village. After destroying Lewiston, General Phineas Riall lead troops along the river toward Lake Erie, burning Fort Schlosser, Black Rock and Buffalo as retaliation for the burning of Newark.

During the following year, skirmishes continued along the Niagara River. On July 3, 1814, American Major-General Jacob Brown, with Brigadier-Generals Winfield Scott and Eleazar Ripley, invaded Fort Erie. After taking Fort Erie, Brown's forces advanced along the

TOP: At the Battle of the Thames, William Henry Harrison led an army to fight against British and Indian forces. The Americans were victorious. Tecumseh was killed in this War of 1812 battle. (Library of Congress, Prints and Photographs Division)

RIGHT: Tecumseh (1768-1813) was a Shawnee chief who worked to unite Indian tribes against white settlement. He was killed at the Battle of the Thames. (Local History Department, Niagara Falls, New York Public Library)

Canadian side of the river and defeated the British at the Battle of Chippawa on July 5.

From Chippawa, the Americans advanced to face the British at the Battle of Lundy's Lane at Niagara Falls on July 25, 1814. After numerous exchanges, the wounding and capture of British General Riall, the wounding of British General Gordon Drummond and American Generals Brown and Scott, the fighting stopped. The British and the Americans were both simply too exhausted to continue fighting, but both sides claimed victory.

The Battle of Lundy's Lane was the bloodiest of the War of 1812 as the Americans lost more than 700 soldiers and the British and Canadians suffered more than 600 casualties.

THE CONCLUSION OF THE WAR OF 1812

The Peace Treaty of Ghent was signed on December 24, 1814 by the United States and Britain, officially ending the War of 1812. The United States had military control of Lake Erie after the war, which was substantiated through the signing of the Rush-Bagot Agreement in 1817. The document severely limited Britain's naval power on the Great Lakes.

MAP: Several battles were fought in the Niagara region during the War of 1812. *(The Pictorial Field-Book of the War of 1812)*

ABOVE RIGHT: The Battle of Lundy's Lane, one of the bloodiest fought on Canadian soil, took place in Niagara Falls, Ontario. A memorial to those who lost their lives stands at Drummond Hill Cemetery.

BOTTOM: Fort Niagara sits at the mouth of the Niagara River on Lake Ontario. The British yielded it to the United States in 1796 and recaptured it in 1813. It was again ceded to the United States at the end of the War of 1812.

5 Settlement

Following native inhabitation, settlement around the Lake Erie basin has continued to this day. The first major wave of settlement on both sides of Lake Erie followed the American Revolutionary War and the War of 1812. Another wave hit as the Erie Canal was completed in 1825 and as other canals were built through the 1840s. Later, railroads, the Industrial Revolution and two world wars brought more people to live and work in the region.

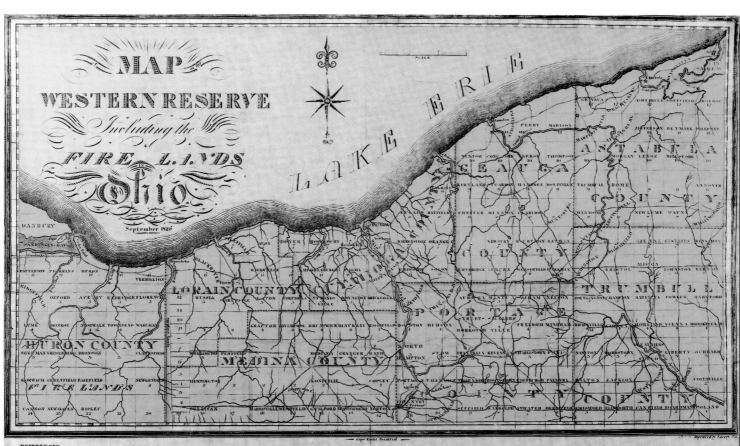

THE HOLLAND LAND COMPANY IN WESTERN NEW YORK

The Holland Land Company owned most of land in western New York. The company, a syndicate of Dutch bankers, hired agents to settle this area and parts of Pennsylvania. The intent was to quickly sell the land at a good profit, but making it attractive to settlers by surveying it and building roads took many years. Robert Morris, who was known as "the financier of the American Revolution," bought this land in 1791, including the land along New York's portion of Lake Erie. A year later he sold it to the Holland Land Company. However, before the transaction could take place, Morris' representatives and those of the Holland Land Company needed to reach an agreement with the Indians. The Big Tree Treaty was signed in 1797 giving the Senecas $100,000 for rights to approximately four million acres. The Senecas reserved roughly 200,000 acres of this land for their own use.

The resident agent in charge of the purchase was Joseph Ellicott. He was initially responsible for surveying the land before it was sold. Ellicott's older brother Andrew, Surveyor-General of the United States, was responsible for carrying out the plan designed for the city of Washington, D.C. Joseph's assistance in the Washington project explains the similar layout seen in Buffalo's street plan.

The Holland Land Company's land was surveyed between 1798 and 1800, and divided into six-square-mile townships, as had been done in the Northwest Territory.

The company built several main roads, but settlement was slow when land sales began in 1801. In 1825, the arrival of the Erie Canal helped increase the flow of settlers. Ellicott, not in good health and facing criticism for some of his practices, resigned his position in 1821. He committed suicide in a New York asylum in 1826. Ellicott is buried in a Batavia, New York cemetery, near the historic Holland Land Company Office Museum. The company liquidated operations in the United States in 1846.

ABOVE: Joseph Ellicott (1760-1826) was employed by the Holland Land Company to survey the tract in western New York. When the survey was completed in 1800, Ellicott was appointed local agent of the company. (Local History Department, Niagara Falls, New York Public Library)

ABOVE RIGHT: Robert Morris (1734-1806), known as the "financier of the American Revolution," was one of the richest men in America. Morris sold a large tract of land to the Holland Land Company. (Library of Congress, Prints & Photographs Division LC-USZ62-48399)

MAP: The western portion of New York State was surveyed and settled by the Holland Land Company. (Holland Land Company Museum)

PAGE 33: An 1826 map of Connecticut's Western Reserve in Ohio. (Western Reserve Historical Society, Cleveland, Ohio)

SETTLEMENT IN PENNSYLVANIA'S ERIE TRIANGLE

New York and Massachusetts ceded their claims to the triangular portion of land north of Pennsylvania, along Lake Erie to the U.S. government in 1781. Following negotiations with the Iroquois, the land was then sold to Pennsylvania in 1792 for 75 cents an acre, giving the Commonwealth a lake port. Immediately after Pennsylvania acquired this land, the General Assembly passed an act to encourage emigration to this new part of the Commonwealth.

After the settlement law was enacted, the Pennsylvania Population Company was formed at Philadelphia to settle the Erie Triangle. In 1793, agents gave 150 acres each to the first 20 families who settled in the Lake Erie territory. The settlers could locate where they wished as long as they built a house and cleared at least 10 acres. After two years, the settlers were awarded a deed for their parcel of land. In all, 30,000 acres in the region were offered for sale to settlers at $1 per acre for up to 300 acres.

Judah Colt, a native of Lyme, Connecticut, arrived in the area in 1795. He offered the Pennsylvania Population Company $1 an acre for a large section of land in the Triangle. The request was denied, but impressed with Colt, the company appointed him as a land agent for Erie County in 1797. Headquarters were set up at Colt's Station, nine miles south of the lakeshore, near French Creek. Soon, Colt built a road from Freeport on Lake Erie (near North East) across the summit to French Creek. In 1804, Colt surmised that land along the

lakeshore was preferable to his settlement in the hills, so he moved to Erie where he died in 1832.

In 1796, another company, the Harrisburg and Presque Isle Company, was formed to settle, improve and populate the land near and along Lake Erie. Additional portions of land were also reserved. The Commonwealth donated land to General William Irvine as a reward for his services during the Revolution. He selected his land while laying out the town of Erie. Another piece of land, a 24-square-mile section around Erie's harbor, became the Erie State Reserve.

The first portion of the Buffalo Road from Erie toward the New York State line was laid out in 1805 and completed in 1812. Once opened, communities began to spring up along the road, which later became U.S. Route 20.

THE CONNECTICUT WESTERN RESERVE IN OHIO

Before the American Revolution, Connecticut laid claim to all of the land from its western border to the Mississippi River. This strip of land included parts of New York and Pennsylvania. Once the U.S. government was set up, Connecticut relinquished claims to these lands with the exception of a 120-mile strip in Ohio. Profits from the sale of Connecticut Western Reserve lands (map on page 33) were to be used to fund public schools in Connecticut. The western portion of this land, currently Ohio's Huron and Erie counties, was used to compensate those Connecticut residents whose property had been burned or destroyed by the British during the American Revolution. These lands were called the "Firelands."

Connecticut sold the rest of the land, about three million acres, to the Connecticut Land Company for about 40 cents an acre. General Moses Cleaveland was hired as the land agent to survey and sell the land. After signing a treaty with the Indians in June of 1796, Cleaveland and a small party made their way to the Reserve, arriving at Conneaut, Ohio on July 4, 1796 (see Chapter 9 profiles of Conneaut, Ashtabula and Cleveland).

The surveying party broke into two groups. Cleaveland took one group and continued down the lakeshore to the mouth of the Cuyahoga River. The other group headed south along Pennsylvania's western border. The teams laid out townships on a grid of ranges in five-mile squares. Before returning to Connecticut, Cleaveland stayed just long enough to survey the land and map out a plan for what later became the city of Cleveland.

MAP: A late 18th century map, which includes the western portion of Pennsylvania before the purchase of the Erie Triangle. *(History of the Mission of the United Brethren among the Indians of North America.* Library of Congress, Geography and Map Division)

LEFT: Judah Colt (1761-1832) was the general agent for the Pennsylvania Population Company, which held the warrants for all the land in the Erie Triangle. (Pennsylvania Historical and Museum Commission)

BOTTOM: General Moses Cleaveland (1754-1806), a director of the Connecticut Land Company, was sent to survey lands within the Western Reserve. In 1796, he established the settlement of Cleaveland (Cleveland) on the banks of Lake Erie at the mouth of the Cuyahoga River. (Western Reserve Historical Society, Cleveland, Ohio)

Within two years, settlers began to arrive in New Connecticut. Families traveled 600 miles to this new land to set up towns and villages. The distinctively New England look can still be seen today. Unlike other villages in the Lake Erie region, these communities, like those in Connecticut, were set up around village squares. Often, these towns were named after the Connecticut towns from which the settlers arrived.

By 1820, the population of the Western Reserve amounted to more than 55,000. Within five years, the opening of the Erie Canal brought an even larger stream of settlers to the area.

THE NORTHWEST TERRITORY OF OHIO AND MICHIGAN

The Michigan Territory was opened to settlement after the British finally gave up control of Detroit and Indians had been forcibly removed from the area. To prevent the United States from developing the Great Lakes area, the British supplied Indians with arms. U.S. military efforts to subdue the Indians were unsuccessful before General "Mad" Anthony Wayne defeated the Indians near Toledo at the Battle of Fallen Timbers in 1794. This military action forced the British to abandon the northwestern forts, and in 1805, the Michigan Territory was organized. The region still was not ready for significant settlement. In 1813, a British force of 1,300 soldiers and Indians attacked the American army at Monroe in the Battle of the River Raisin. Later that year, U.S. forces returned to drive the British from Michigan's soil.

ABOVE: General "Mad" Anthony Wayne (1745-1796) defeated the Indians at the Battle of Fallen Timbers. The Northwest Territory was then opened to white settlement. (Independence National Historical Park)

TOP: General Moses Cleaveland's party traveled along the shoreline of the Lake Erie while surveying the lands of Connecticut's Western Reserve. The shoreline pictured is near North Perry, Ohio.

BOTTOM: "Charge of the Dragoons at Fallen Timbers" painted by R.F. Zogbaum. (The Ohio Historical Society)

After the war, Michigan's growth was slow until the Erie Canal was opened in 1825. As was the case with the Western Reserve in Ohio, the canal brought a steady stream of immigrants, mostly from New York and New England. In 1837, Michigan became the nation's 26th state.

THE TALBOT SETTLEMENT IN UPPER CANADA

Perhaps the most colorful story of settlement occurred along the north shore of Lake Erie, centered on the eccentric Irish-born Colonel Thomas Talbot. From 1791 to 1794, Talbot explored the wilderness with John Graves Simcoe, the Lieutenant-Governor of Upper Canada. After retiring from the British army in 1803, Talbot was granted 5,000 acres of land for his services. Simcoe assisted Talbot in making a special deal with the Crown, where Talbot would receive 200 additional acres of land for every family he established on his plot. Families would receive a 50-acre parcel and Talbot would be granted additional land elsewhere for his efforts. Talbot's interpretation of this arrangement eventually helped him accumulate 60,000 acres of his own. Talbot made sure that he settled newcomers far away from his own property.

Talbot made his base west of Kettle Creek at Port Talbot, living the life of a hermit in a log home. From his perch, high above the shores of Lake Erie, Talbot was visited by immigrants and others interested in settling in the area under his control. The area extended from the Long Point region to the Detroit River.

Talbot was particular about who would be allowed to settle. Those looking for land had to travel for many miles to see Talbot at his residence. There, he sat behind a special sliding window to hear requests for land. If Talbot deemed the visitor acceptable, he would pull out a map and write the settler's name on a parcel in pencil, so that it could be easily erased. If the colonel deemed someone unfit, he would refuse to do business with him and would turn his dogs on anyone who did not leave immediately.

By 1826, Talbot claimed to have 26,000 in his settlement. He built mills, settled 27 townships and cleared more than one-half-million acres in his non-governmental land settlement program.

The eccentric Talbot left his name and mark on the area. He oversaw the construction of the Talbot Trail (today's Highway 3). This 200-mile-plus road, located north of the Lake Erie shoreline, attracted new settlers and made travel easier for those who had moved to the area. His name is seen throughout the region on local streets, roads and villages. Talbot controlled the settlement of London, and in 1817 the city of St. Thomas was also named for him. Known as the "Lake Erie Baron," Thomas Talbot died in 1853.

TOP LEFT: Colonel Thomas Talbot (1771-1853) settled much of the land on Lake Erie's northern shoreline. (James B. Wandesford, Collection of McIntosh Gallery, The University of Western Ontario. Gift of Judge Talbot MacBeth, 1941)

ABOVE: The scenic and historic Talbot Trail is marked to represent the woods settlers had to cut down to build the road. The Emerald green represents Colonel Talbot's birthplace, the amber color represents the maize grown by the Neutral Indians. (St. Thomas-Elgin Tourist Asscoiation)

6 Connections

Growth around Lake Erie was rapid following the War of 1812. Settlements spread quickly as manmade connections were created to move people onto the Holland Land Company's parcels in New York, Pennsylvania's Erie Triangle, the Western Reserve in Ohio, the Northwest Territory of Michigan and Talbot's settlement in Upper Canada.

Rivers provided excellent connections to Lake Erie, but faster, safer and more reliable means of travel were developed to meet demands of transporting people and goods throughout the region. Paths worn by natives turned into roads. Then bridges, canals and railroads were built. Later, air connections further contributed to the Lake Erie region's strength as a leading industrial, agricultural and residential center in North America.

ENTRANCE TO WELLAND CANAL, PORT COLBORNE, ONT.

CLOCKWISE FROM LEFT: The *Walk-in-the-Water* was the first steamship on Lake Erie. (Local History Department, Niagara Falls, New York Public Library)
Native Americans cross the Niagara River near Fort Niagara in this painting by Robert Griffing. (Robert Griffing/Paramount Press)
A passenger steamer in the Cuyahoga River at Cleveland.
A recent view of the *Walter J. McCarthy Jr.*, passing the *Oglebay Norton* on the Detroit River. (U.S. Army Corps of Engineers, Detroit District)

PAGE 38: Five modes of transportation can be seen in this view of the Miami & Erie Canal in Ohio.

PAGE 39: The Roebling Suspension Bridge at Niagara Falls was opened in 1855. (Library of Congress, Prints & Photographs Division LC-USZC2-3301)

An early 20th century view of a lakeboat passing through the lock at the entrance to the Welland Canal at Port Colborne, Ontario.

CONNECTING RIVERS

The early inhabitants of the Lake Erie region used dugout and bark canoes to travel along the lakeshore and to the interior via rivers and streams. The main connecting rivers are the Detroit River, connecting with the upper Great Lakes; the Maumee River, flowing through northern Indiana and Ohio to the lake; the Cuyahoga, meeting Lake Erie in Ohio; and the Niagara, which is the lake's exit to the east. On the Canadian side, the Grand River winds its way southward through Ontario to Lake Erie. These rivers and other smaller tributaries were the main thoroughfares for natives of the region. Today, these rivers continue to provide vital transportation and recreational connections to Lake Erie.

CONNECTING ROADS

Many of the roads encircling Lake Erie have a long and rich history that is actually tied to the very formation of the lake. As the glaciers advanced and retreated, beach ridges formed and flat lake plains were also exposed. Early inhabitants of the Lake Erie region wore paths along these ridges. Later, European explorers followed these routes.

By the early 1800s, stagecoach routes developed along these trails, carrying settlers westward along the very same thoroughfares. Along U.S. Route 20 in Western New York, Pennsylvania and Ohio, several taverns and inns dating to as far back as 1805 remain. These establishments served as resting points along the Cleveland-Buffalo stage route. Similar routes along the lakeshore followed ancient paths through western Ohio, and between Toledo and Detroit in what is now Michigan. These lakeshore routes were also used by the military during the War of 1812.

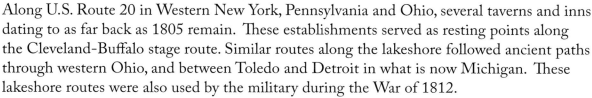

Natives had also worn paths along Lake Erie's northern shoreline in Canada. Later, Colonel Thomas Talbot, the "Lake Erie Baron," began his work of settling the north shore. Talbot's team of surveyors and workers cut what would, by the 1820s, become a more than 200-mile-long road stretching from one end of Lake Erie to the other. Originally a "corduroy" road made by laying logs across the roadbed, tolls were added in 1826 and regular stagecoach service began in 1830. Ontario's Highway 3 was designated in 1925 and parallels much of what was Talbot's road.

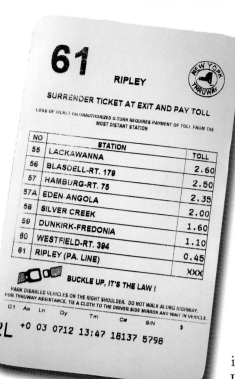

During the early 20th century, a number of highway firsts occurred near the shores of Lake Erie in the automobile capital of Detroit. One of the world's first concrete roads was built in the Motor City in 1909. It was a section of Woodward Avenue between Six Mile and Seven Mile roads. Detroit was home to the first traffic light, and by the mid-1930s, the city had more than 900 automatic traffic lights.

The road passing along Lake Erie's western shore in Michigan and Ohio was designated as the Dixie Highway in 1916. The U.S. route system was established in 1926 as more vehicles hit the road; thoroughfares around Lake Erie were improved and officially given route numbers. The key routes around Lake Erie became known as U.S. 20, U.S. 6 and U.S. 24. Ohio's State Route 2 also became a significant route along Lake Erie during this period. During 1930s and 1940s, arteries were built in the Lake Erie region in Cleveland and Detroit. The Cleveland Shoreway opened in 1938. During a visit by King George VI and Queen Elizabeth in June 1939, a new superhighway between Niagara Falls and Toronto was officially designed as the Queen Elizabeth Way (QEW). It was eventually connected with the Peace Bridge at Fort Erie. In the boom years after World War II, many roads became choked with traffic, especially in the

TOP: Rider's Inn at Painesville, Ohio served travelers headed west to settle. The establishment on the stage route from Buffalo to Cleveland was opened in 1812 and remains in business today.

LEFT: A New York State Thruway toll ticket. The section of the highway between Buffalo (Lackawanna) and Ripley, New York at the Pennsylvania border follows the Lake Erie shoreline. (New York State Thruway Authority)

industrial cities around the lake. To alleviate the congestion, more expressways were built. The Ohio Turnpike Commission was created in 1949, and in 1952 ground was broken on the 241-mile superhighway. The thoroughfare was completed and opened in 1955. The portion of the Ohio Turnpike between Cleveland and Toledo follows a route just a few miles south of Lake Erie's shoreline.

The first spade of dirt was turned to start construction of the New York State Thruway in 1946. The roadway between New York City and Buffalo was completed in 1954. The section of the Thruway along Lake Erie, between Buffalo and the Pennsylvania Line, was opened in 1957. Ultimately, the New York State Thruway and the Ohio Turnpike were incorporated into the Interstate Highway System, as parts of I-90 and I-80, following President Dwight D. Eisenhower's signing of the Federal-Aid Highway Act of 1956.

In 1960, Pennsylvania's 46-mile section of I-90 along Lake Erie opened and connected to Ohio's portion of the interstate highway when it was completed shortly thereafter. The construction of I-79 between Erie and Pittsburgh was completed in 1972. Ohio and Michigan's Detroit-Toledo Expressway was opened by 1959 and officially designated as I-75 in 1962. The stretch of I-75 connecting the Ambassador Bridge opened in 1967. By 1970, I-75 had been completed through midtown Detroit.

TOP LEFT & RIGHT: A postcard shows the exits and regional attractions along the newly opened Ohio Turnpike. When the roadway opened in the 1950s, in addition to the gateways at the eastern and western boundaries of the state, the Ohio Turnpike had 15 interchanges. (Ohio Turnpike Commission)

MIDDLE: The concrete ribbons of the New York State Thruway ended at fruit orchards and grape vineyards at the Pennsylvania border in 1957. Pennsylvania's section of Interstate 90 was completed in 1960, connecting to the Thruway. (New York State Thruway Authority)

BOTTOM: A 1920s-era postcard of U.S. Route 20's crossing of Elk Creek at Girard, Pennsylvania.

On the quieter Canadian side, most of the traffic between Toronto-Hamilton-Niagara Falls and Windsor-Detroit was diverted well to the north of the lakeshore and the Talbot Trail, when Highway 401 was completed in 1968.

Roads continue to be developed around Lake Erie. In 1999, a new highway, Interstate 86, was linked with I-90 at Erie, Pennsylvania. This road provides a more direct route from the Erie area to New York City, traversing the Southern Tier of New York State. Another new artery, the Bayfront Connector on Erie's east side, now carries traffic into the city from I-90.

CONNECTING CANALS

Spans and Tunnels: Bridging Nations

Bridges replaced ferry service across the Detroit and Niagara rivers. The Ambassador Bridge, connecting Detroit and Windsor, was the longest suspension bridge in the world when it opened in 1929. In 1930, the Detroit-Windsor Tunnel was completed. On the eastern end of Lake Erie, the Peace Bridge opened in 1927, linking Buffalo, New York with Fort Erie, Ontario. Further down the Niagara River at Lewiston, the first of several spans to cross the Niagara River was opened in 1851.

The Erie Canal: Clinton's Ditch Across New York

While other canals connected Lake Erie with the interior and the world, the Erie Canal is the best known. This early towpath route crossed New York State, slipping through a gap in the Appalachian Mountains to connect Lake Erie with the Hudson River and the Atlantic Ocean. The Erie Canal was the spine of a system of canals that included connections to Lake Ontario at Oswego, the St. Lawrence River from Lake Champlain, the Susquehanna River via the Chenango Canal, the Southern Tier of New York through the Genesee Valley, the Finger Lakes and the northern part of the state via the Black River Canal.

ABOVE: The Ambassador Bridge was opened to traffic in 1929, connecting the U.S. and Canada at Detroit. (U.S. Army Corps of Engineers, Detroit District)

BOTTOM: Dewitt Clinton (1769-1828) served as State Senator, U.S. Senator, Mayor of New York City and Lieutenant-Governor before being elected Governor from 1817 to 1823 and from 1825 until his death in 1828. Clinton was the leading proponent of the building of the Erie Canal. (Library of Congress, Prints & Photographs Division LC-USZ62-50394)

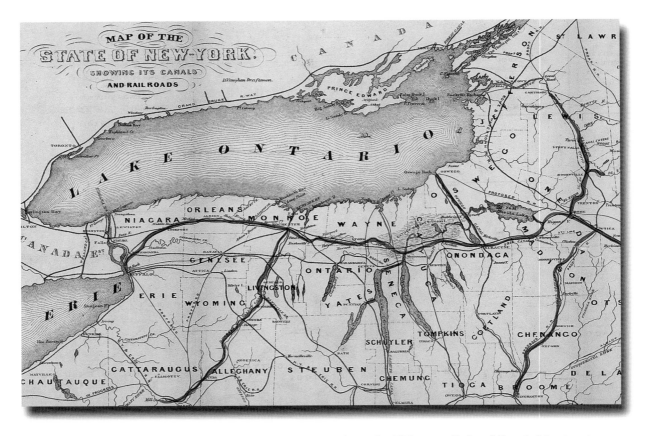

The history of the Erie Canal dates to 1792, when the Western Inland Lock Navigation Company was chartered. The company set out to create a water route from the Hudson River to Lake Ontario via the Mohawk River, Oneida Lake and the Oswego River. The company was only able to build a bypass of Little Falls on the Mohawk River before running into financial problems.

Even with these difficulties, many leaders urged the state to build a canal to link the Hudson River with Lake Erie. Dewitt Clinton, who became governor of New York in 1817, was most prominent in this effort. Ground was broken for the Erie Canal on Independence Day in 1817. The canal crossed rivers, swamps, and hills on its 363-mile route across New York State. The channel was originally 4 feet deep, 40 feet wide at the surface and 28 feet wide at the bottom. The canal used 83 locks to handle ups and downs totaling 685 feet. Eighteen aqueducts carried the canal over rivers and streams and many bridges spanned the waterway. Irish immigrants and local laborers worked 10- to 12-hour days to build the Erie Canal, earning 80 cents a day.

MAP: An 1858 map of the canal system in New York State. (C. Van Benthuysen, Albany, 1860)

BOTTOM: Old lock chambers on the Erie Canal at Lockport, New York. The locks were replaced when the canal's route was revitalized as the New York State Barge Canal in 1918.

On November 4, 1825, Governor Dewitt Clinton poured a keg of Lake Erie water into New York Harbor to mark the opening of the Erie Canal. The canal was a success from a commercial standpoint, cutting travel time and the cost of moving goods from Lake Erie to New York from $90-$125 a ton to $4 per ton. The Erie Canal brought

a steady stream of New Englanders and immigrants to work and settle farmland in western New York, northwestern Pennsylvania, Ohio and Michigan. Crops were sent eastward along the route, while manufactured goods were sent to the newly settled areas in the west. Even after the arrival of the railroad, the Erie Canal continued to be successful.

The Erie Canal was responsible for the early exponential growth of Buffalo, other cities around Lake Erie and the region's farmland. Between 1836 and 1862, the canal was enlarged, increasing the amount of cargo able to be transported. Tolls were removed in 1882. The Erie Canal and other main branches were enlarged after 1905 and collectively became known as the New York State Barge Canal System in 1918. Instead of being towed by mules, boats and barges were moved by steam or diesel-powered tugboats. Operation of the locks was converted to electricity. The canal, which paralleled the Niagara River to its terminus at Buffalo, later simply joined the river at the twin cities of Tonawanda and North Tonawanda. The canal carried commercial traffic until 1994. Today, the canal is primarily used for recreation.

Ohio's Canals: The Ohio & Erie and the Miami & Erie

The building and opening of the Erie Canal in New York State began a canal craze that spread around Lake Erie. With an agriculturally based economy, Ohio also needed a way to get its goods to eastern markets. Ohio's goods could easily be transported along Lake Erie and down the Ohio River, but getting the crops to the river and lake from the agricultural interior was difficult.

The state legislature commissioned a study to examine the possibility of bringing canal travel to Ohio in 1822. On July 4, 1825, four months before the Erie Canal opened, Dewitt Clinton was on hand to see the first spade of dirt turned as work began on the Ohio & Erie Canal at Newark, east of Columbus. Work also was underway from Akron at Portage Summit to Cleveland. Within two years, the canal was completed between Akron and Cleveland. By 1832, the Ohio & Erie Canal was open from Lake Erie to the Ohio River, a distance of 308 miles.

TOP: The Pine Street Bridge and locks on the Erie Canal at Lockport, New York. The image is from the late 1890s.

BOTTOM: The Miami & Erie Canal runs behind the business district of St. Marys, Ohio. The scene is much the same today.

In the meantime, to the west, the Miami & Erie Canal slowly took shape. It started as a route between Middletown and Cincinnati in 1828. Two years later, the canal was extended to Dayton. The Miami & Erie Canal was not completed until 1845, when the entire 250-mile route was opened to traffic between the Ohio River and Lake Erie. More canals were completed through the state and across Indiana. Lake Erie was also connected to the Wabash River, which joins the Ohio River near Evansville, Indiana. This route was completed in 1853. The canal through Indiana was completed after the railroads had already gained their foothold. As a result, Indiana nearly went bankrupt. Toledo, however, flourished as a shipping port at the western end of Lake Erie.

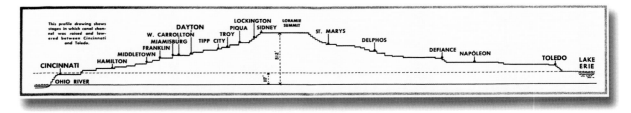

The successes of the Miami & Erie and Ohio & Erie canals were short-lived after their completion but their contributions to the development of Ohio were significant. Canal revenues peaked in 1855. By that time, the railroad was becoming a formidable competitor. Heavy snows during the winter of 1912-1913 and a rainstorm in March of 1913 finally put an end to Ohio's canal system. Sections of canal became impassable as locks and aqueducts were ruined and banks collapsed. Several sections of Ohio's historic canals have been restored and today provide numerous recreational opportunities.

Pennsylvania's Erie Extension Canal

Pennsylvania was not to be left out of the canal craze. The Pennsylvania Mainline Canal, completed in 1834, crossed the Commonwealth from Pittsburgh to Philadelphia and leaders in Northwestern Pennsylvania wanted a canal that would connect Lake Erie with the Mainline and the Ohio River.

Two routes were considered. One would use the Allegheny River and French Creek to reach the divide between the Ohio River and Lake Erie, and the other route would use the Beaver and Shenango rivers. The Beaver-Shenango route was chosen and construction of the Erie Extension Canal began on the Ohio River at Beaver, Pennsylvania in 1838. As was the case with New York State's Erie Canal, Irish laborers and local workers dug the 136-mile-long canal. Workers lived in shantytowns, were paid low wages and given an allocation of whiskey for their toils.

TOP: An 1842 image of the Miami & Erie Canal from the *Ladies Repository*. (The Ohio Historical Society)

DIAGRAM: The elevations along the route of Ohio's Miami & Erie Canal between Toledo on Lake Erie and the Ohio River at Cincinnati.

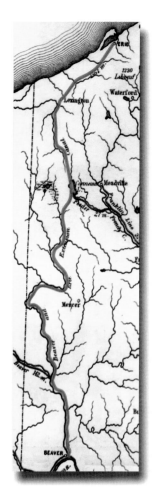

The Pennsylvania & Ohio Canal connected the Erie Extension Canal to the Ohio & Erie Canal. Begun in 1835 and completed in 1840, the Pennsylvania & Ohio (P & O), also known as the Mahoning Canal, extended from Akron, Ohio through Warren and Youngstown, Ohio to join the Beaver division of the Erie Extension Canal at a point just south of New Castle, Pennsylvania. This 83-mile-long canal was abandoned and the land sold by 1877.

In 1844, the Erie Extension Canal was opened for shipping from the Ohio River to the Port of Erie on Lake Erie. The canal followed Lee's Run into Presque Isle Bay on Erie's west side. The *Queen of the West* and the *R.S. Reed* were the first boats to make the trip from Pittsburgh to Lake Erie. One boat brought passengers and the other brought coal, iron ore and merchandise.

The history of the Erie Extension Canal was short. In operation for less than 30 years, the canal's viability came to an abrupt end in 1873 when the aqueduct across the Elk Creek Gorge, not far from Lake Erie, was destroyed. The collapse of this structure, which carried canal boats across the deep gorge, was controversial. Some felt that those with railroad interests had caused the aqueduct to collapse. In any event, much of the Erie Extension Canal's former bed was used as a base to lay railroad track. Some portions of Pennsylvania's Erie Extension Canal are still visible today.

The Welland Canal: Lake Erie's Link to the World

Niagara Falls was a barrier that made Canadian settlement of the Lake Erie region more challenging. Before the Welland Canal was built, settlers and goods from Lake Ontario made the 326-foot climb to Lake Erie by taking the Niagara River to a portage at Queenston. The portage led to Chippawa Creek above the falls, where the journey continued on the Niagara River to Lake Erie. Much like the Erie Canal, the idea of building a canal was on the minds of Canadians for many years before the first Welland Canal was built. There have actually been four Welland Canals.

The canal project was set into motion under the leadership of the Honorable William Hamilton Merritt. Merritt believed that by using the valley of Twelve-Mile Creek from Lake Ontario, a canal could be built to meet Chippawa Creek, which connects to Lake Erie via the upper Niagara River. The Welland Canal Company was incorporated in 1824 by the passage of an act in the legislature of Upper Canada. Ground was broken for the first of the four Welland Canals on Nov. 30, 1824. Exactly five years later, the first Welland Canal was complete. On Nov. 30, 1829, the Canadian schooner *Annie and Jane* of York (Toronto), Ontario and the *R.H. Boughton* of Youngstown, New York arrived at Chippawa.

MAP: The Erie Extension Canal routed traffic from Lake Erie at the harbor of Erie, Pennsylvania to the Ohio River, a few miles downstream from Pittsburgh. Conneaut Lake and several creeks and rivers along its route fed the canal.

BOTTOM: A tug and barge enter the Flight Locks of the Welland Ship Canal at Thorold, Ontario.

The Welland Canal's original route followed the Twelve-Mile Creek valley from Port Dalhousie on Lake Ontario to the foot of the Niagara Escarpment. From there, locks raised vessels to Port Robinson. At this point, a feeder canal from the Grand River flowed northeast from Dunnville to supply water at the summit of Welland Canal route. Two locks connected the Welland Canal to Chippawa Creek at Port Robinson.

With the feeder canal and Chippawa Creek, two routes were available to Lake Erie from Port Robinson, one by way of the feeder to Dunnville on the Grand River, and the other via Chippawa Creek to the Niagara River. Both routes had their drawbacks, as the feeder had only a 4-foot draft and sailing vessels that used the Chippawa Creek route required eight to 14 yoke of oxen to pull them to Lake Erie against the Niagara River's strong current. It was decided that one direct route between Lake Ontario and Lake Erie would be built to overcome these problems. Gravelly Bay, as Port Colborne was called at the time, became the Lake Erie terminus. The extension directly to Lake Erie was completed in 1833. The 27 1/2-mile-long canal had 40 locks, which were 110 feet in length, 22 feet wide and 8 feet deep.

Just a few years later, a second Welland Canal needed to be built. Larger boats had outgrown the canal and the wooden lock chambers had to be replaced with those made of stone. The route selected for the second canal was basically the same as the first. By increasing the lift of each lock, the number of locks was reduced from 40 to 27. The new locks were larger, 150 feet long, 26 1/2-feet-wide and 9 feet deep over the lock sills. The feeder canal was also enlarged and a connection was made to Port Maitland on Lake Erie. The feeder was the only route available from 1845 to 1850 while the main canal was being

ABOVE: William Hamilton Merritt (1793-1862) led the effort to build a canal connecting lakes Erie and Ontario. In 1824, Merritt formed the Welland Canal Company to carry out his project. The Welland Canal was opened in 1829. (St. Catherines Museum - N4101)

TOP: The Welland Canal's former terminus on Lake Ontario at the harbor of Port Dalhousie, Ontario. The canal now connects with Lake Ontario at Port Weller.

BOTTOM: Algoma Central Corporation's *Algocen*, which was launched in 1968, navigates the Welland Canal at Port Colborne, Ontario.

reconstructed between the junction of the feeder and Port Colborne.

It wasn't long before steamers were replacing sailing vessels and a third Welland Canal had to be constructed. To increase the depth, the whole canal would be fed directly by Lake Erie instead of using the feeder canal. The locks were increased in size to 270 feet in length and 45 feet in width with

a 14-foot draft. The third Welland Canal followed the same route as the second canal but left the Twelve-Mile Creek route to follow a more direct line to Port Dalhousie. The 26 3/4-mile-long third Welland Canal was opened in 1881.

Again, as ships increased in size and number, a much larger fourth canal was needed. Construction of the Welland Ship Canal began in 1913 and continued until 1916, when shortages of labor and materials resulting from World War I suspended work. Efforts resumed in 1919 and the Welland Ship Canal was completed in 1932. The route was the same above the Niagara Escarpment, but from Thorold to the north, the canal flowed to the Ten Mile Creek Valley to join Lake Ontario at Port Weller. There, an artificial harbor was created by the construction of breakwaters extending into Lake Ontario.

The Welland Ship Canal is now 27 miles long, 310 feet wide at water level and 200 feet wide at the bottom. Seven lift locks and one guard lock do the work that had been done by 40 locks on the first Welland Canal. The current locks are 859 feet long, 80 feet wide and have 30 feet of water over the lock sills. Each of the seven locks has a lift of approximately 46 1/2 feet. The Welland Ship Canal was further improved between 1965 and 1972, when a wider section was completed to bypass Welland, Ontario. This portion is 350 feet wide and 30 feet deep. It takes roughly eight hours to navigate the canal, which is usually open from early April to the end of December.

The Welland Ship Canal is part of the St. Lawrence Seaway, which was opened in 1959 to connect Lake Erie and the middle of the North American continent with the Atlantic Ocean. The Seaway's canals and locks bypass Niagara Falls and rapids on the St. Lawrence River and on the St. Mary's River at Sault Ste. Marie.

CONNECTING RAILS
New York State: Lake Erie's Eastern Rail Hub

Just after completion of the Erie Canal, the railroad arrived in New York State. In the 1830s and 1840s, eight short-line railroads were built across the state. Many of these railroads ran parallel to the Erie Canal but had restrictions imposed upon them to control their competitive effect on the state's investment in the canal. These restrictions were in place until 1851. By 1853, these railroads were consolidated to become the New York Central Railroad and the railroad business gained more momentum. The Buffalo & Niagara Falls Railroad was built in 1836, later becoming part of the New York Central and extending to Lewiston.

Running across New York State's Southern Tier, the Erie Railroad opened between

TOP: A 1940s-era postcard view of a Welland Canal lock chamber.

BOTTOM: The Roebling Bridge spanned the Niagara River Gorge from 1855 until 1897, when it was replaced. (Local History Department, Niagara Falls, New York Public Library)

49

the New York City area and Dunkirk on Lake Erie in 1851. It wasn't long before the western terminus of the Erie Railroad was moved to Buffalo, where it would compete more directly with the New York Central Railroad. Locomotives continued to be produced at Dunkirk. In 1852, the Buffalo & State Line Railroad was established, later becoming part of the Lake Shore & Michigan Southern Railroad. By 1854, rails running along New York State's portion of this route had been connected all the way to Chicago with a uniform gauge.

New York State's rails were connected with Canada at Niagara Falls in 1855 and Buffalo in 1874 with the opening of the International Railroad Bridge. In 1882, the New York, Chicago & St. Louis Railroad, known as the Nickel Plate, was completed between Buffalo and Chicago. Buffalo became the second largest railroad center in the United States in the early 20th century with 11 main railroad lines running to the city.

The first street railway in the Lake Erie region of New York State operated between Buffalo and Black Rock, opening in 1834. Soon other lines were built in the city of Buffalo. New York State had several interurban trolley companies, which ran between the towns along Lake Erie and into Pennsylvania during the late 19th and early 20th centuries. The Buffalo & Lake Erie Traction Company was incorporated in 1906 to join the companies and operate the trolley line to Erie, Pennsylvania. The line ran through Hamburg, Silver Creek, Fredonia, Westfield and Ripley before heading into Pennsylvania. The Buffalo & Lake Erie Traction Company line ceased operations in 1934 after a short history, as autos became the preferred mode of travel.

TOP LEFT: The New York Central Terminal in Buffalo was one of the finest examples of art deco architecture when it was built in 1929.

TOP RIGHT: The Brooks Locomotive Works was formed in 1869 and merged with other companies to become the American Locomotive Company in 1901. The company produced steam locomotives in Dunkirk, New York until 1928.

BOTTOM: The Chautauqua Traction Company operated interurban cars between Jamestown and Westfield, New York from 1904 until 1926.

Trolleys ran on the streets of Buffalo until 1950, before tracks were removed or covered. In 1986, light rail returned to Buffalo, as the NFTA's Metro Rail system was completed from the downtown area to the campus of the State University of New York at Buffalo.

Today, many freight trains and some passenger trains can still be seen following New York State's Lake Erie shoreline.

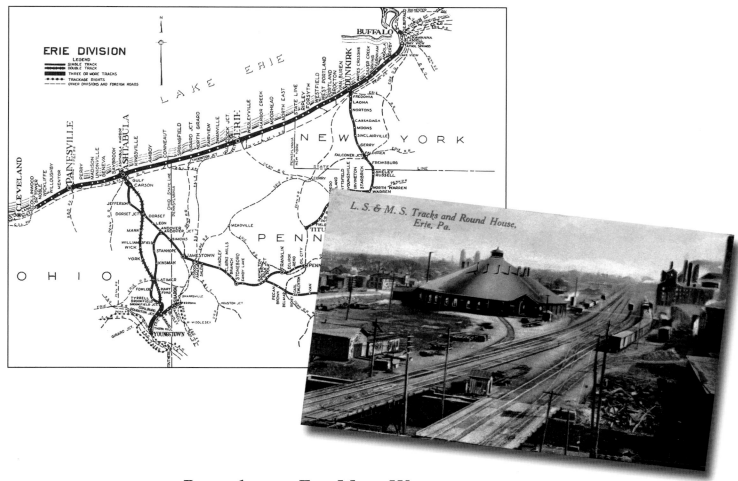

ERIE DIVISION
LEGEND
SINGLE TRACK
DOUBLE TRACK
THREE OR MORE TRACKS
TRACKAGE RIGHTS
OTHER DIVISIONS AND FOREIGN ROADS

L. S. & M. S. Tracks and Round House, Erie, Pa.

Pennsylvania: East Meets West

Rail transportation between New York and Ohio along Lake Erie was joined in Pennsylvania. The Erie & North East Railroad opened a 6-foot gauge track between Erie and the New York State line in 1852. That same year, another railroad line was extended from Erie, westward to the Ohio border, to connect with yet another line to Cleveland. This line, built by the Franklin Canal Company, had a different gauge, which meant that passengers would have to transfer at Erie. This inconvenience was averted in 1853 when the Erie & North East Company reached an agreement with the New York Central Railroad to change to a gauge of 4 feet and 10 inches. At the same time, a line was being built from Buffalo to the Pennsylvania border, creating a uniform gauge between Buffalo and Cleveland. Some, however, were not happy with this convenience. Residents of Erie were upset to see their city become a mere stop as opposed to a railroad terminus. A series of riots, known as the "Peanut War," broke out in late 1853 before federal agents put an end to the unrest.

Over the years, the New York Central, Pennsylvania, Nickel Plate and Bessemer & Lake Erie Railroads have served Erie. Successors have included the Norfolk & Western and Conrail. The Bessemer & Lake Erie Railroad continues to operate. Some of its tracks were built on the Erie Extension Canal's bed.

Several branches of railroads meet Lake Erie just over the state line in Ohio at Conneaut and Ashtabula, continuing to bring loads of iron ore and other materials southwest into the Commonwealth, supporting industry in the Shenango, Beaver and Ohio valleys of western Pennsylvania. For many years, travelers could see newly built locomotives being tested on tracks east of Erie.

The interurban trolleys of Conneaut & Erie Electric Traction Company began rolling in 1903. The Buffalo & Lake Erie Traction Company operated between 1906 and 1924.

MAP: A map showing the Erie Division of the New York Central Railroad. The stations from Springfield to North East are part of Pennsylvania's section of the line.

ABOVE: A circa-1910 image of the Lake Shore & Michgan Southern tracks and roundhouse at Erie, Pennsylvania.

Ohio: Exchanging Coal for Ore

Ohio's railroad history is rich, with roots dating back to 1832. At that time, the entire United States had a total of only 229 miles of railroad and Ohio had a special charter to build a 156-mile line from Dayton to Sandusky on Lake Erie. Known as the Mad River & Lake Erie Railroad, the line was completed in 1844. In 1836, a 32-mile-long line between Toledo and Adrian, Michigan, part of the Erie & Kalamazoo Railroad, was completed as the first operating railroad in the state. Horses pulled the first cars on this railroad. By the time of the Civil War, Ohio had more miles of railroad than any other state in the Union.

The Cleveland, Painesville & Ashtabula Railroad opened from Erie, Pennsylvania to Cleveland in 1852, before it became part of the newly formed Lake Shore & Michigan Southern Railroad in 1869. This gave railroad tycoon Cornelius Vanderbilt a continuous route between New York City and Chicago. The Nickel Plate Railroad was completed and opened in 1882. The Cleveland, Lorain & Toledo Railroad connected Lorain in 1872. By 1884, Cleveland had an electric street railway.

In 1892, iron ore began to arrive on Lake Erie's Ohio shores from ranges in Michigan and Minnesota. Ore boats transferred their cargo to awaiting Pittsburgh, Shenango & Lake Erie Railroad cars at Conneaut. Pennsylvania and West Virginia coal ran in the opposite direction, heading north to the lake. This railroad later became part of Andrew Carnegie's Bessemer & Lake Erie Railroad. In 1895, railroad cars full of coal began to be transported across the lake from Conneaut to Port Dover, Ontario. Other railroad connections were made at Toledo, Sandusky, Lorain, Cleveland, Fairport Harbor, Ashtabula and Conneaut as coal and iron ore to support industry on the Great Lakes was shipped through these ports. The Chesapeake & Ohio Railroad brought coal to the lake at Toledo beginning in the early 1900s.

During the 1890s an interurban system of electric railways for passengers began to take hold. The trolley routes ran between towns on Lake Erie's shore and were built to provide transportation between towns that had been bypassed by conventional railroads. This era was short-lived, however, as roads were improved and automobile travel began to take greater hold in the 1920s.

Among many changes in the 20th century, the Norfolk & Western Railroad took over the Nickel Plate Railroad in 1964, assumed the lease of the Wheeling & Lake Erie Railroad and acquired the Sandusky Line and Sandusky Coal Docks of the Pennsylvania Railroad. The Norfolk & Western merged into Norfolk Southern Corporation in 1992.

Trolleys ran on the streets of Toledo until 1952 and busses replaced Cleveland's trolleys shortly thereafter. Cleveland has a light rail rapid transit system operated by the RTA. Trains continue to follow Ohio's North Coast and commuter trains carry thousands in and out of Cleveland daily.

ABOVE: Cornelius Vanderbilt (1794-1877) was a financier and businessman who pioneered the nation's transportation system. By 1873, his New York Central Railroad stretched from New York City to Chicago. (Library of Congress, Prints & Photographs Division LC-USZ62-69657

TOP: A view of the unloading operation at Conneaut, Ohio during the early 1900s. The large arms of the Hulett unloading machinery can be seen reaching into the holds of a lakeboat. Coal and ore were dumped into waiting rail cars.

BOTTOM: Railroad cars have carried Pennsylvania and West Virginia coal to waiting lakeboats and moved ore to steel mills for many years. This circa-1905 photo shows a Bessemer train making its way along the Conneaut River.

Michigan: Rails Moving Autos

The first railroad charter in the Northwest Territory was issued to the Detroit & Pontiac Railroad in 1830. In 1836, the year before Michigan became a state, the Michigan Southern (Erie & Kalamazoo) Railroad began operation, providing horse-driven train travel between Adrian and Toledo, Ohio. By the 1850s, several lines made their way along Michigan's portion of Lake Erie's shoreline to Detroit.

In 1873, the Canada Southern Railway completed construction of a freight route that was to be a part of a more direct route between Buffalo and Chicago. This route crossed the Detroit River at Trenton. Bridges brought the trains across to Grosse Ile and Stony Island. From there, the cars would be taken across the river on a ferry to Amherstburg, Ontario. The Canada Southern ran into financial difficulties and the line did not remain in business for long.

In 1883, William M. Vanderbilt, president of the Michigan Central Railroad, began ferry service between Detroit and Essex Centre, Ontario. The Trenton to Amherstburg river crossing was abandoned in 1888.

In 1891, the Grand Trunk Railway completed a tunnel under the St. Clair River between Port Huron and Sarnia, Ontario. Detroit, desiring to protect its status as an international rail connection, completed the Michigan Central Railroad tunnel under the Detroit River in 1910. The growth of the auto and related industries in the early 20th century meant more railroads were built in and around Detroit. Rows of tracks were laid from the downriver cities to the automotive plants in Detroit's industrial core.

Streetcars ran on Detroit thoroughfares until 1956. Today, trains continue to travel within a few miles of the western shore of Lake Erie between Detroit and Toledo on CN North America and CSX tracks.

TOP: Detroit's grand Michigan Central Depot served from 1913 until its closing in 1988.

BOTTOM: The Michigan Central Railroad Tunnel connects Detroit with Windsor, Ontario. It opened in 1910 and is still in use today.

Loading Fish at Port Stanley, Ont., Canada

Ontario: Rails along the North Shore

Canada's Great Western Railway opened its main line between Windsor and Niagara Falls in 1854, completing the route along Lake Erie's northern shoreline. This railroad was connected to the American side with the completion of Roebling's suspension bridge at Niagara Falls in 1855. The Michigan Central Railroad was connected to Canada's Great Western Railway at both Niagara Falls and Detroit.

Further south, the Canada Southern Railway built a track to create a more direct route between Fort Erie and Amherstburg. This line was opened in 1873 and connected the Detroit area with Buffalo by way of Canada. The line ran across the Niagara River to Buffalo over the International Railroad Bridge.

Another railroad, the Grand Trunk Railway, had extended its line to Chicago in 1880 and was merged with the Great Western Railway in 1882.

In addition to these main routes across Southern Ontario, some other significant railroads connected to Lake Erie's northern shoreline. These lines carried passengers to summer resorts and met cars full of West Virginia and Pennsylvania coal coming off ferries at Lake Erie's Canadian ports.

The London & Port Stanley Railway was opened in 1856. The Port Stanley Terminal Rail uses a portion of this route today for passenger excursions (see profile of Port Stanley in Chapter 11). In 1875, the Port Dover & Lake Huron Railway connected Simcoe and Woodstock with Lake Erie at Port Dover. The Erie & Lake Huron Railway met docking and harbor facilities on Rondeau Bay at Erieau in 1889, heading through Blenheim to the lake before closing in 1974.

The Hamilton & Lake Erie Railway ran between Hamilton and Port Dover from the late 1800s until 1935. Other railroads, including the Lake Erie, Essex & Detroit River Railway,

POSTCARDS: Fish were transported by rail to market. Excursion trains took passengers to several of Canada's Lake Erie ports. Both postcards are early 1900s views of Port Stanley, Ontario.

MAP: The Great Western Railway opened its main line, Niagara Falls-Hamilton-London-Windsor, in 1854. In 1882, the Great Western Railway merged with the Grand Trunk Railway, joining forces to be more competitive with U.S. railroads.

made their way to the lake. Famed distiller Hiram Walker built this railroad to connect his agricultural holdings with his Walkerville industry. The route was completed through Kingsville to Leamington by 1889, carrying passengers for summer excursions to Lake Erie.

Completed in 1889, the South Norfolk Railway Company's railroad made its way from Simcoe through St. Williams and to Lake Erie at Port Rowan. In 1896, the Tillsonburg, Lake Erie & Pacific Railway met the lake at Port Burwell.

Tunnel, Windsor, Canada.

A number of passenger and trolley railroads were built along the northern shore of Lake Erie. In 1903, the Sandwich, Windsor & Amherstburg Railway opened between hose communities. The Windsor, Essex & Lake Shore Rapid Railway, with trolleys running along country roads to Kingsville and Leamington, was completed in 1907. That same year, the electric London & Lake Erie Railway brought passengers from London to Port Stanley, also running next to rural roads.

The Chatham, Wallaceburg & Lake Erie Railway was built for passengers heading to Erie Beach in 1908. In 1916, the Toronto, Hamilton & Buffalo Railway was completed to Port Maitland, where coal was picked up from boats crossing Lake Erie from Ashtabula, Ohio. Service commenced on the Lake Erie & Northern Railway to Port Dover as part of the Canadian Pacific Electric Lines.

The Great Gorge Route was a scenic rail line that made a loop around the U.S. and Canadian sides of the Niagara River between 1895 and 1935.

CN continues to operate a line between Buffalo and Detroit through southern Ontario.

TOP: The Great Gorge Route operated as a scenic railway along the Niagara River beginning in 1895. The attraction closed in 1935 when a rock fall destroyed a section of track. (Local History Department, Niagara Falls, New York Public Library)

MIDDLE: The 2 1/2-mile-long Michigan Central Railroad tunnel between Windsor and Detroit was completed in 1910.

BOTTOM: The International Railroad Bridge between Buffalo and Fort Erie, Ontario was completed in 1873 and is still in use today.

TOP: A 1940s view of Buffalo-Niagara Falls International Airport. Two hundred acres of farmland were purchased in 1925 to build the airport. The terminal was built by the W.P.A. in 1938 and expanded several times before being razed in 1997. A modern terminal building opened that same year and the airport was renamed Buffalo-Niagara International Airport.

BOTTOM: Detroit has used several airports during its history, including City Airport and Willow Run. Detroit's Wayne County Airport opened in 1929 and by the 1960s all commercial traffic had moved there. At what is now known as Detroit Metro, a new 97-gate state-of-the-art terminal opened in 2002.

Air Connections

The major airports around Lake Erie continue to be developed. New runways and terminal facilities have been built recently in Detroit, Cleveland and Buffalo.

The Toledo Express Airport, opened in 1954, replaced the municipal airport. Also a major hub for cargo, the airport has undergone recent improvements. Erie International Airport (now also known as Tom Ridge Field), dedicated in 1968, has plans for expansion. Opened as Walker Airport in 1928 by distiller Hiram Walker, Windsor Airport recently extended its runway to 9,000 feet. London International Airport, opened in 1939, has new terminal buildings and ranks as the 12th busiest passenger airport in Canada.

Auto, rail, water and air connect the Lake Erie region to the rest of North America and the world.

TOP: Erie International Airport, now known as Tom Ridge Field, is located 5 miles southwest of the city. The airport serves general aviation, charters and scheduled airline flights.

MIDDLE: Cleveland Municipal Airport became known as Hopkins International Airport in the 1950s. It is named for City Manager William Hopkins, who was a leader in the founding of the airport in 1925.

BOTTOM: Toledo Express Airport is located in western Lucas County about 20 miles from downtown Toledo.

7 New York State Shoreline

New York State's portion of the Lake Erie shoreline begins in Buffalo at the entrance to the 35-mile-long Niagara River. Here, Lake Erie's outflow rushes northward under the arches of the Peace Bridge, a span joining two great nations. The American side of the river is heavily populated and industrialized along much of its journey toward Niagara Falls. Along the way, the river is split by the residential and agricultural Grand Island. At the twin cities of Tonawanda and North Tonawanda, the river passes the entrance to the New York State Barge (Erie) Canal. After a few more miles, the water picks up speed before tumbling over the mighty cataract of Niagara.

After a turbulent trip over the falls and down a seven-mile-long gorge, the Niagara flows past Lewiston and for another seven miles at a more relaxed pace, across Lake Ontario's plain. This is a tranquil spot, known for its fruit orchards and rich farmland. The Niagara River completes its work here, handing Lake Erie's water over to Lake Ontario, the next stop on its journey out to sea.

The Empire State's shoreline along Lake Erie runs roughly 70 miles to the southwest from Buffalo to the Pennsylvania border. At Buffalo, large breakwaters protect the Erie Basin, the mouth of the Buffalo River, and Buffalo's outer harbor. The breakwaters extend southward to Lackawanna.

Much of the lakeshore between the town of Hamburg and the Pennsylvania line includes shale cliffs of various heights, punctuated by creeks winding to the lake through deep ravines. Along this southwestern route, the beach ridges of Lake Erie's predecessors, Lake Whittlesey and Lake Warren, can clearly be seen to the south. These ancient shorelines run parallel to Lake Erie's present shoreline and also mark the northern boundary of the Allegheny Plateau.

Most of New York's shoreline is agricultural and especially well known for its abundant grape vineyards and fruit orchards. There are several small villages along the way, with Dunkirk being the only industrial city between Lackawanna and the Pennsylvania border.

TOP: The mouth of the Niagara River opens into Lake Ontario. Youngstown, New York is in the foreground and Niagara-on-the-Lake, Ontario is at left.

BOTTOM: An aerial view of Buffalo at the eastern end of Lake Erie. The Peace Bridge crosses the Niagara River to Fort Erie, Ontario. The Niagara River flows northward from Lake Erie to Lake Ontario in the distance. Grand Island, New York is at the upper right.

PAGE 59: The shoreline at Lake Erie State Park near Brocton, New York.

OLD FORT FROM TOWER, NIAGARA.

YOUNGSTOWN

YOUNGSTOWN, New York (population 1,957) is a quiet village situated at the northern end of the Niagara River, where Lake Erie's waters flow into Lake Ontario.

There was a small Neutral Indian village here until 1650, when the Iroquois Indians forced them out. Later this site was part of lands awarded to the British as reparation for the Devil's Hole Massacre in 1763. The attack occurred when John Stedman, the keeper of the portage around Niagara Falls, and 24 other men were ambushed by a band of Seneca Indians of the Iroquois Confederacy. Stedman and one or two others were the only survivors. Sixty-five soldiers who later came to the rescue were also killed.

The French built Fort Niagara here in 1678 and originally called it Fort Conti. It was later rebuilt by the French and called Fort Denonville. In 1726, it was rebuilt once again and named Fort Niagara. It was captured and controlled by the British until 1796, when it was taken over by the United States. The British took it over during the War of 1812, but the United States regained control of the fort with the signing of the Treaty of Ghent in 1815. Fort Niagara was restored in 1934 and is open to the public as a New York State Park.

The village of Youngstown was named for John Young in 1808. Young, a Loyalist, also owned businesses across the river in Newark (Niagara-on-the-Lake, Ontario). Youngstown was burned in 1813 in retaliation for the American burning of Newark, during the War of 1812.

Shipbuilding and the shipment of lumber and grain were the principal industries beginning in the 1800s. A gristmill, docks, ferry to Canada and commercial fishing were important aspects of the settlement's history. Youngstown was incorporated as a village in 1854.

Three railroads served Youngstown. The first railroad was the Niagara Falls & Lake Ontario in 1853, and the Canandaigua arrived here in 1856. Both had a brief existence. The electric Youngstown Frontier Railroad was built in 1896. Its tracks were torn up in 1950.

The Fort Niagara Lighthouse was built here at the mouth of the Niagara River in 1872 and was made 11 feet taller to a height of 61 feet in 1900. It continues to stand as a local attraction. Today, the peaceful village of Youngstown is also home to marinas, shops, bed & breakfast establishments, a U.S. Coast Guard station and Old Fort Niagara.

TOP LEFT: An early 20th century postcard view of Fort Niagara at Youngstown, New York. Lake Ontario is in the background.

TOP RIGHT: The 50-room Eldorado Hotel, opened in 1891, was a landmark in Youngstown through the 1930s.

LEWISTON

LEWISTON, New York (population 2,781) is 7 miles north of Niagara Falls at the base of the escarpment over which the Niagara Falls were formed some 12,000 years ago. The view from the top of the escarpment includes the village, the lower Niagara River and the Lake Ontario plain. On a clear day, Toronto, Canada can be seen in the distance across Lake Ontario. Lewiston is a quiet residential village with numerous historic buildings and homes.

A Franciscan missionary discovered a Neutral Indian settlement here in 1626. The Senecas destroyed the village in 1651. In 1678, René Robert Cavalier de La Salle built a storehouse and established a portage around Niagara Falls from what is now Lewiston. The portage was improved when the British took control of the area in 1759. In 1764, the British improved the fortification of the Niagara Portage and constructed a machine to move supplies up the hill. A counter-balance railway known as "The Cradles" lifted freight to the top of the escarpment where it would be placed on wagons for the trip around the falls. After the British had surrendered Fort Niagara in 1796, the village of Lewiston, named for Governor Morgan Lewis, was settled.

During the War of 1812, Lewiston was the American army's headquarters during the Battle of Queenston Heights. In 1813, the British burned the village, but it was quickly rebuilt.

TOP: A postcard view of the suspension bridge crossing the Niagara River at Lewiston. This bridge was used from 1899 until 1962, when the steel arch Lewiston-Queenston Bridge replaced it.

BOTTOM: An early 1900s view of the busy landing on the lower Niagara River at Lewiston, New York.

Following the opening of the Erie Canal in 1825, the portage became less important, but the village continued to prosper as a shipping point for ports on Lake Ontario. Lewiston's present village was laid out in 1835 and incorporated in 1843. A horse-drawn railroad was opened in 1836, followed by a steam railroad in 1851 and the Great Gorge Route (a Niagara Falls scenic railroad) in 1895. Railroads carried passengers to and from Lewiston, where steamers would arrive at the landing on the Niagara River. Steamers made their way down the Niagara from Lewiston and across Lake Ontario to Toronto until the early 20th century.

The Frontier House, a three-story inn constructed from gray stone, was built in 1824. It remains today on the village's main street. The Frontier House is believed to be where James Fenimore Cooper wrote *The Spy*.

A suspension bridge to Queenston, Ontario was completed in 1851 and destroyed in a storm in 1864. A second suspension bridge was built in 1899 and replaced upriver by the arched Lewiston-Queenston Bridge in 1962. The waterfront was often plagued by ice jams as Lake Erie ice made its way down the Niagara River. An ice jam in 1909 did heavy damage to Lewiston's dock area, hotels and other waterfront establishments. Since an ice boom was placed at the entrance to the Niagara River in the 1960s, ice jams are no longer a problem. Artpark, an indoor/outdoor amphitheater for the visual and performing arts, was opened in Lewiston in 1974.

TOP IMAGES: Current and historic images of the 1824 Frontier House at Lewiston, New York.

BOTTOM: A view from the top of the Niagara Escarpment, looking north over Lewiston, New York. The Niagara River, rich farmland of the Niagara Peninsula, Lake Ontario and Toronto, Ontario can be seen in the distance.

Niagara Falls: The Cataract City

ABOVE: The skyline of the city of Niagara Falls, New York includes a casino in the building with the arched roof and several hotels. The round object at center is a tethered balloon, which takes tourists aloft for a view of the area.

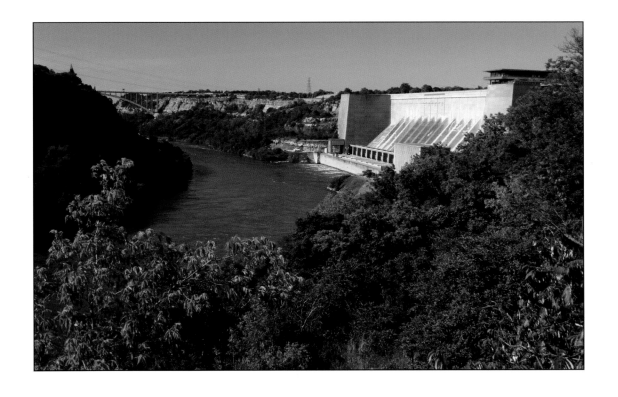

TOP: A scene at Three Sisters Islands in the Niagara Reservation State Park.

BOTTOM: The hydroelectric Robert Moses Power Plant at Niagara Falls, New York went on line 1961. The facility generates 2.4 million kilowatts.

NIAGARA FALLS, New York, (population 55,593) located 15 miles north of Buffalo, sits in the shadow of one of the world's most famous natural wonders. The city is framed on the south and west by the Niagara River, which makes a turn at the cataract.

The Niagara River divides at Goat Island, forming two main waterfalls. The Horseshoe (Canadian) Falls curve around a 2,215-foot crest, dropping water 177 feet. Although the American Falls, with a 1,075-foot crest, is higher at 184 feet, a large pile of rock at its base breaks the water's drop. The falls were originally formed 7 miles north of their present location about 12,000 years ago as a glacial lake poured over the ridge of the Niagara Escarpment into Lake Iroquois (Lake Ontario's glacial predecessor), near what is now Lewiston, New York and Queenston, Ontario. The falls have since carved a gorge to their current location on the 35-mile-long Niagara River, midway between Lake Erie and Lake Ontario.

The city of Niagara Falls has heavy industrial roots. Factories line the upper Niagara River along Buffalo Avenue. The main business district extends along Falls Street and Pine Avenue, and to the north along Main Street. The residential areas are located primarily to the north and east of the downtown area.

TOP: An 1882 panoramic map of Niagara Falls, New York. (Library of Congress, Geography and Map Division)

BOTTOM: Father Louis Hennepin viewed Niagara Falls for the first time in 1678.

Ancestors of the Seneca Indians inhabited the area around Niagara Falls for centuries before Europeans first saw the cataract. The Indian name *Niagara* is translated to mean the "Thunderer of Waters." The first published view of Niagara Falls was based on the recollections of Father Louis Hennepin from a visit he made in 1678. The area was of strategic importance to the French because of the seven-mile portage around the falls. Over the years, the French built log forts at the mouth of the Niagara River at Lake Ontario (see Youngstown), with construction of the present structure beginning in 1726.

The French also built two forts near the falls in 1745 and 1750 to guard the upper terminus of the portage. As the British approached the area in 1759, the French master of the portage burned the two forts near the falls before retreating. The British took over what was left of the forts and built Fort Schlosser. That same year, the British gained control of the region when the French surrendered Fort Niagara. The British remained in control of Fort Niagara and the region until 1796, when the U.S. government took possession.

Augustus Porter, a surveyor, first visited the falls in 1795. His vision of building a manufacturing center brought him back to the area a few years later with his family. He became the master of the portage and named the settlement Manchester after its industrial counterpart in England. The British burned Fort Schlosser on the upper Niagara River and most of the settlement of Manchester during the War of 1812.

With the completion of the Erie Canal in 1825, business along the portage quickly faded, and Porter looked to the falling water and its potential to power industry. The railroad arrived in 1840, and soon mills and factories were well established along the upper rapids and on the rim of the Niagara Gorge. The Roebling Bridge was built across the gorge in 1855, providing a more direct route for rail traffic across southwestern Ontario to Detroit and beyond to Chicago, the shortest possible route to the expanding west. A canal, diverting water from the upper river to the mills along the gorge wall, was completed in 1862. In 1877, Jacob F. Schoellkopf, whose family later merged their holdings with the Niagara Falls Power Company, purchased the canal. By 1881, electricity was being generated. In 1892, Niagara Falls was incorporated as a city. Four years later, lines carried electricity to Buffalo. In 1901, Niagara Falls power lit the Pan-American Exposition in Buffalo.

The availability of electricity brought more industry. Factories sprung up to produce abrasives, food products, paper, foundry materials and machinery. The electricity also powered the development of technology to begin the production of aluminum, carbide, graphite and chemicals. Niagara Falls was an important manufacturing center during both world wars.

In 1956, a rockslide destroyed most of the Schoellkopf Generating Station along the

TOP: Jacob Schoellkopf (1819-1899) owned the hydraulic canal at Niagara Falls. His canal provided power for several mills and an early electric generator. (Local History Department, Niagara Falls, New York Public Library)

ABOVE: Augustus Porter (1769-1849) established a gristmill along the Niagara River and a settlement called Manchester. (Local History Department, Niagara Falls, New York Public Library)

TOP LEFT: Factories using the power of the Niagara River lined the gorge wall through the early 20th century.

BOTTOM: In 1896, Niagara Falls Power Company lines began transmitting electricity 20 miles away to Buffalo. (Local History Department, Niagara Falls, New York Public Library)

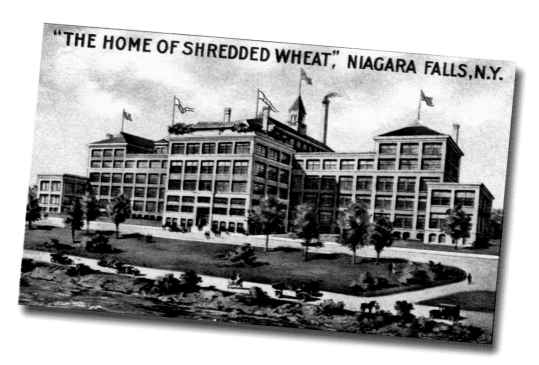

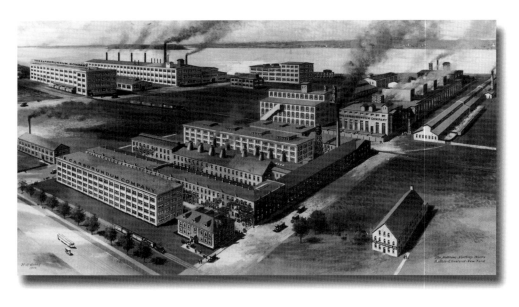

ABOVE: Robert Moses (1888-1981), a powerful public official, oversaw construction of the Niagara Power Project. (Local History Department, Niagara Falls, New York Public Library)

TOP: The Shredded Wheat plant, built in 1901, was known as "The Palace of Light." It closed in 1954.

BOTTOM: In 1895, the Carborundum Company built a plant on the upper Niagara River to manufacture abrasives. (Local History Department, Niagara Falls, New York Public Library)

river's gorge. The crisis led Congress to pass the Niagara Redevelopment Act in 1957. Under the direction of Robert Moses, crews began construction of the Niagara Power Project. When completed in 1961, the project was the largest hydroelectric power complex in the western world.

For nearly a century, there was little civic planning to control the furious growth of industry and the larger problem of the disposal of industrial wastes. Dumps in the area quickly filled, including one at the site of the never completed and abandoned Love Canal, several miles above the falls. A brew of the most toxic chemicals known to man was dumped into Love Canal through the 1940s, seeping into the ground and surfacing in area homes and a school built on the dump. In the 1970s, as the chemicals surfaced, the area was closed and the federal government moved hundreds of residents elsewhere.

Much of the city's central core was demolished in the 1960s and 1970s for urban renewal. Vacant buildings and open spaces exist, despite some development taking place from the 1960s through the 1980s, including the large Niagara Falls Convention Center (now housing a casino), and several retail establishments.

The falls may be viewed from the Niagara Reservation, New York State's oldest State Park dating to 1885. The Reservation includes Goat Island and Prospect Point on the American side of the river. A parkway, beginning several miles upriver from Niagara Falls and extending to Lake Ontario, sliced through the Niagara Reservation as part of Robert Moses's legacy. The portion of the parkway near the falls was later closed, allowing for easier access to the park and rejoining the city with its natural wonder.

During the off-season for tourists and during nighttime hours year-round, more than half of the water in the Niagara River is diverted from the river above the falls to drive turbines in power plants on both sides of the river. More than 90 percent of the remaining water drops over the Horseshoe Falls.

Niagara Falls' area attractions include the Cave of the Winds trip, Schoellkopf Geological Museum, Niagara Falls Aquarium, state parks and the Niagara Power Project Visitor Center. For automobile traffic, three bridges link the U.S. and Canadian sides of the river.

TOP LEFT: An early 20th century view of Niagara Falls from the Steel Arch Bridge.

TOP RIGHT: Tourists were allowed to venture onto the ice bridge until 1912, when ice suddenly broke up, carrying three people to their deaths.

BOTTOM: A nighttime view of Niagara Falls from the Rainbow Bridge.

DAREDEVILS AND SURVIVORS

Niagara Falls has been a lure for those in search of fame and fortune, while others have unintentionally become part of the lore of the falls. In 1829, Sam Patch leaped from a 100-foot-high platform into the water at the foot of the falls. French tightrope walker Charles Blondin crossed the gorge several times in 1859 and 1860 and a number of people made the trip over the falls in various contraptions. Perhaps most famous was Annie Edson Taylor, who survived the plunge in a barrel in 1901.

Only three people are known to have survived the plunge over the falls without the aid of a barrel or any other device. In October 2003, Kirk Jones, 40, of Canton, Michigan, went over the Canadian Horseshoe Falls. Tourists were stunned as Jones quietly jumped into the water just above the falls, floating past on his back before going over headfirst. He pulled himself out of the water onto the rocks below. Jones was immediately arrested and taken away for psychiatric evaluation. In March of 2009, a man survived the plunge in an apparent suicide attempt.

One survivor's trip over the cataract was unintentional. Roger Woodward, a seven-year-old boy, went over the falls in the summer of 1960 after the 12-foot aluminum boat in which he was riding with his sister, Deanne, and family friend, James Honeycutt, was sucked into the upper rapids. After hitting a shoal upstream from the falls, the shear pin on the 7.5 horsepower motor snapped, immobilizing the craft and sending it toward the cataract. In the rapids above the falls, the boat capsized, dumping the trio into the torrent. Two tourists from New Jersey pulled Woodward's sister from the water just feet from the brink. The boy clad only in bathing suit and lifejacket was pulled from the water below the Horseshoe Falls by the crew of the *Maid of the Mist* tour boat. Honeycutt's body was found four days later near the *Maid of the Mist's* Canadian dock.

CLOCKWISE FROM LEFT: French tightrope walker Charles Blondin (1824-1897) made numerous trips across the Niagara River gorge. In 1901, Anna Edson Taylor survived a trip over the falls in a barrel. Taylor with her barrel. Young Roger Woodward was rescued below the falls after plunging over the cataract in 1960. (Local History Department, Niagara Falls, New York Public Library)

Island Club, Grand Island, Buffalo, N. Y.

GRAND ISLAND

GRAND ISLAND, New York (population 18,621) is four miles upstream from Niagara Falls in the Niagara River. The southern tip of the 17,000-acre island extends south nearly opposite Buffalo.

The Senecas called the island *ga-we-not*, meaning "the great island." Father Louis Hennepin referred to *d'une grand ile* in his book about the New World in 1697. He wrote of the *Griffin's* trip past the island to its anchorage close to the entrance of the Niagara River at Black Rock.

In 1796, following the Revolutionary War, the British ceded control of Fort Niagara to the United States and the Iroquois claimed control of the islands in the Niagara River. Representatives of New York State met with the Indians at Buffalo Creek in 1815 and purchased Grand Island and several other islands in the Niagara River for $1,000. By the late 20th century, the Senecas made claim to Grand Island and other islands in the Niagara River.

Between 1817 and 1819, a few people settled on the island, but they were later evicted. In 1824, a large tract of land on the island was purchased by Major Mordecai Noah as a "City of Refuge for Jews." It was later decided that transportation between the island and the mainland was inadequate and the community was never realized.

In 1833, the East Boston Company purchased most of Grand Island to harvest white oak. The lumber was used to build ships in Boston and New York. Once the timber supply was depleted, the land was sold to farmers.

Grand Island, along with Buckhorn and Beaver islands, became the Town of Grand Island in 1852. A post office was established in 1877. The island became a resort for Buffalonians. Several hotels and private clubs were built, and ferries departed from Buffalo to bring passengers to the island.

Before World War I, most of the resorts on Grand Island went out of business as the popularity of the automobile grew, making other destinations more accessible. Additionally, several hotels were destroyed in disastrous fires, and a large dock collapsed in 1912, killing 37.

In the early 20th century, the state purchased Beaver and Buckhorn islands to create parks, connected by bridges to Grand Island. Since the 1820s, ferries had served Grand Island but the need for a bridge grew. After several attempts to have a bridge built, two bridges were finally opened in 1935. One bridge was constructed from the island to Tonawanda and the other from the island to the City of Niagara Falls. The bridges were twinned in the 1960s to become part of the Niagara section of the New York State Thruway. Grand Island and adjacent Beaver Island are home to an amusement park, golf courses and a popular state park and beach.

TOP LEFT: The Island Club was one of several resorts on Grand Island. Grand Island's golden era took place in the late 19th and early 20th centuries when it grew as a town of clubs, hotels and mansions.

TOP RIGHT: Access to the island was greatly improved with by the opening of the North and South Grand Island Bridges in 1935. The bridges were twinned in the early 1960s, becoming part of the New York State Thruway system.

NORTH TONAWANDA

NORTH TONAWANDA, New York (population 33,262) is located along the northern bank of the New York State Barge Canal at its terminus on the Niagara River, four miles southeast of Niagara Falls, opposite Grand Island. The city's business district, along several blocks near the canal, is comprised of two, three and four-story brick buildings dating to the late 19th and early 20th centuries. Most of the homes in the area are from the same era, with some newer housing in developments north and east of the city.

By 1805, a small settlement had been built at the mouth of Tonawanda Creek. The opening of the Erie Canal in 1825 made the area a prime location for the shipment of lumber from the dense forests of the upper Great Lakes. In 1857, the settlement was incorporated as *Tonawanda* from the Seneca language, meaning "swift waters." It consisted of four wards, with the first ward (North Tonawanda) seceding as a result of a battle with the other wards over the use of gravel for paving streets. North Tonawanda was incorporated as a village in 1865. The Twin Cities of North Tonawanda and Tonawanda across the canal were jointly known as "The Lumber City." By 1900, the area became the largest lumber supply center in the world, holding this title for a brief period. Over the years, North Tonawanda has also been a center for the production of iron and steel products, furniture, spark plugs, shingles, paper and amusement park carousels. For many years, jukeboxes, organs, pianos and other musical instruments were produced at the Wurlitzer factory, which opened in 1910.

North Tonawanda has become a bedroom community for both Buffalo and Niagara Falls, and today tourism is a growing part of North Tonawanda's economy. In 1998, Gateway Park was opened, featuring cobblestone streets and a recreational and business section. The city is home to the restored Riviera Theater (1926) with its "Mighty Wurlitzer" organ and the Herschell Carrousel Factory Museum. Canal Fest, an annual eight-day celebration of the history of the Twin Cities, is held during July.

TOP: Looking east along the New York State Barge Canal. North Tonawanda is at left.

BOTTOM: The Rudolf Wurlitzer Company made pianos, organs and jukeboxes at North Tonawanda. A larger factory was built in 1910.

The Lumber District, North Tonawanda, N. Y.

Birds—eye view of some of the dockage at Twin Cities. Tonawanda and N. Tonawanda, N. Y.

TONAWANDA

TONAWANDA, New York (population 16,136) lies along the south bank of the New York State Barge Canal, at its entrance to the Niagara River, 10 miles north of Buffalo. Tonawanda was incorporated as a village in 1854. Similar in appearance to North Tonawanda, the village shared the distinction of being the world's prime lumber supply center with its neighbor across the canal. Tonawanda was incorporated as a city in 1903, separating itself from the residential and industrial township to the south, which bears the same name.

In addition to being a thriving lumber center on the river and canal, Tonawanda also became a transportation center served by several railroads and has been a producer of office furniture, motorboats, shingles, manufactured wood-board and paper.

TOP RIGHT: An early 20th century view of Tonawanda and North Tonawanda.

MIDDLE LEFT: Lakeboats made their way down the Niagara River to Tonawanda Iron & Steel in the early 20th century, while lumber was loaded in the foreground.

MIDDLE RIGHT: Looking west over Tonawanda, New York circa 1905. The Niagara River and Grand Island are in the background.

BOTTOM: Unloading lumber at Tonawanda in an early 20th century view. The Tonawanda communities were jointly known as the "Lumber City."

Buffalo: Queen City of the Great Lakes

PANORAMA: Buffalo, New York from the Erie Basin Marina.

BOTTOM: Buffalo's Main Street also carries the tracks of a light rail public transit system.

MIDDLE: The Peace Bridge connects Buffalo with Fort Erie, Ontario.

BOTTOM: The Darwin Martin House (1904) is one of several examples of the works of famed architect Frank Lloyd Wright in Buffalo.

ABOVE: The skyline of Buffalo, New York includes the classic art deco city hall, modern office buildings and upscale waterfront residences.

BUFFALO, New York (city population: 292,648, metro population: 1,170,111) lies at the eastern end of Lake Erie, where the lake empties into the Niagara River.

Buffalo, the "City of Good Neighbors" and the "Queen City of the Great Lakes," is well known for lake-effect snow, chicken wings and its industrial heritage. But the city's story goes much deeper. Buffalo's location on Lake Erie assured its position as one of America's transportation and industrial giants. The city was carefully planned by one of America's leading landscape architects, and the wealth from its early industrial prowess remains showcased in its architectural, cultural and civic assets.

Indians had inhabited this region for hundreds of years by the time French explorer René Robert Cavalier de La Salle's ship, the *Griffin*, was towed up the Niagara River in 1679 to what is now Buffalo. The French settled in the area in 1758 at the mouth of Buffalo Creek (River), but a year later the British burned the settlement. With the exception of British

troops, who occasionally camped along the river, white settlement of the area did not occur again for several years. The Seneca Indians inhabited the area until they sold their lands after the American Revolution.

The Holland Land Company purchased a large tract of the land in Upstate New York, which included Buffalo. Joseph Ellicott mapped the site of

Buffalo in 1799, calling the settlement New Amsterdam. He divided the land in 1803, modeling it after plans his brother, Major Andrew Ellicott, assisted in laying out for Washington, D.C. The name New Amsterdam did not take hold as residents preferred Buffalo. There are several theories as to why this place is called Buffalo, the most common being a mispronunciation of the French *beau fleuve*, or "beautiful river."

Buffalo was an organizing point for troops during the War of 1812. In December of 1813, a British force burned the settlement, but most of Buffalo's 500 inhabitants returned a few months later to rebuild. In 1814, American troops captured Fort Erie, across the Niagara River from Buffalo, and continued down the river to Chippawa and finally Lundy's Lane, where they were defeated by the British. Buffalo was incorporated as a village in 1816. By 1819, the first steamboat to ply the Great Lakes, the *Walk-in-the-Water*, had been built here.

Buffalo's exponential growth began in 1825 following the opening of the Erie Canal. As the western terminus of the canal, Buffalo was the transition point for the shipment of farm products from the west and manufactured goods from the east. In 1832, the village of 12,000 was incorporated as a city. The expanding commerce drove Buffalo into manufacturing, as foundries opened and the Buffalo Steam Engine Works was incorporated.

The scourge of Asiatic cholera had spread through Europe in 1831 and arrived by ships bringing immigrants up the St. Lawrence River and through the Great Lakes. A cholera epidemic in Buffalo killed 120 people in 1832, and other epidemics hit the city in 1834, 1849 and 1854.

William G. Fargo helped start the Wells-Fargo Company in 1841 and Joseph Dart invented the steam-powered grain elevator here in 1843, assuring Buffalo's position as a grain port. The University of Buffalo was founded in 1846 under the leadership of Millard Fillmore, who became President of the United States in 1850.

By 1850, the rapid development of railroads threatened Buffalo's position as the key transition point in the east-west trade route. However, the threat was eliminated as the city became a railroad center. By the mid-20th century, Buffalo was the second largest railroad center in the United States.

During the Civil War period, Buffalo was a key terminus on the Underground Railroad, with the freedom of Canada in view just across the Niagara River.

In 1870, the population had swelled to more than 150,000 as industries were fueled by the coal brought by railroads from Pennsylvania and ore transported by boats from the Lake Superior region. During this decade, Samuel Longhorn Clemens, better known as Mark Twain, was editor of the *Buffalo Express*. Water, sewer and gas pipes were laid under newly paved streets. Irish and German immigrants arrived to work in the burgeoning industries. Grover Cleveland was elected mayor in 1881 and in 1884, he became the second Buffalo resident to

ABOVE: Joseph Ellicott (1760-1826) was a surveyor for the Holland Land Company and laid out the city of Buffalo. (Local History Department, Niagara Falls, New York Public Library)

ABOVE LEFT: Millard Fillmore (1800-1874) was the 13th President of the United States and a resident of Buffalo. (Library of Congress, Prints & Photographs Division LC-USZ62-48559)

BOTTOM: Grover Cleveland (1837-1908) was the Mayor of Buffalo and the 24th President of the United States. (Library of Congress, Prints & Photographs Division LC-USZ61-89)

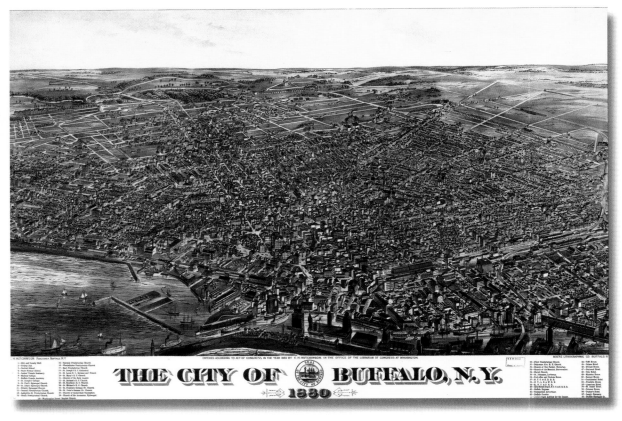

become President of the United States. Buffalo's 19 independent breweries expanded, using vast amounts of barley stored in the city's grain elevators. In the meantime, Buffalo's industrial barons showcased their accumulated wealth by building mansions along Delaware Avenue and other nearby streets. These showplaces were similar to those on "Millionaire's Row" along Cleveland's Euclid Avenue.

Frederick Law Olmstead, who laid out New York's Central Park, redesigned the urban landscape of Buffalo between 1870 and 1898, laying out parkways, planning grounds for civic buildings and designing five parks.

Buffalo's growth as an industrial giant continued as nearby Niagara Falls was harnessed to produce abundant inexpensive electricity near the turn of the century. The city was the eighth largest in the U.S. in 1890. By 1900, Buffalo had surpassed Chicago as the nation's largest inland port. Buffalo also became the second largest rail and livestock-processing center. In 1901, the miracle of electricity was highlighted at the Pan-American Exposition, but Buffalo's fair was tarnished by the assassination of the visiting president, William McKinley.

In the early 20th century, immigrants continued to arrive in great numbers to work in the city's factories and mills. Poles and Germans settled in parts of Buffalo's East Side; Italians on the West Side; Irish in South Buffalo; African-Americans near the downtown area around Michigan Street; a Hungarian community and another Polish settlement grew in the Black Rock section, along the Niagara River.

ABOVE: President William McKinley was assassinated at Buffalo's Pan-American Exposition in 1901. (Library of Congress, Prints & Photographs Division LC-USZ62-8198)

TOP: A panoramic map of Buffalo from 1880. (Library of Congress, Geography and Map Division)

The city produced automobiles, furniture and many other products. Ford, General Motors, Dunlop Tire and Rubber, DuPont and Republic Steel built plants here. The World Wars kept Buffalo at work with mills and factories operating at capacity along the lakeshore and on the Buffalo and Niagara Rivers Aircraft factories contributed to war efforts. The city's population peaked at 580,132 in 1950 and Buffalo was the 15th largest city in the country. Flight to the suburbs and a shifting economic base led to the loss of nearly half of the city's population between 1950 and 2000.

Main Street from Shelton Square.

Delaware Park. Buffalo. N.Y.

Buffalo today continues to produce glass, rubber, automotive parts, plastics, electronics and aircraft parts, and has a growing high-technology sector. The city possesses community assets usually associated with much larger cities. It is home to several colleges and universities. The renowned Buffalo Philharmonic Orchestra performs at Kleinhans Music Hall. The world-class Albright-Knox Art Gallery includes sculptures and paintings dating back to 3,000 B.C. along with the works of Cézanne, Willem de Kooning, Van Gogh, Matisse, Monet, Picasso, Renoir, Marc Chagall, Jackson Pollock and Andy Warhol. Buffalo's architectural assets include John J. Wade's 32-story Art Deco City Hall, Louis Sullivan's Prudential Building, six Frank Lloyd Wright homes including the Darwin Martin House and Martin's summer home known as Graycliff at Derby on Lake Erie, Eliel and Eero Saarinen's Kleinhans Music Hall and Charles B. Atwood's Ellicott Square Building. Many prominent people are buried at Buffalo's historic Forest Lawn Cemetery, including President Millard Fillmore; Red Jacket, Chieftain of the Senecas; William Fargo, founder of the Wells-Fargo Express; and Willis Carrier, inventor of air conditioning.

Other attractions include The Buffalo Zoological Gardens, Buffalo and Erie County Historical Society, Frederick Law Olmstead's Park and parkway system, the Buffalo Museum of Science, Shea's Performing Arts Center, Studio Arena Theatre and the Naval and Military Park on the waterfront. A new terminal building and gates were opened at Buffalo-Niagara International Airport in 1997. The Buffalo Bills (NFL) play at the 75,339-seat Ralph Wilson Stadium in suburban Orchard Park, and the Sabres (NHL) play in the 18,595-seat HSBC Arena, which opened in 1996. Baseball's AAA-class Buffalo Bisons (International League) play in the 21,050-seat Dunn Tire Park, built in 1988.

TOP LEFT: Main Street in Buffalo, circa 1905.

TOP RIGHT: An early 20th century view of Buffalo's Delaware Park. The Albright (Albright-Knox) Art Gallery is at left. The Buffalo and Erie County Historical Society is at right.

BOTTOM: Buffalo's busy inner harbor, circa 1910.

LACKAWANNA

LACKAWANNA, New York (population 19,064) is situated four miles south of Buffalo on the eastern shore of Lake Erie. Originally known as Limestone Hill and incorporated as a city in 1909, Lackawanna is named for the Scranton, Pennsylvania steel company that moved its operations here in 1905.

In 1922, Bethlehem Steel Company acquired the Lackawanna Steel Company, doubling its capacity by 1930. The unmistakable odor of the smoke of steel making billowed across the city and Buffalo's southern suburbs every day until 1982, when Bethlehem ended steel production at Lackawanna.

The road through the city reveals the ghosts of its industrial heyday as N.Y. Route 5 (Hamburg Turnpike) passes the 1,300-acre site of Bethlehem Steel's mills. Most of the more than 50 long, narrow buildings have been torn down, but train tracks and power lines continue to mark the landscape. Over the years, African-Americans and Europeans of mostly Polish and Hungarian descent and others made up a workforce often numbering more than 20,000, to labor in the hot and grimy mills.

The city is much cleaner today than during much of the 20th century when Bethlehem Steel Company was in full operation, but the rows of plain looking houses stand as a reminder of a day when Lackawanna's Bethlehem works produced 5 percent of the nation's steel.

Lackawanna is the site of the Basilica of Our Lady of Victory, a white limestone structure with a Byzantine dome. The structure originally included two 165-foot towers, which were

ABOVE: Father Nelson H. Baker (1841-1936) helped the underprivileged and built Our Lady of Victory Shrine. (Our Lady of Victory Institutions)

TOP RIGHT: Bethlehem Steel's massive plant at Lackawanna was once the world's largest producer of steel. (Lackawanna Steel Plant Museum)

MIDDLE: A 1930s view of the rows of company-owned homes, which housed Lackawanna's steelworkers. (Lackawanna Steel Plant Museum)

BOTTOM: Our Lady of Victory Basilica & National Shrine was the second in the U.S. to receive a basilica designation in 1926. Its copper-topped dome and twin bell towers can be seen for miles.

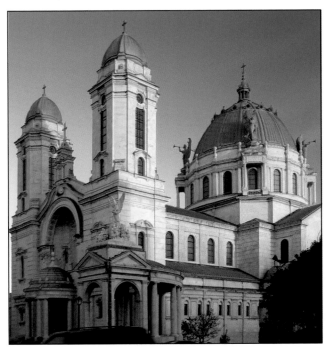

shortened after one of the towers was damaged by lightning. The shrine, which took five years to build, was completed in 1926 at a cost of nearly $3 million. It was the crowning achievement of Msgr. Nelson Henry Baker (1841-1936), who was well known for his social work. The interior of the shrine is decorated with 48 varieties of marble, and the work of the finest craftsmen from around the world is represented at this National Shrine.

A modern sight has replaced the rust-belt panorama of smokestacks in Lackawanna. Several 400-foot-tall windmills used to generate electricity were built and put on line in 2007 on the former site of the Bethlehem Steel Company's works (photo on page 91).

HAMBURG

HAMBURG, New York (town population: 56,259 village population: 10,116) is 11 miles south of downtown Buffalo. The town borders on Lake Erie's shoreline, with the busy village of Hamburg set back four miles from the lake. Bluffs 50 to 100 feet high mark the lakeshore. Eighteen-Mile Creek, well known among fossil collectors, skirts the southern part of the town, on its way to Lake Erie. The area was first settled in 1804 and named for Hamburg, Germany in 1812. Hamburg was incorporated in 1874.

Hamburg claims to be the birthplace of the hamburger. Two brothers, Charles and Frank Menches, traveled between fairs and farmers' picnics in the early 1880s. They sold sandwiches made of pork sausage, fried egg and liverwurst. In 1885, while vending at the Erie County Fair (also known as the Hamburg Fair), they ran out of pork sausage. The brothers used beef as a substitute and made patties out of the meat. The hamburger was born.

The Erie County Fair began in 1819 in the city of Buffalo and was moved to Hamburg in 1868. Also known as America's Fair, the Erie County Fair is the largest independent county fair in North America. The 11-day event takes place each August on the 265-acre fairgrounds.

A suburb of Buffalo, Hamburg is also home to Woodlawn Beach State Park and Buffalo Raceway, a harness racing facility.

TOP: Buffalo Raceway, located in Hamburg, began operations in 1942.

MIDDLE: The cliffs along Lake Erie shoreline at Wanakah in the town of Hamburg.

BOTTOM: Hamburg, New York's Main Street, circa 1905.

ANGOLA

ANGOLA, New York (population 2,226) is 20 miles southwest of Buffalo, set back two miles from Lake Erie. Big Sister Creek skirts the eastern side of the village.

Settlement of the village now called Angola began in 1852, as the Buffalo & State Line Railroad laid tracks and built a station here. Originally called Evans Station, the settlement was renamed Angola in 1855. The railroad, mills and other businesses brought growth to the community.

Angola was the site of a tragic railroad accident in 1867 on the Lake Shore & Michigan Southern Railroad. A train headed for Buffalo derailed on the bridge over Big Sister Creek. Passenger cars fell into the creek below and fires from potbelly stoves rapidly spread, killing more than 50 people in what was known as the "Angola Horror."

With more than 600 residents, Angola incorporated as a village in 1873. In 1881, the Buffalo, Pittsburgh & Western Railroad (Nickel Plate) was built through the southern part of the village. Trolleys ran through Angola between 1908 and 1932. Passengers were able to depart for Erie or Buffalo every 40 minutes on Buffalo & Lake Erie Traction Company trolleys.

Willis H. Carrier, the engineer who developed many processes of air conditioning, was born here in 1876. Key industries in Angola have included the manufacture of bicycles, tile and brewing equipment. A canning company, established in 1928, continues operation today. Several public beaches and residential areas along Lake Erie are nearby.

ABOVE: Two historic post-cards of Angola's Main Street during the early 20th century.

SILVER CREEK, N.Y.

SILVER CREEK

SILVER CREEK, New York (population 2,896) is located 30 miles southwest of Buffalo where two creeks, Walnut and Silver, join to meet Lake Erie.

The first settlers arrived here from Massachusetts in 1803 and built a gristmill. Less than 20 years later, the harbor was developed and wharves, shipyards and a warehouse were built.

The settlement was originally named Walnut Creek for a giant black walnut tree that had fallen here in 1822. The trunk of the tree, with a 31-foot circumference, was said to be the biggest tree east of the Rockies. A local grocer transformed a section of the tree into an addition for his store by hollowing it. The tree was sold several times to various people who wished to exhibit it. First, it was sent to Buffalo, then down the Erie Canal to New York, and finally to a museum in London where it was destroyed in a fire. The name Silver Creek was adopted from the other creek that flows through the community. Silver Creek was incorporated as a village in 1848. Silver Creek's shipping industry declined with the arrival of the railroad in 1852.

Silver Creek was the site of two disasters during the 19th century. In 1841, the steamer *Lake Erie* caught fire and sank a mile off shore with nearly 200 German and Swiss immigrants aboard. The bodies of 175, who were unable to make the swim, washed ashore or were picked up later by passing ships. In 1886, 20 people were killed in a head-on train collision.

During the late 19th and early 20th centuries, Silver Creek grew because of its location at the northeastern end of Lake Erie's grape-growing belt. Today, the village features quiet shaded streets and a business district running along U.S. Route 20 and N.Y. Route 5. The Skew Arch, a unique stone railroad bridge built in 1869, is located on Jackson Street.

TOP LEFT: The S. Howes Company, circa 1910. The business, established in 1856 to produce equipment used to clean grain, continues to operate in the village. A baking company also operates in the village.

TOP RIGHT: An early 20th century view of the beach and Lighthouse Point at Silver Creek, New York.

BOTTOM: An 1892 panoramic map of Silver Creek, New York. (Library of Congress, Geography and Map Division)

DUNKIRK

DUNKIRK, New York (population 13,131) is 40 miles southwest of Buffalo. Point Gratiot and a breakwater protect the harbor. The industrial city is located along the eastern grape-growing belt of Lake Erie.

In 1809, the settlement was founded as Chadwick's Bay, named for Solomon Chadwick, an early settler. The settlement was renamed Dunkirk in 1817 by Elisha Jenkins, a proprietor of the village who had done business in Dunkerque, France. Chadwick's Bay reminded Jenkins of the harbor at Dunkerque. Dunkirk was incorporated as a village in 1837 and as a city in 1880. A lighthouse on Point Gratiot was established in 1827, with the present structure dating to 1875.

Beginning as a fishing community, the city grew around the harbor. Factories also sprang up, producing oil-refining machinery, shovels, glass, boilers, radiators, tools and silk. In 1869, the Brooks Locomotive Company was formed by Horatio G. Brooks and by 1884 had produced 1,000 locomotives. The company merged with several other locomotive firms in 1901 to form the American Locomotive Company. The last steam locomotive was produced at Dunkirk in 1928, but the Dunkirk operation continued to produce thermal products before closing in 1962. Dunkirk's Metz Brewery was established in 1870, later becoming the Fred Koch Brewery, which operated until 1980.

The smokestacks of the NRG power plant (formerly Niagara-Mohawk) on Point Gratiot can be seen for miles up and down the lakeshore, marking Dunkirk's position along the horizon. Along with its industrial base, grape vineyards, farms, tourism and recreational opportunities such as boating, fishing and swimming also support Dunkirk's economy. The Dunkirk Historical Lighthouse and Veterans Park Museum is located on Point Gratiot along with a public beach and park.

TOP LEFT: Dunkirk, New York, circa 1910.

TOP RIGHT: The 61-foot Dunkirk Lighthouse on Point Gratiot was built in 1875, replacing the original lighthouse, which was established in 1827.

BOTTOM: An aerial view of Dunkirk, New York. The NRG power plant is at left. New York State's Route 5, left to right, follows the shore of Lake Erie. (Ken Winters, U.S. Army Corps of Engineers, Buffalo District)

FREDONIA

FREDONIA, New York (population 10,706) is three miles south of Dunkirk in the heart of the grape belt. The attractive village is set around Barker Commons, a large town square with fountains and a gazebo.

Originally known as Canadaway for the creek that runs through the village, the settlement became known as Fredonia in the 1820s and was incorporated in 1830.

Fredonia claims a number of "firsts." The first natural gas well in the U.S. was established and the first Grange was built here during the 1860s. In 1873, the first meeting of the Women's Christian Temperance Union was held at the Fredonia Baptist Church to fight against the fermentation of local grapes.

The Fredonia Academy was established in 1826, changing its name to the Fredonia Normal School, later the Fredonia State Teachers College, and finally today's State University of New York at Fredonia (SUNY Fredonia).

The production of grapes continues to be a driving force in the area's economy. The Red Wing Company (Carriage House Companies) operates a processing plant in the village.

TOP LEFT: The Baptist Church at Fredonia was the birthplace of the Women's Christian Temperance Union in 1873.

TOP RIGHT: Fredonia's Historic District includes an attractive village green known as Barker Commons.

BOTTOM: Main Street, Fredonia, New York during the 1920s.

BROCTON

BROCTON, New York (population 1,547) is seven miles southwest of Fredonia along U.S. Route 20.

Deacon Elijah Fay arrived here from Massachusetts and found the area particularly fit for growing grapes. He began to raise grapes on his farm here in 1818. Fay tried a number of varieties before planting Isabella and Catawba grapes in 1824. He produced more than 300 gallons of wine annually until his death in 1860. Elijah Fay's son, Joseph, and others purchased land from the elder Fay, starting a wine house that increased annual production to 16,000 gallons within a few years.

Other businesses grew, including sawmills, a gristmill, a cider mill and a tannery. Brocton was also the terminus of the Buffalo, Corry & Pittsburgh Railroad. Completed in 1866, the railroad operated for a few years before it went bankrupt.

The bustling Brocton incorporated as a village in 1894. In 1913, to commemorate the centennial of the Town of Portland, a double arch was erected at Brocton's main intersection. The landmark Brocton Arch remains the most prominent feature of the village's business district.

TOP LEFT: Main Street, Brocton, New York, circa 1919.

TOP RIGHT: A grape juice label from Huntley Manufacturing Company, one of several Brocton area grape juice producers.

BOTTOM: The Crandall Panel Factory, Brocton, New York.

In 1933, businessman Jack Kaplan purchased a grape processing plant here and formed the National Grape Corporation. This organization helped revive the declining Concord grape growing business. During World War II, the government imposed price ceilings on commodities and the National Grape Corporation. Many growers began to form their own small cooperatives to avoid the controls and get higher prices. Kaplan sold the Brocton plant to the growers with the understanding the growers would form a single, large cooperative. The growers agreed and formed The National Grape Cooperative Association Inc. in 1945. Today, the cooperative operates in five states and in Canada.

Scene from Barcelona Light House along Lake Erie, Westfield, N. Y.

BARCELONA

BARCELONA, New York is a small hamlet on the shore of Lake Erie, 10 miles east of the Pennsylvania border. Grape vineyards and the sheer cliffs along Lake Erie's shore surround Barcelona, part of the town of Westfield.

Barcelona was a busy harbor community in the early 1800s as salt, grain and lumber were moved over land on the Portage Trail, a commerce route for goods between the lake and points to the south. The U.S. government designated the settlement an official U.S. Port of Entry in 1827.

The Barcelona Light was erected in 1828, initially lit by oil lamps. In 1830, escaping natural gas was discovered in the area along the lake and the lighthouse became the first in the world to be illuminated by natural gas. The gas was channeled through wooden pipes from the bed of Chautauqua Creek, three quarters of a mile away.

By 1831, three large docks and four warehouses operated in Barcelona. The village grew as a fishing center into the early 20th century, as local boats pulled in catches of herring, trout, suckers, blue pike and whitefish. When the commercial fishing industry died, Barcelona became a quiet place. Today, the harbor supports recreational fishing and boating, and the historic lighthouse is a private residence.

TOP: An early 20th century view of Barcelona, New York.

MIDDLE: A circa-1908 view of the historic lighthouse at Barcelona. The 1828 lighthouse was the first in the world to be lit by natural gas. Today it is a private residence.

BOTTOM: Barcelona was a very active fishing port on Lake Erie from the 1800s through the early 20th century. Fish houses and drying nets were a common sight in this settlement.

WESTFIELD

WESTFIELD, New York (population 3,481) is 17 miles southwest of Dunkirk, set back two miles from the lakeshore and the harbor hamlet of Barcelona. Like other towns in the area, the village borders numerous grape vineyards. In September, the fragrance of ripened grapes fills the air.

Cross Roads, as Westfield was originally known, was first settled by white men in 1802, when James McMahan of Pennsylvania cleared land and planted his first crop. By 1804, mills were operating and more settlers arrived. The village was incorporated within the town of Westfield in 1833.

Westfield lies on the eastern grape belt, which is between five and seven miles wide, extending from the Cattaraugus and Chautauqua County border nearly to Erie, Pennsylvania. The clay soil and the climate tempered by Lake Erie make the area favorable for grape vineyards. In 1818, Deacon Elijah Fay planted his first vineyard in nearby Brocton. By 1859, Fay's son had opened the area's first winery. The grape growing industry flourished, acreage increased and the grape growers' union was formed in 1866. Production peaked in the 1890s. Overproduction and pressure from the Women's Christian Temperance Union, which battled against the fermentation of local grapes, destroyed the

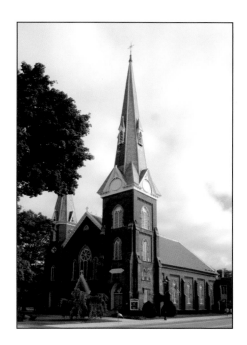

market. But dentist Dr. Thomas B. Welch revived it, creating a new market for the grapes as he learned to preserve the juice in an unfermented form. Welch and his son, Charles E., also a doctor, opened the world headquarters of Welch's Grape Juice Company here in 1896, after operating for a time in Watkins Glen, New York. To support the business, shops were built to manufacture baskets to package the grapes.

By the early 1970s, winemaking had made a comeback through family-owned operations. Welch's moved its headquarters to Concord, Massachusetts in 1983, closing its general offices in Westfield in 2002, but some employees remain at the processing plant. The area's vineyards also continue to produce grapes for the company.

Today, the Westfield's Main Street is lined with shops. Concord grapes still cover the landscape along with newer winemaking varieties like Niagara, Seyval and Chambourchin. The area's harvest also includes apples, cherries, sweet corn, peaches, pumpkins, raspberries, tomatoes and blueberries. Maple syrup is also produced in the area. Westfield is home to several food-processing companies along with a fabricating and machining company. The seven-mile-long, 100-foot-deep Chautauqua Gorge between here and Mayville at the northern end of Chautauqua Lake, attracts hikers. Attractions also include the McLurg Museum (an 1820 mansion), the William Seward Inn and the nearby Chautauqua Institution.

TOP LEFT: The First Presbyterian Church at Westfield was built in 1879 in the High Victorian Gothic style.

TOP RIGHT: Looking east along Main Street in Westfield, New York, circa 1905.

BOTTOM: A 1910-era view of Westfield, New York from the western side of the village.

Main St. looking East, Ripley, N. Y.

RIPLEY

TOP: Ripley, New York circa 1905.

BOTTOM: The view from the ridge overlooking the grape vineyards at Ripley, New York. Lake Erie is in the background.

PAGE 91 CLOCKWISE: The silhouette of a lakeboat from New York State's shoreline. The Peace Bridge links the U.S. and Canada at the entrance of the Niagara River. Windmills generate electricity at Lackawanna. The old Buffalo Main Lighthouse was built in 1833.

RIPLEY, New York (population 1,030) is a small village just inside the New York-Pennsylvania line, 10 miles west of Westfield on U.S. Route 20.

Alexander Cochran, an Irish immigrant, settled what is now Ripley in 1802. The township was known as Quincy in 1816 and was named Ripley in 1873 for General Eleazar Wheeler Ripley, a veteran of the War of 1812.

The town grew after the opening of the Erie Canal and continued with the arrival of the Buffalo & State Line Railroad in 1852 and the Nickel Plate Railroad in 1881. Trolleys running between Erie and Buffalo came through the village beginning in 1905. In 1917, U.S. Route 20 was paved between Silver Creek and the Pennsylvania line, running through Ripley.

Two men from Ripley gained different kinds of fame in two different centuries. Benjamin Franklin Goodrich, born in 1841, founded the nation's first rubber manufacturing company. TWA pilot John J. Testrake was at the controls when his plane was skyjacked to the Middle East during a 17-day ordeal in 1985.

Ripley was known as the "Marriage Capital of the World" between the 1880s and 1937. Before passage of an "anti-hasty" marriage law, many out-of-state couples came to Ripley to tie the knot. Justices competed for business, erecting large neon signs in front of their homes. Many were open for business 24 hours a day.

Today, Ripley's largest business is grape growing. Vineyards were first planted here in the middle of the 19th century. In the early 20th century, two companies produced baskets to hold the grapes harvested here. Other types of farming are also important to Ripley's economy, and several wineries operate in the area.

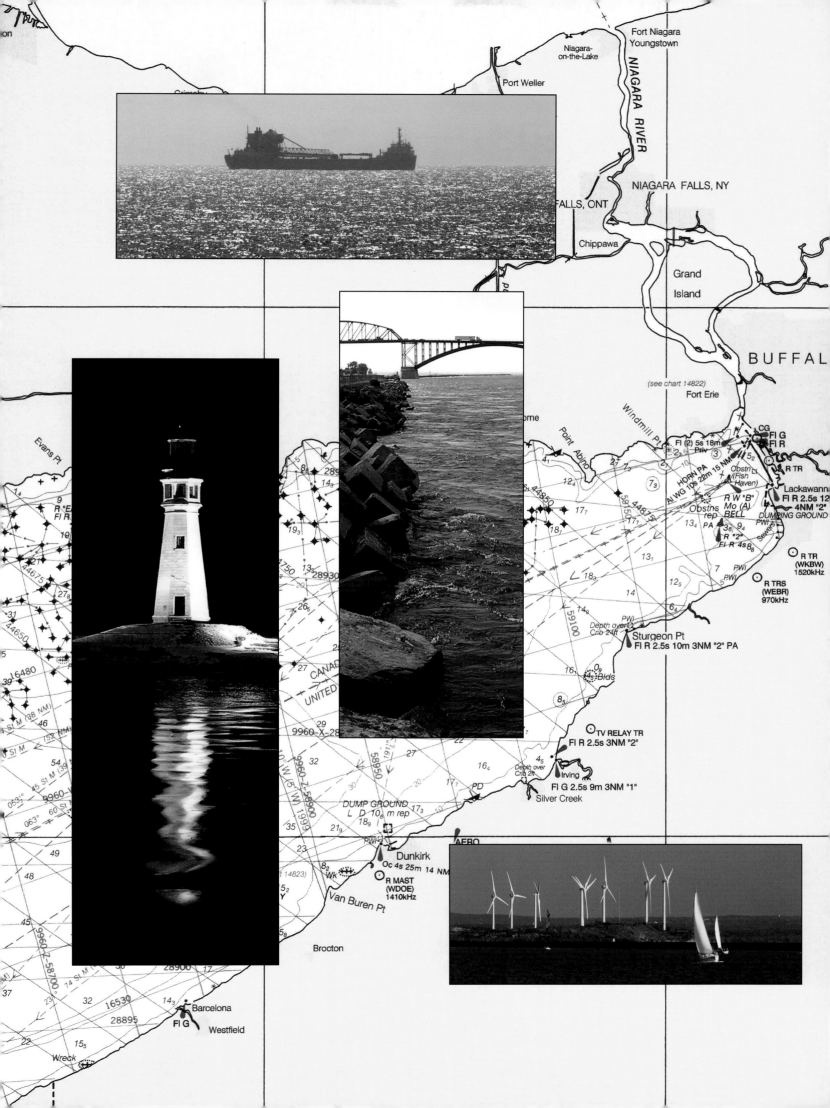

8 Pennsylvania Shoreline

The Commonwealth of Pennsylvania has 45 miles of Lake Erie shoreline. The lake plain is only a few miles wide in this area, with the Allegheny Plateau and terraced ancient shorelines of Lake Erie's predecessors clearly visible paralleling the lakeshore to the south. This is a region of vineyards, apple and cherry orchards and produce farms. Halfway along Pennsylvania's shoreline is Presque Isle, a 3,200-acre sandy peninsula, whose arm gently reaches into Lake Erie. The seven-mile-long sand spit is attached to the mainland four miles west of downtown Erie and protects Presque Isle Bay, a deep and wide harbor for the city of Erie.

TOP: An aerial view of Presque Isle, which protects Pennsylvania's lone port on Lake Erie. (Ken Winters, U.S. Army Corps of Engineers, Buffalo District)

MAP: Historically, Erie has been well connected to Cleveland to the west, Pittsburgh to south and Buffalo to the east.

BOTTOM: Waldameer Park in Erie, one of the nation's oldest amusement parks, opened in 1896.

PAGE 93: A dramatic sky over Lake Erie and Presque Isle State Park at Erie, Pennsylvania.

Pennsylvania received land in the northwestern part of the state through a treaty with the Six Nations, but the triangular portion that includes most of the current frontage on Lake Erie was not part of the acquisition. The 42nd parallel, forming the northern boundary of Pennsylvania, intersects Lake Erie just three miles east of the Ohio border. This appeared to be the only frontage Pennsylvania would have on Lake Erie while other states had claims to various portions of northwestern Pennsylvania. The other states eventually ceded these lands to the U.S. Government. In 1788, Pennsylvania made a plea to Congress to obtain additional frontage on the lake. Following a negotiation with the Iroquois, the Erie Triangle was subsequently sold to Pennsylvania in 1792 for 75 cents an acre to be settled by the Pennsylvania Population Company and others.

Except for Erie and its suburban communities, there are really only two boroughs of significant size near the lake: North East, near the New York State border, and Girard, which lies between Erie and the Ohio border. The numerous creeks that drain into Lake Erie between the New York State line and the city of Erie are named for their distance from Erie, starting with Twenty-Mile Creek.

NORTH EAST

NORTH EAST, Pennsylvania (population 4,601) is a quiet borough on U.S. Route 20, four miles west of the New York State border and 16 miles east of Erie. It is named for North East Township, which is in the northeast section of the Erie Triangle, the portion of Pennsylvania that extends north to Lake Erie. The village contains numerous Victorian-era mansions and well-maintained homes, tree-lined Main Street and Gibson Park. The downtown business district with its intact grouping of original commercial and residential buildings is listed on the National Register of Historic Places. Sixteen-Mile Creek skirts the western edge of the village.

North East was settled in 1801. By 1809, traffic between Buffalo and the west was heavy enough to support two taverns. Originally called Burgettstown and later called Gibsonville, the village was incorporated as the Borough of North East in 1834. The first grapevines were planted here in 1850, and by 1869, the South Shore Wine Company was formed, followed by others.

Today, North East Township has five wineries and thousands of acres of vineyards. Concord, Portland and white Niagara grapes are used to make jelly and wine, with much of the harvest processed at the Welch's grape juice plant located here. Grapes are so much a part of life in North East that the public schools' sports teams are called the "Grapepickers."

Other industries include the manufacture of industrial storage systems, commercial frozen pizza, copper products and auto/truck brake components. North East is home to the Lake Shore Railway Museum and a branch campus of Mercyhurst College. North of the borough lies a beach and park named after North East native Halli Reid, who in 1993 became the first woman to swim across Lake Erie.

TOP LEFT: The method of harvesting grapes has changed in the days since this circa-1905 image, but the backdrop of Lake Erie remains at North East, Pennsylvania.

MIDDLE RIGHT: Looking south on Lake Street at the corner of Main Street. The buildings in this early 1900s view remain today in North East, Pennsylvania's historic downtown district.

BOTTOM: A familiar sight at North East, Pennsylvania, circa 1905, along the grape belt of Pennsylvania and New York State.

Erie: The Gem City

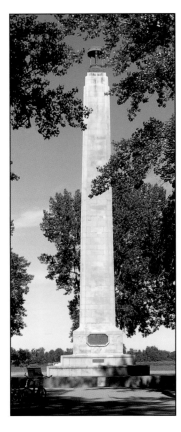

TOP: The *Adam E. Cornelius* of the American Steamship Company unloads gravel at the Erie Sand & Gravel Company's dock in Erie's well-protected harbor. The boat has been working the Great Lakes since 1973.

LEFT: Perry Monument on Presque Isle honors Commodore Oliver Hazard Perry, victor in the Battle of Lake Erie during the War of 1812.

RIGHT: Family houseboats, which have been passed through generations, have been allowed to remain at Presque Isle State Park.

TOP: Erie's Bayfront District includes the Erie Maritime Museum, Public Library and the Erie Intermodel Transportation Center.

MIDDLE LEFT: Jerry Uht Park is the home to baseball's Erie SeaWolves.

MIDDLE RIGHT: Opened in 1931, the historic Warner Theater was built by the Warner Brothers. Seating 2,500, it hosts concerts, plays and is the home of the Erie Philharmonic.

BOTTOM: The North Pierhead Lighthouse is a beacon for boats heading for the protection of Presque Isle Bay, which serves as Erie's Harbor.

ERIE

ERIE, Pennsylvania (city population: 103,717, metro population: 280,843) is located on the shores of Lake Erie, midway between the New York and Ohio borders, in the northwestern portion of Pennsylvania. Erie is the Commonwealth's only port on the lake.

ABOVE: General "Mad" Anthony Wayne (1754-1796) defeated the Miami Confederacy in the Battle of Fallen Timbers. He died at the Erie blockhouse.

TOP: Erie, State Street, circa 1910. The thoroughfare is the city's main street.

MIDDLE RIGHT: An 1870 panoramic map of Erie, Pennsylvania. (Geography and Maps Division, Library of Congress)

BOTTOM: The *Niagara* was one of six vessels in Commodore Oliver Hazard Perry's fleet. The reconstructed brig's home berth is on Erie's harbor.

The city stretches from east to west on a plain above the lake and extends southward to higher ground along ridges that were once the shorelines of Lake Erie's predecessors, Lake Warren and Lake Whittlesey. The city's well-protected harbor is nearly landlocked by the curving seven-mile-long Presque Isle Peninsula. The French name *presque ile* means "almost an island." Geologists have determined the peninsula was built by the action of the eastward-moving winds, waves and currents and was likely located three miles west of its present location when it first formed. According to Eriez Indian legend, the peninsula was created when a group from the tribe ventured out into the lake to see where the setting sun went. This angered the spirits of the lake, causing a great storm. To protect the Eriez from the storm, the "Great Spirit" stretched his left arm out into the lake to shelter the Eriez. The Eriez, from which the city and lake were named, inhabited the area until 1654, when the Senecas of the Iroquois Confederacy killed most of the tribe and scattered the survivors.

The French, attracted by the shelter of the peninsula, established a fort at Presque Isle in 1753. The fort, abandoned in 1759, was taken over the following year and garrisoned by the British. In 1763, the Seneca Indians, fearful of further infringement from the white man, captured Fort Presque Isle and burned it to the ground.

Birds-Eye View of Erie, Pa.

Indians continued to inhabit the region, but their spirit was broken after General "Mad" Anthony Wayne launched a campaign and won the Battle of Fallen Timbers near Toledo. During the summer of 1795, treaties were signed with tribes at western end of Lake Erie; by the fall, a treaty was signed with the Six Nations, opening the Erie Triangle to settlement.

General William Irvine and Major Andrew Ellicott, the surveyor and engineer who helped design Washington, D.C., laid out the town of Erie across the bay from Presque Isle. The settlement was incorporated as a borough in 1805, growing slowly around lumber mills, gristmills, brickyards and foundries.

The fleet used in the Battle of Lake Erie was built here, making Erie pivotal during the War of 1812. The British had military posts along the Canadian border and controlled Lake Erie with a strong provincial navy. In 1813, Colonel Oliver Hazard Perry arrived at Lake Erie to take command of the small fleet being constructed to defend the south shore of the lake. As part of Perry's mission to gain naval control of Lake Erie, his squadron skirmished with the British in the lake just beyond the protected waters of Presque Isle Bay. The British retreated after the brief encounter and were later conquered by Perry and his men in the Battle of Lake Erie near Sandusky, Ohio.

During the 1820s, steamboats plied the waters between Erie and Buffalo, where passengers and goods could connect with the Erie Canal. This spurred more rapid development. In 1833, the Erie Iron Mill had begun operation. By 1844, the Erie Extension Canal had opened, linking Erie with Pittsburgh and the Ohio River. In 1851, Erie was incorporated as a city and continued

ABOVE: Major Andrew Ellicott (1754-1820) oversaw construction of the fort at Presque Isle. In 1795, he laid out the town of Erie.

TOP LEFT: The Presque Isle Lighthouse at Erie was completed in 1873, followed by the keeper's residence in 1876. The tower was built of brick, "five courses thick," to provide protection from the storms of Lake Erie.

MIDDLE: Looking northward along State Street toward Presque Isle Bay in the early 20th century.

BOTTOM: The view of Erie looking south, circa 1905.

TOP LEFT: An early 20th century view of the Public Dock at Erie. It is now known as Dobbins Landing for Daniel Dobbins (1776-1856) who, along with Oliver Hazard Perry, oversaw construction of the fleet used to defeat the British at the Battle of Lake Erie.

TOP RIGHT: The observation tower of the Tom Ridge Envronmental Center at the entrance to Presque Isle State Park.

BOTTOM: A modern view of Erie's Harbor.

to grow in the late 19th and early 20th centuries as Germans, Russians, Poles and Italians were drawn to work in various industries. Erie's population peaked in 1960, at 138,440.

Until recently, the city also was a major producer of paper products. Today, Erie's largest employer, GE Transportation Systems, is a manufacturer of locomotives. Other significant and diverse industries include plastics, metal work, fabricating and machine shops. Erie's economy is also tied to education. Gannon University, Mercyhurst College, Behrend College of Penn State University and other institutions of higher learning are located here. The surrounding area in western Pennsylvania is also home to several colleges and universities.

Recent development in the city's core and Bayfront District includes the Erie Maritime Museum with a berth for the reconstructed and seaworthy U.S. Brig *Niagara*. The museum houses exhibits on the construction of the fleet of ships in the War of 1812, including a full-scale reconstruction of the side of the *Lawrence*, Commodore Oliver Hazard Perry's original flagship. The 187-foot Bicentennial Observation Tower at Dobbins Landing was built in 1995 to commemorate Erie's 200th birthday. The Tom Ridge Environmental Center at the entrance to Presque Isle opened in 2006. It includes interactive exhibits and educational opportunities. The Bayfront Convention Center opened in 2007.

Erie is home to numerous attractions, including the restored Warner Theater, Erie Playhouse, Lake Erie Arboretum, Waldameer Park, Erie Zoo and Botanical Gardens, the Discovery Square Museum complex, Erie Historical Museum and Planetarium, Dobbins Landing, Lake Erie Welcome Center and the several miles of sandy beaches at Presque Isle State Park. The AA-class Erie SeaWolves baseball team plays in the 6,000-seat Jerry Uht Park. The Erie Otters hockey (Ontario Hockey League) club plays at the 5,486-seat Louis J. Tullio Arena. Erie also has an NBA Development League franchise, the Erie Bayhawks. The team began play during the 2008-09 season.

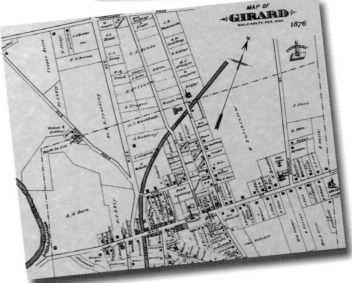

GIRARD

GIRARD, Pennsylvania (population 3,164) is located midway between Erie and the Ohio border. The borough sits on the ridge, two miles south of Lake Erie. Girard's business section reflects the 19th century, with its brick and frame buildings, flowers and tree-lined streets.

Settlement of the area occurred before 1800. It was named for Stephen Girard, a Philadelphia merchant who owned land in the area. Girard was incorporated as a borough in 1846.

Dan Rice, credited by many for originating the Uncle Sam character, operated a circus that made its winter home in Girard from the 1850s to 1875. Every spring, the circus was floated down the Erie Extension Canal to perform in towns along the Ohio River system and other localities in the interior. In the fall, townspeople waited to see the return of Rice's troupe marching in a full circus parade from the canal. Rice also commissioned the first memorial to those lost in the Civil War. Erected in 1865, the pillar remains on Girard's Main Street.

A factory producing wrenches opened here in 1874. The Louis Marx Toy Company operated between 1928 and 1986, retooling during World War II to support the war effort.

Today, Girard is residential and remains an agricultural center for the surrounding area. To the west, Elk Creek, popular with anglers in search of steelhead and other sport fish, winds its way through a deep ravine to Lake Erie.

TOP: Dan Rice (1823-1900), a circus operator and performer, was a famous resident of Girard.

ABOVE LEFT: Girard, Pennsylvania's Main Street looking west, circa 1909.

MAP: The Erie Extension Canal (center), which connected Lake Erie with the Ohio River, ran through Girard. The canal bed was later filled and became a route for the railroad.

MIDDLE RIGHT: Looking east along Main Street, Girard. Dan Rice's Civil War monument stands in the island on the street.

BOTTOM: Uncle Sam Poster. (Library of Congress, Prints & Photographs Division LC-USZC4-595)

101

Rice Avenue, North Girard, Pa.

LAKE CITY, PLATEA & SPRINGFIELD TOWNSHIP

LAKE CITY, Pennsylvania (population 2,811) was originally known as Miles Grove. It was named North Girard in 1926 and renamed Lake City in 1954. The village is two miles north of Girard.

Miles Grove did not get the canal, but instead benefited from the arrival of the Cleveland, Painesville & Ashtabula Railroad, which was laid through the village. Girard's circus operator Dan Rice had a road built called Rice Avenue to make his way from Girard to the Miles Grove depot.

For many years, the Otsego Works operated in North Girard, producing handles for forks; its successor company made anchors for railroad ties. The depot remains as a restaurant near the attractive downtown park.

TOP LEFT: Girard Station as it was known on this 1876 map is now called Lake City.

TOP RIGHT: The Erie Extension Canal is long gone and Lockport is now known as Platea, Pennsylvania.

BOTTOM: Rice Avenue, North Girard (Lake City), Pennsylvania.

PLATEA, Pennsylvania (population 474) is five miles south of Girard. The small borough was settled in 1840 when work was begun on the Erie Extension Canal.

The settlement was originally known as Lockport, for the 28 locks within a two-mile stretch in the area. The divide between the Lake Erie watershed and the Ohio River drainage basin is nearby, so the locks were built to lift canal boats nearly 200 feet to the summit.

Lockport grew with the canal, incorporating as a borough in 1870, but a few years previously, in 1864, the Erie & Pittsburgh Railroad laid track parallel to the canal. This began to spell the end for the canal, as shipping by rail was more efficient. Before plans to make the canal wider

and deeper could be realized, the canal line was sold to the railroad. On the night of September 5, 1871, the canal aqueduct over Elk Creek Gorge, just north of Lockport, collapsed. Canal traffic from Lockport to Erie never resumed. The section of the canal between Lockport and Beaver remained in use for a few more years before the Erie Extension Canal faded entirely into history, displaced by the Erie & Pittsburgh Railroad. From the 1880s to 1952, theatrical groups headquartered in the community. Lockport changed its name to Platea in 1902. Traces of the old Erie Extension Canal may still be seen in the area.

SPRINGFIELD TOWNSHIP, Pennsylvania (population 3,378) is at the northwestern most corner of the Commonwealth. In 1796, Captain Samuel Holliday was the first to settle in the area and the township was organized in 1803. In 1824, stage service was established between Erie and Cleveland. Springfield saw daily stage runs by 1827 and the railroad arrived in 1852.

Springfield Township was comprised of North Springfield, where Holliday and his family settled; West Springfield, at the Ohio border; and East Springfield. East Springfield was the largest settlement, with its post office established in 1836. East Springfield was incorporated as a borough in 1887 and dissolved in 1979 when the township returned to a single government entity.

Resorts sprang up along Lake Erie during the late 1800s, some of which remain today. The Conneaut & Erie Traction Company established trolley service through the township in 1903. Agriculture, fishing and recreation support Springfield's economy today.

TOP LEFT: Lockport, Pennsylvania was a busy place when the Erie Extension Canal was in operation. It later became a quiet farming community under its new name, Platea.

TOP RIGHT: The West Springfield Store building, pictured circa 1905, is still standing in this Pennsylvania hamlet.

BOTTOM: Main Street looking west, East Springfield, Pennsylvania.

9 Ohio Shoreline

Most of the southern shoreline of Lake Erie belongs to Ohio. Some 185 miles of Ohio lakefront stretches from Conneaut to the Maumee River estuary at Toledo. The Western Reserve, a strip surveyed by Moses Cleaveland for the Connecticut Land Company, extends westward from the Pennsylvania border along the south shore of Lake Erie for 120 of those miles. The Buckeye State's connection to Lake Erie is varied. Often called "Ohio's North Coast," this portion of Lake Erie's shoreline includes small to large cities, yet also features miles of quiet beaches, peaceful marshes and islands. Historic and newer resort areas have also made this a favorite vacation place.

Part of Lake Shore Dock, Ashtabula, Ohio.

Interstate 90, several sets of railroad tracks, strings of power lines and U.S. Route 20 all cross from Pennsylvania into the Buckeye State, two miles east of Conneaut. The thoroughfare that is now U.S. Route 20 was used by the Iroquois Indians during their extermination of the Eriez Indians and later by hundreds of settlers making their way onto Connecticut's Western Reserve. A few homes and taverns from this period remain along the roadway.

Along the lake in northeastern Ohio, ridges marking the shorelines of Lake Erie's predecessors are very apparent, creating a narrower plain to a point just west of Cleveland. From this point and westward, the lake plain widens greatly, joining the flat midwestern portion of the U.S. The Allegheny Plateau disappears off to the south. The stretch of lakeshore from the Pennsylvania border to Cleveland is very similar in appearance to the region between Buffalo and the Pennsylvania border. Scenes of grape vineyards, fruit orchards and creeks with deep gorges are repeated along the route.

West of Cleveland, the scene shifts to more general farming, with several industrial towns and resort areas dotting the lakeshore. North of Sandusky, the Marblehead Peninsula shelters Sandusky Bay and points toward Lake Erie's western islands. On a map or from a plane, these islands look like stepping stones placed across a giant pond.

Past the islands, more vineyards, orchards and farms appear before the shoreline becomes more marsh-like as it approaches the mouth of the Maumee River at Toledo. The Maumee winds through northeastern Indiana and northwestern Ohio before emptying into Lake Erie at Maumee Bay. The Lake Erie shoreline immediately north of Toledo belongs to Michigan.

BIRD'S-EYE VIEW OF CHERRY STREET BRIDGE. TOLEDO. OHIO.

TOP: Cleveland's Terminal Tower was the second-tallest building in the world when it was completed in 1930.

MIDDLE RIGHT: Linwood Park was established at Vermilion, Ohio in 1884.

MIDDLE LEFT: Toledo's Cherry Street Bridge, now known as the Martin Luther King Bridge, opened in 1914.

BOTTOM: Port Clinton, Ohio is located in the rich agricultural belt along lake Erie's shoreline.

CONNEAUT,
OHIO.
1896.

CONNEAUT

CONNEAUT, Ohio (population 12,485) is at the mouth of Conneaut Creek in the north-easternmost part of the state, 70 miles northeast of Cleveland.

The small city has two separate business districts. The larger main district is south of the lake, and the smaller harbor district is at the mouth of Conneaut Creek. Conneaut has a fine harbor and excellent railway connections, making it a significant shipping center. The city features a mixture of businesses and neatly kept neighborhoods with tree-lined streets.

On July 4, 1796, Moses Cleaveland stopped here while surveying the Western Reserve for the Connecticut Land Company. Cleaveland, accompanied by 48 men and two women from New England, stopped here briefly, toasting, making speeches and drinking "several pails of grog." They named this place, their first stop west of Pennsylvania, "Port Independence." Before continuing on their journey, the group erected a log cabin. Actual settlement of the area did not occur until 1799, when early settlers adopted the name *Conneaut*, from the Seneca Indian word, believed to mean "snow place."

Conneaut was incorporated in 1832 and grew quickly thereafter as the natural harbor and railroads attracted shipping of all kinds. Soon, planing mills, flourmills, brick works, tanneries and the manufacture of electric and gas fixtures and tungsten gas lamps added to Conneaut's economy. Growth continued as Conneaut became a shipping port for millions of tons of coal and ore used to make steel in the plants of eastern Ohio and western Pennsylvania. Conneaut became a city in 1898. The area attracted Finns who worked around the busy docks in the harbor area.

MAP: An 1896 panoramic map of Conneaut, Ohio. (Geography and Map Division, Library of Congress)

108

Fleet of Whalebacks, Conneaut Harbor, Ohio.

By the middle of the 20th century, metal cans were being produced for the growing canning business, along with the manufacture of leather goods, farm tools, communications equipment, light bulbs, cutlery and clothing. Conneaut also established railroad shops, molding sandpits and fisheries.

Today, Conneaut's industries include fishing, recreation and tourism. The area is home to the Conneaut Historical Railroad Museum, marinas, cottages, golf courses and several wineries.

TOP: A 1901 panoramic view of the harbor at Conneaut, Ohio. (Prints and Photographs Division, Library of Congress)

MIDDLE LEFT: Main Street at Conneaut, looking east, circa 1905.

MIDDLE RIGHT: The busy harbor at Conneaut in the 1930s.

BOTTOM: Whalebacks at Conneaut, circa 1905.

ASHTABULA

ASHTABULA, Ohio (population 20,962) is at the mouth of the Ashtabula River, 55 miles northeast of Cleveland.

Known for its harbor area, Ashtabula is quartered by the Ashtabula River from south to north and by the east-west ridge that separates the main business district from the harbor area below. Ashtabula Harbor's focal point is the Bascule Lift Bridge. The views in this area are mixed, from the sights of the massive train yards, freighters and gigantic cranes for loading and unloading freighters and a coal conveyor that arches across the river, to views of pleasure boaters and a harbor area business district with shops and restaurants. Ashtabula's main downtown business district on the ridge 75 feet above Lake Erie is now relatively quiet, having yielded to chain restaurants and retail establishment built along U.S. Route 20.

Ashtabula is an Indian phrase believed to mean "river of many fishes." Moses Cleaveland discovered the natural harbor here in 1796. Two men from his party decided to remain, founding the town. The rest of Cleaveland's party continued on along the lakeshore to the mouth of the Cuyahoga River, where they laid out a town square, storehouse and cabins in what became the city of Cleveland. Ashtabula was incorporated in 1831, and the population of mostly New Englanders quickly grew to more than 1,800.

A strong abolitionist sentiment in Ashtabula, combined with its location on the lake, made it an important terminus of the Underground Railroad. The Hubbard Homestead is the best-known "station" on this route. The home became known as Mother Hubbard's Cupboard and The Great Emporium, code names used by fugitive slaves. The slaves followed the route north to the house, a final stop on the Underground Railroad, before leaving on boats bound for the freedom of Canada.

The city was the site of a horrible train disaster in December 1876, when the bridge carrying a train on the Lake Shore & Michigan Southern Railroad collapsed into the Ashtabula River. Some 160 passengers were aboard as the train dropped 75 feet into the icy water, killing 92 people. The wrecked train immediately caught fire in the river and ravine below

TOP: A modern view of Ashtabula's harbor. The lift bridge was built in 1925 to replace a swing bridge.

ASHTABULA HARBOR,
OHIO
1896

Upper Harbor, Ashtabula, Ohio.

when lighted oil lamps in the cars smashed. The spreading flames killed many of the passengers who survived the fall.

Growth in Ashtabula continued in the latter part of the 19th century as Swedish and Finnish immigrants arrived, settling in the harbor area to work in the fishing industry. By the 1880s, immigrants from Italy began to arrive. Ashtabula became a city in 1891.

In the harbor area, ore was transferred from monstrous lake freighters into railroad cars to be transported south to the steel mills in the Pittsburgh and Youngstown areas. Eight Hulett unloaders operated at Ashtabula Harbor, unloading more than four billion tons during their 72-year history. In the harbor area, fishing boats passed the arms of steel cranes and the massive piles of coal and ore, while the sounds of rowdy sailors and dock workers echoed from the taverns along Bridge Street.

Ferries bound for Canada, filled with railroad cars loaded with coal, waited their turn to head out past the breakwaters to cross the lake. Shipyards and fisheries were built. Factories sprung up, producing foundry castings, farm implements, hydraulic presses, leather goods and clothing. Other industries developed, including oil refineries and the production of oxygen and communications equipment. The mass cultivation of vegetables in greenhouses began in the 1880s and continues today.

Ashtabula remains a major coal and iron port and a manufacturing center. It is a waterfront resort community and is home to a branch campus of the Kent State University system. Ashtabula Harbor is an historic district with its well-known Bascule Lift Bridge. The bridge was built in 1925 and restored in 1986. The area is also home to 16 covered bridges, the Ashtabula Arts Center, Hubbard House Underground Railroad Museum, Walnut Beach, Lake Shore Park and the Great Lakes Marine & U.S. Coast Guard Memorial Museum.

TOP: An 1896 panoramic view of Ashtabula Harbor, Ohio. (Division of Maps, Library of Congress)

MIDDLE: Ashtabula's Main Street, circa 1905.

BOTTOM: An early 20th century view of the busy harbor at Ashtabula.

GENEVA-ON-THE-LAKE

GENEVA-ON-THE-LAKE, Ohio (population 1,545) is seven miles west of Ashtabula. It was established as a public picnic grounds on July 4, 1869 and named "Sturgeon Point." A few years later, a horse-powered carousel was added. By 1900, numerous cottages, boarding houses and dance halls had been built. The well-to-do frequented the village. The Firestones, Fords and Rockefellers relaxed here, choosing to camp rather than stay in hotels or cottages. The village was incorporated in 1927.

With the advent of automobile travel, Geneva-on-the-Lake began to attract the working class. Before World War II, the Pier Ballroom was the largest ballroom between Buffalo and Sandusky. The Big Band sounds of Tommy Dorsey, the Glenn Miller Orchestra, Duke Ellington and others spilled out onto the mile-long strip during the 1940s and 1950s.

By the 1960s, the lake was polluted and families stopped coming as the village gained a rowdy reputation, frequented by motorcycle gangs and throngs of teens who came from nearby Pennsylvania to take advantage of Ohio's younger drinking age. The village raised the legal drinking age to 21 in 1970.

Today, the lake is much cleaner and the village has returned to its focus on entertainment and recreation. In the early 1990s, a marina and small boat harbor were built. Attractions include Geneva State Park, The Strip, the Jennie Munger Gregory Museum (home of the Ashtabula County Historical Society), beaches and Erieview Amusement Park.

TOP LEFT & RIGHT: Images of the popular entertainment district at Geneva-on-the-Lake, Ohio.

BOTTOM: An aerial view Geneva State Park and the marina, which was created in 1989. (Ken Winters, U.S. Army Corps of Engineers, Buffalo District)

Broadway and Main Streets, Geneva, Ohio

Champion Safety Lock Works. Geneva. Ohio.

GENEVA

GENEVA, Ohio (population 6,595) is three miles south of Lake Erie along U.S. Route 20, eight miles west of Ashtabula and 45 miles east of downtown Cleveland.

Geneva occupies land that belonged to Caleb Atwater, Gideon Granger and William Hart in 1798. The settlement was founded as Mills Corners in 1805, during the time other nearby settlements were forming on the Western Reserve. It was renamed Geneva in 1806, when Major Levi Gaylord came to the area and stated, "This is the prettiest place I've seen since I left Geneva, New York."

Geneva was built at the intersection of the north-south route between Lake Erie and Windsor and the east-to-west route that later became U.S. Route 20. It was incorporated as a township in 1816 and by the 1820s had a general store, post office, gristmill, tannery, distillery and a blacksmith shop. Geneva developed as a stop on the railroad upon its arrival in 1852. Two years later, Norman S. Caswell started a business that was later known as the Geneva Tool Company and True Temper. When Geneva's population grew to 1,000 in 1866, it was incorporated as a village. In 1895, an armory was built here for the Ohio National Guard.

Just after the turn of the century, Geneva was manufacturing automobiles. Geneva Steamers were built here before the company was sold to General Motors, moving to Michigan. Automotive legend Ransom E. Olds, the son of Geneva Brass owner Pliny Olds, was born here in 1864. He moved to Lansing in 1904, later producing the "REO." and the Oldsmobile.

The armory was converted into governmental offices in 1934. Over the years, Geneva has supported large numbers of greenhouses and been home to a milling company and factories producing farm implements, metal wheels, safety locks and other goods.

Geneva became a city in 1958. Today, the area is home to several wineries and the annual "Grape Jamboree," which is held during the last weekend of September. Tourists visit numerous historic covered bridges located nearby.

TOP LEFT: Not far from Geneva is the Harpersfield Covered Bridge, which was built in 1868. At 228 feet, it is the longest covered bridge in Ohio.

TOP RIGHT: Geneva's Enterprise Manufacturing Company started in 1877. It became the Champion Safety Lock Company in 1902, producing garden and household equipment, carpenter tools, games, toys and holiday goods.

BOTTOM: Geneva, Ohio's main intersection, U.S. Route 20 and Broadway.

Pavilion, Madison on the Lake.

MADISON

MADISON, Ohio (population 2,921) is west of Geneva along Ohio State Route 84, three miles south of Lake Erie.

A group of 25 settlers left their larger lake vessel and landed at the mouth of Cunningham Creek in 1798. They called the place Harper's Landing until 1811, when the name was changed to Harpersfield, for Colonel Alexander Harper, who brought his family with the group to this area. The Harper family arrived from Harpersfield, in Delaware County, New York. The name Harpersfield was later given to a hamlet a few miles to the east. The "new" Harpersfield is home to an historic covered bridge on the Grand River.

The settlement had several other names, including Chapintown and Centerville, before being called Madison. It was incorporated as a township in 1811. Bog iron was found in the area and provided work for many in the township in processing and shipping of the material. By 1834, between 1,000 and 1,500 tons of iron were produced at Arcole Furnace.

The village of Madison has a number of homes on The National Register of Historic Buildings and the downtown section is recognized as a National Historic District.

The Harper Homestead, located between Madison and Geneva, is maintained by the Western Reserve Society of Cleveland. Unionville, east of Madison, is known as the scene of a slave chase and escape. The bounty hunters were put on trial in Madison. The story is the basis for Harriet Beecher Stowe's book *Uncle Tom's Cabin*. Stowe was a visitor at Unionville's Old Tavern.

TOP LEFT: An early 20th century view of the pavilion at Madison-on-the-Lake. Today, the settlement continues as a summer resort.

TOP RIGHT: The Main Street business district of Madison, Ohio looks much the same today as it did in this 1920s-era view.

BOTTOM: The Old Tavern in Unionville was a stop on the Underground Railroad. Escaping slaves would enter tunnels under the tavern. After being fed and rested, a wagon came to take them to the Madison docks to board boats bound for Canada.

PERRY & NORTH PERRY

PERRY, Ohio (population 1,195) is 40 miles east of Cleveland. The settlement served as a stop along the stage route between Buffalo and Cleveland.

The Lake Shore & Michigan Southern Railroad was built through the town in the mid-1800s, operating today as the Norfolk & Southern Railroad. The interurban trolley ran through here during the early 1900s and the community grew. Perry was incorporated as a village in 1913.

Today, Perry is a residential and agricultural community and is home to a number of smaller manufacturing companies.

NORTH PERRY, Ohio (population 838) is 38 miles east of Cleveland on U.S. Route 20. Eleazor Parmly and his wife, Hanna, settled the area in 1817. They followed their daughters who had arrived a few years earlier. After the family opened a mill here, other settlers arrived. The area was known for its harvest of onions and grapes in the 1800s. Later, summer homes were built here for residents of Cleveland.

North Perry was incorporated in 1925. Today, the community is known as a nursery center, with plants being shipped from here throughout the northeastern U.S. The Perry Nuclear Power Station on the lakeshore went on-line in 1987.

TOP: The cooling towers of the Perry Nuclear Power Station can be seen for miles along Ohio's portion of the Lake Erie shoreline. The plumes of steam can even be seen from the Canadian side of the lake.

BOTTOM: The view to the northeast at Lakeshore Reservation Metropolitan Park in North Perry, Ohio.

FAIRPORT HARBOR

FAIRPORT HARBOR, Ohio (population 3,180) is at the mouth of the Grand River, just north of Painesville. A breakwater protects the harbor and a jetty extends far out into the lake. Though smaller, it has a similar feel and heritage to Ashtabula and Conneaut. The population here also includes the descendents of the Finns and Hungarians who moved here to work on the docks.

Archaeologists have discovered that Indians inhabited a major village here. The Grand River was once called *kichisibi*, which is an Indian word meaning "big river." It was also called the Geauga River, from the Indian word *sheauga* meaning "raccoon."

Abraham Skinner, who called it Grandon for the Grand River, arrived here in 1812 as part of the settlement of the Connecticut Western Reserve. Fairport had a population of 300 when the first wooden lighthouse was built in 1823. Samuel Butler, an active abolitionist, was the first lighthouse keeper. Fairport was officially named in 1836 and by 1845 had four hotels and several saloons to serve the busy port.

In the period leading up to the Civil War, slave hunters from the South rested in upper floors of hotels, while slaves were hidden a few floors below in cellars waiting until they could be whisked away on their journey to Canada along the Underground Railroad.

Fairport Harbor's continued growth resulted from salt production, fishing and the shipment of iron ore. Slovenians and Slovaks arrived here in the late 1800s and early 1900s to work in the growing industries. By 1910, commercial fisheries landed nearly two million pounds of fish a year, with fish processing plants lining the Grand River for a mile inland. Fish was transported via rail to New York, Chicago and St. Louis. By the early 1960s, the annual catch had declined to less than 30,000 pounds, and by the late 1960s the fishing industry was dead.

Fairport's location on top of large salt deposits was ideal for an alkali plant, which operated here between 1912 and 1975. Some 3,000 to 5,000 workers produced chlorine-based chemical products. Brine was made when water was pumped into the salt beds, and used to make chlorine and other products. The Morton Salt Company has operated the

TOP: The 42-foot-high Fairport Harbor West Breakwater Lighthouse went into service in 1925.

Light House on the Hill.   Painesville, Ohio.

Break Water at Fairport Harbor, Ohio.

Coast Guard Station, Fairport, Ohio

deepest salt mine in the nation here since the 1950s. This 2,000-foot deep mine extends two miles under Lake Erie with numerous tunnels crisscrossing throughout the subterranean complex. The rock salt deposits were formed during the Silurian Period, more than 400 million years ago, when a warm saltwater sea covered much of the region, which included northeastern Ohio. As the sea evaporated, salt was precipitated to form layers up to 200 feet thick. A similar mine, primarily producing rock salt for road de-icing, operates under Lake Erie just offshore from downtown Cleveland.

Back on the surface, the quiet village focuses on recreation and residential development. The Fairport Marine Museum is housed in the lighthouse quarters at the mouth of the Grand River. The original lighthouse, built in 1825, was improved with a new foundation in 1835 and replaced in 1871 with the present sandstone lighthouse, which operated until 1925. Across the harbor is Grand River, a village of 345 inhabitants, with roots in the fishing industry. Nearby is Headlands Dunes and Headlands Beach State Park.

TOP LEFT: Built in 1871, the 60-foot Fairport Harbor Lighthouse is now home to the Fairport Marine Museum. In 1925, a light and foghorn station on the west breakwater pier head replaced the light on the hill at Fairport Harbor.

TOP RIGHT: The view of the breakwater at the mouth of the Grand River at Fairport Harbor, circa 1905.

BOTTOM: The U.S. Coast Guard Station at Fairport Harbor was built in 1876 and remains active today.

PAINESVILLE

PAINESVILLE, Ohio (population 17,503) is situated on the ridge, two miles above the mouth of the Grand River (Fairport Harbor) and 30 miles northeast of Cleveland. Painesville's business district is attractive, featuring brick buildings dating from the late 19th and early 20th centuries, and also includes an historic courthouse.

Painesville had its beginning in two Western Reserve settlements: New Market, established in 1803, and Champion, founded in 1807 in honor of Henry Champion, an early Ohio pioneer. The community was later named Painesville for General Edward Paine, a native of Connecticut who was a heroic officer in the American Revolution and representative to the Northwest Territorial Legislature. Paine passed through here in 1800, establishing a settlement known as "The Openings" between Lake Erie and the Grand River. The settlement grew and was incorporated in 1832. In 1840, Painesville became the county seat of Lake County when the county was organized.

Western Reserve architect Jonathan Goldsmith was one of the early pioneers who came to the area, living in Painesville from 1811 until his death in 1847. He built structures in Painesville and the neighboring communities of Mentor, Willoughby and Cleveland.

When the Cleveland, Painesville & Ashtabula Railroad was built here in 1852, the community grew. A business was established to build machinery used to produce veneer and another company opened to deal in seeds and nursery stock.

Today, Painesville is primarily residential, but the community is also home to Lake Erie College, a small liberal arts institution founded in 1856 as a school for women. Originally in Willoughby, the school was moved to Painesville and was called the Lake Erie Female Seminary. The college became coeducational in 1985.

Painesville became a city in 1902 and new industries arrived in the early 20th century, including an alkali plant, rayon manufacturer and soybean processing plant. Other industries produced concrete building blocks, resin, iron powder, baskets, castings and bindings.

Nurseries and chemical production industries are key employers here today. The Indian Museum of Lake County is located on the campus of Lake Erie College.

ABOVE: The Lake County Courthouse at Painesville, Ohio, circa 1910.

TOP RIGHT: An early 20th century view of the railroad bridges crossing the Grand River at Painesville.

BOTTOM: Painesville's Main Street, 1905.

MENTOR & MENTOR-ON-THE-LAKE

MENTOR, Ohio (population 50,278) and MENTOR-ON-THE-LAKE, Ohio (population 8,127) are 20 miles east of Cleveland. The city of Mentor is five miles south of Lake Erie.

Charles Parker, a surveyor for the Connecticut Land Company, arrived in the area in 1797. Parker built a cabin at Mentor Marsh, establishing the settlement. The name Mentor came from Greek literature and was inspired by America's fascination with the ancient world.

Mentor Township was formed in 1815 with 460 people. The Cleveland, Painesville & Ashtabula Railroad reached Mentor in 1851, and in 1855 Mentor Centre was incorporated as Mentor Village.

A nut-and-washer factory was built in Mentor in 1868 and later served as a knitting mill. The remote town's residents were farmers, nurserymen or shop workers. Mentor resident James A. Garfield was elected as the 20th President of the United States in 1881. He was assassinated later that year. In 1898, the first commercial block of buildings was constructed in Mentor.

Mentor was the scene of a terrible train accident in 1950 when the Lake Shore & Michigan Southern's Twentieth Century Limited crashed into a freight station, killing 19.

Mentor Village was incorporated as a city in 1963. Today, Mentor is part of suburban Cleveland and Mentor-on-the-Lake is a residential and resort community.

A temple in nearby Kirtland was the first house of worship for the followers of Joseph Smith Jr., who founded the Latter Day Saints movement in western New York in 1830. The Kirtland Temple was dedicated in 1836.

ABOVE: James A. Garfield (1831-1881) was the 20th President of the United States and a Mentor resident. He was assassinated four months after being sworn in and died 80 days after the shooting. (Library of Congress, Prints & Photographs Division LC-USZC4-595)

TOP: The Mentor Lagoons were constructed in 1924 as part of a planned upscale development, which was never realized. The marsh is located in what was an ancient channel of the Grand River. Today, the lagoon and marsh are part of a 450-acre park.

BOTTOM: James A. Garfield acquired the Mentor home, known as Lawnwood, in 1876. It was the site of the first successful front porch campaign in 1880. The National Park Service and the Western Reserve Historical Society now operate the site.

119

Drawn by Henry Howe in 1846.
PUBLIC BUILDINGS IN WILLOUGHBY.

ERIE STREET.
WILLOUGHBY, OHIO.

WILLOUGHBY

WILLOUGHBY, Ohio (population 22,621) is 15 miles east of Cleveland. It is a bedroom community of Cleveland on the Chagrin River.

Willoughby's roots are tied to early Indians and the settlement of the Western Reserve. The Eriez dug for clams along the banks of the Chagrin River. The name *sha-ga-rin* is translated to mean "clear water." The name was later modified to Chagrin to express disappointment felt when Moses Cleaveland confused the river with the *crooked* or Cuyahoga River, of which he was searching while surveying the Western Reserve.

David Abbott was the first known permanent settler in Willoughby, establishing a gristmill in 1798. A public square was built and the name Chagrin was changed to Willoughby in 1835 in honor of the founder of a medical college who willed his estate to the village. The Willoughby Female Seminary operated between 1847 and 1854 before shifting to Painesville as Lake Erie Female Seminary, later to be known as Lake Erie College.

The Cleveland, Painesville & Eastern Railroad offices were established in Willoughby in 1895. This electric rail system connected the village with downtown Cleveland and Painesville. Euclid Avenue was paved through Willoughby in 1911.

Willoughby became a city in 1950 when the population hit 5,000, as many post-war homes were built. Today, Willoughby's business district, which was built around a town square, is listed on the National Register of Historic Places.

TOP LEFT: Like many other communities on Connecticut's Western Reserve in Ohio, Willoughby was built around a public square.

TOP RIGHT: An early 20th century view of Willoughby, Ohio's business district. Downtown Willoughby is listed on the National Register of Historic Places.

BOTTOM: The Willoughby viaduct carried traffic over the Chagrin River.

CLEVELAND

CLEVELAND, Ohio (city population: 478,403, metro population: 2,250,871) is centered at the mouth of the winding Cuyahoga River.

The industrialized ravine of the Cuyahoga River divides the city into a West Side and an East Side. The major downtown buildings are located around three main areas: the Mall, running inland from Lake Erie, which includes government and civic buildings; Public Square, an area of monuments surrounded by the city's tallest buildings; and Erieview Plaza, which began as an urban renewal project in the 1960s. The city and suburbs spread to the east, south and west.

Indians named the river *Cuyahoga*, meaning "crooked river" before Moses Cleaveland's surveying team arrived here on July 22, 1796. Standing on the bluff overlooking the river, the plain and Lake Erie, the group named the area after Cleaveland. Bitten by mosquitoes and plagued by other maladies, they platted the town around a square and built a storehouse and some cabins. Moses Cleaveland then quickly returned east, leaving a few hearty souls to develop his namesake town on the Western Reserve. In 1800, the settlement had just seven residents, while most of Ohio's 45,000 people lived in the southern part of the state along the Ohio River.

During the War of 1812, two of Colonel Oliver Hazard Perry's ships, the *Porcupine* and the *Portage*, were built here on the Cuyahoga River. In 1818, the arrival of the first steamship on Lake Erie, *Walk-in-the-Water*, signaled the future growth of the area. That growth, however, was very slow until the Erie Canal was opened through New York State in 1825. The Erie Canal's opening, along with the completion of the Ohio & Erie Canal from Cleveland to the Ohio River in 1832, brought a huge influx of settlers to the area. The town's name "Cleaveland" became "Cleveland" in 1831 when the compositor of the town's new newspaper,

ABOVE: A nighttime view of Cleveland's skyline. The Great Lakes Science Center is in the center of the image.

LEFT: Moses Cleaveland (1754-1806) was a director of the Connecticut Land Company. In 1796 he led a party to the mouth of the Cuyahoga River. The site was named after Cleaveland. In 1831, the spelling changed to "Cleveland." (Western Reserve Historical Society, Cleveland, Ohio)

Cleveland: The New American City

TOP: The skyline of
Cleveland, Ohio. The Key
Tower is the tallest building
in Cleveland. The historic
Terminal Tower is at right.

BOTTOM: Built in 1931,
Severance Hall is the home
of the Cleveland Orchestra.

TOP: The Fountain of Eternal Life, also known as the War Memorial Fountain, is located on the Cleveland Mall in honor of those who served in World War II.

MIDDLE LEFT: The Soldiers' and Sailors' monument was built in 1894 to honor those from northeastern Ohio who served in the Civil War. The names of 9,000 are engraved on the interior walls of the monument on Cleveland's Public Square.

BOTTOM: A view of the Cuyahoga River and The Flats at Cleveland.

EUCLID AVENUE, CLEVELAND, OHIO.

The Cleveland Gazette and Commercial Register, chose to drop the first "a" in Cleaveland so the masthead of the paper could fit on the page.

Cleveland was chartered as a city in 1836, and by 1840 boasted 6,000 residents. In the next few years, the railroad came, the Lake Erie Telegraph Company arrived and record industrial growth brought more people to Cleveland. In 1855, the opening of the canal at Sault Ste. Marie, Michigan between Lake Superior and Lake Huron brought a steady stream of rich ore to Cleveland's burgeoning iron industry. Coal was brought up the Ohio & Erie Canal, meeting the ore at Cleveland to rapidly grow the city's industrial roots.

The Civil War divided the nation and Ohio over the issue of slavery. In the 1860s, much of the state's population continued to be centered along the southern boundary on the Ohio River. This group's southern roots clashed with Cleveland's New England stock, which strongly opposed slavery. A sympathetic Cleveland became an important stop on the Underground Railroad, as the Ohio & Erie Canal brought escaping slaves northward on their journey to Canada and freedom. Bounty hunters came to Cleveland to prowl the docks to catch runaways waiting to board steamers.

Following the Civil War, the city's success followed that of the nation moving into the Industrial Revolution. Cleveland's rapid development continued as foreign immigrants arrived. The iron industry grew, and shipping, railroads, manufacturing and oil business all expanded during this period. The barons of these industries built mansions along a mile-plus long section of Euclid Avenue known as "Millionaire's Row."

The flats of the Cuyahoga River became the center of a vast body of steel mills and manufacturing plants. The steel and shipping industries were growing exponentially as cargoes of ore continued on their route from the ranges of Lake Superior down the lakes to Cleveland, while coal was routed upward. Samuel L. Mather developed the Cleveland-Cliffs Iron Company. Jeptha Wade's telegraph lines stretched westward, later resulting in the formation of the Western Union Company. The Standard Oil Company, which is now Cleveland-based British Petroleum America, was organized in 1870, making Cleveland the oil center

TOP LEFT: A 19th century view of Cleveland's harbor at the mouth of the Cuyahoga River.

TOP RIGHT: Euclid Avenue was known as "Millionaire's Row" during the 19th century. Here stood the homes of Cleveland's industrial barons.

BOTTOM: Samuel L. Mather (1817-1890) was the key founder of the Cleveland Iron Mining Company, which later became the Cleveland-Cliffs Iron Company.

of the nation. John D. Rockefeller made a fortune through Standard Oil during an era that built the wealth of the Vanderbilt family and others. Marcus Hanna, who made his fortune in the iron, coal and shipping industries, was also a powerful political boss in the late 19th century. Charles F. Brush lit Cleveland's Public Square, and in 1881 a central power station went on-line. Arc lamps were erected around the city. Parks given to the city by wealthy

business leaders were later joined to form the present 19,000-acre Metroparks system.

Meanwhile, during the late 19th century, workers toiling in the industries of Cleveland were aware of the opulence on "Millionaire's Row." Many of these workers lost trust in the giant companies and formed labor unions. Some 500 workers on the Lake Shore Railroad struck to protest working conditions, including a 12-hour day, seven-day week shift. Other major strikes ensued as labor fought for better working conditions.

Specialized educational institutions came into existence to support growing industry. The Case School of Applied Science and Western Reserve College (which later merged to become Case Western Reserve University), Adelbert College of the University Group and St. Ignatius College (which later became John Carroll University), were among the first institutions of higher learning.

The early 20th century saw continued industrial growth. The shortage of labor was stressed by the demands of the steel industry. This demand sparked mass immigration primarily from Europe's Slavic nations, while others migrated from the southern United States. During this period, the Cleveland Museum of Art was built in 1916 and the Cleveland Orchestra was organized in 1918. Cleveland grew to become the fifth largest city in America by 1920. The Mall Plan of the 1920s was realized through the construction of City Hall, the County Courthouse, Federal Building, Public Library, Board of Education Building and the Municipal Auditorium. The Federal Reserve Building and the Plain Dealer Building also were constructed nearby. The skyline was taking shape, crowned in 1930 by the landmark 52-story Union Terminal Tower.

Cleveland was not immune to the effects of the Great Depression, as nearly one third of the workforce was unemployed in 1933, but the Great Lakes Exposition celebrated the city's

ABOVE: Jeptha H. Wade (1811-1890), founder of the Western Union Company, began with a network of telegraph lines between Detroit, Milwaukee, Buffalo, Cleveland, Cincinnati and St. Louis. Wade was a resident of Cleveland. (Library of Congress, Prints & Photographs Division LC-USZ6-1855)

TOP: An 1877 panoramic view of Cleveland and the winding Cuyahoga River. (Geography and Map Division, Library of Congress)

LEFT: John D. Rockefeller (1839-1937), a Cleveland resident, founded Standard Oil and built it into the largest oil refining business in the world. For a time, he was the richest man in the United States. (Library of Congress, Prints & Photographs Division LC-USZ62-123825)

centennial in 1936-37. World War II sent thousands into the service and put the city back to work. Steel mills, the manufacture of airplane engines, electrical parts factories, the Cleveland Bomber Plant and other Cleveland industries supported the war effort.

Following the war, GIs returned to jobs and starter homes in the suburbs. The city's population topped out in 1950 at 914,808 as Cleveland was the seventh largest city in the nation.

The 1960s and 1970s were marked by more flight to the suburbs. The shift to dependence on foreign oil and the lower labor costs associated with production of steel abroad were major blows to Cleveland's industrial economy. A burning oil slick on the Cuyahoga River in 1969 attracted national attention. By the late 1970s, Cleveland became the first major city in America since the Depression to default on its obligations.

Diversification of industry, a stronger economy and a reorganized city government helped Cleveland recover. In the 1980s, as steel mills closed, the downtown area began to revitalize. The Flats area was converted into an entertainment center. The Sohio (BP) building was constructed on Public Square; other construction followed and the city emerged from default in 1987. The 1990s continued to be a renewal period for Cleveland as Key Tower and other large office buildings reshaped the skyline. Tower City continues to be developed in the 21st century. The Cavaliers (NBA) moved from the suburbs, bringing basketball back downtown to the 22,562-seat Gund Arena (now called Quicken Loans Arena) in 1994. Jacobs Field, now called Progressive Field, became the new home of baseball's Indians (AL) in 1994, seating 43,545 fans. The Rock and Roll Hall of Fame, the William G. Mather Lakeboat Museum and other attractions opened as part of the lakefront's redevelopment. In 1999, a new expansion Browns (NFL) football team moved into a new 73,200-seat stadium on the lakefront.

Today, professional theater continues at Playhouse Square in the Cleveland Play House, founded in 1915 as the nation's first resident theater program. The city boasts Severance Hall, built by philanthropist John Long Severance for the renowned Cleveland Orchestra.

TOP LEFT: Cleveland Municipal Stadium, built in 1931, was the longtime home of the baseball's Indians and football's Browns. It was demolished in 1996. Cleveland Browns Stadium was opened on the same site in 1999.

TOP RIGHT: Cleveland's Pubic Square in the 1930s. The square was originally laid out in 1796 by Moses Cleaveland's surveying party.

TOP: An early 20th century view of Cleveland's waterfront.

MIDDLE LEFT: Cleveland's busy Cuyahoga River, circa 1908.

MIDDLE RIGHT: The Arcade, built in 1890, is comprised of two nine-story towers with a 100-foot-high skylight. In 2001, it was redeveloped into a Hyatt Regency hotel.

BOTTOM: The Great Lakes Exposition was held during the summers of 1936 and 1937 to commemorate the centennial of the city's incorporation. The 135-acre fairgrounds extended from Public Hall to the lakeshore.

127

TOP LEFT: The Rock and Roll Hall of Fame museum was opened in Cleveland in 1995.

TOP RIGHT: The Cleveland Museum of Art, opened in 1916 on land donated by Jeptha Wade, is known for collections of Western paintings, Medieval European and Oriental art.

BOTTOM: Cleveland Browns Stadium was built in 1999 at the lakefront on the site of the old Cleveland Municipal Stadium.

Cleveland is home to numerous museums, including the Cleveland Museum of Art, the Great Lakes Science Center and the Western Reserve Historical Society. The Cleveland Clinic, revered for its advanced medical treatments, Case Western Reserve and Cleveland State universities and the Cleveland Metroparks Zoo are some of Cleveland's important assets.

10682

SCENE ON LAGOON, ROCKY RIVER, CLEVELAND, O.

ROCKY RIVER

ROCKY RIVER, Ohio (population 20,735) is nine miles west of Cleveland, where the river of the same name meets Lake Erie.

Rocky River, a bedroom community of Cleveland, was incorporated in 1903. Most of the city's homes were built in the early part of the 20th century. A number of affluent neighborhoods surround Rocky River's attractive business district.

Rocky River is home to the Cleveland Yachting Club, a number of swimming pools, an indoor ice rink and eight city parks. Rocky River lies between Lakewood and Bay Village.

Lakewood, a city of 57,000, is part of "The Gold Coast" and known for its turn-of-the-century mansions. Settled in the 1880s, the community was known as Rockport before being incorporated as Lakewood in 1889. The residential community of Bay Village was settled in 1811, incorporated in 1903 and it became a city in 1950; it now has more than 16,000 residents.

TOP: The Detroit Road Bridge at Rocky River was built in 1910 as the world's longest non-reinforced concrete arch bridge. The span was replaced in 1980.

MIDDLE: A view of Rocky River in the early 1900s.

BOTTOM: The marina at Rocky River is adjacent to the scenic Rocky River Reservation, which is part of the Metroparks system.

AVON LAKE & AVON

AVON LAKE, Ohio (population 18,145) and AVON, Ohio (population 11,446) are 15 miles west of Cleveland in the township of Avon.

First settled in the early 1800s along French Creek and originally called Troy, the area was renamed Avon in 1824. The community grew around a sawmill and gristmill. During the 1860s, land along the lakeshore sold for $300 an acre as the grape business grew.

Tom L. Johnson, who built what later became the U.S. Steel plant in Lorain, also built the interurban trolley system through Avon Township in 1898. It operated until 1938. In 1917, Avon Lake was incorporated as a village and separated from Avon, the community in the southern part of the township.

The Avon Isle Dance Pavilion on French Creek was built in Avon Township in 1926. The venue was very popular when dancing was outlawed in nearby Lorain and Elyria. That same year, the Cleveland Electric Illuminating Company built a plant along the lakeshore in Avon Lake. Other industry followed, and Avon Lake grew as a residential community, incorporating as a city in 1952.

Avon Township also includes Avon to the south, which was incorporated as a city in 1961. These bedroom communities for Cleveland and Lorain are also home to a chemical plant and the 230-acre Ford Motor Company Ohio Assembly Plant, which opened in 1974.

TOP: The Cleveland Illuminating Company built a power plant on Lake Road in Avon Lake in 1926.

BOTTOM: A view to the east along Lake Erie's shoreline at Sheffield Lake, Ohio.

SHEFFIELD LAKE & SHEFFIELD

SHEFFIELD LAKE, Ohio (population 9,371) and SHEFFIELD, Ohio (population 2,949) are five miles east of Lorain.

Originally called Sheffield Village, it was shown on maps as Township 7 of Range 17 of the Western Reserve. In 1815, Captain Jabez Burrell and Captain John Day arrived here from Sheffield, Massachusetts. After surveying the area, they chose lots for themselves.

The township was organized in 1824, the first to do so in Lorain County. In 1846, German settlers arrived and settled around the eastern edge of the community. After the Civil War, the railroad arrived. In 1872 the Baltimore & Ohio Railroad passed through the southwestern part of township. In the 1880s the New York, Chicago & St. Louis Railroad was built through the northern section of Sheffield.

The Johnson Steel Company built a mill along the Black River in 1895, and the city of Lorain annexed a third of the township, including the land on which the mill was built. In 1920, the section east of the Black River separated from the township. The new village was called Sheffield Lake. The southern portion became Sheffield Village.

The township grew as a residential area during World War II when people came to work in mills in nearby Lorain. Today, Sheffield and Sheffield Lake feature a mix of commercial and residential development.

TOP: Sheffield Lake features impressive homes along Lake Erie's shoreline.

BOTTOM: A view to the east at Sheffield Lake, Ohio.

Steel Plant Furnaces. Lorain, O.

Lorain, Ohio. View of Lorain looking North toward Lake Erie.

Boat Launching, Lorain, Ohio.

LORAIN

LORAIN, Ohio (population 68,652) is at the mouth of the Black River, 25 miles west of Cleveland. Lorain boasts one of the finest harbors on Lake Erie and the river is dredged to allow lake freighters to travel well inland. While some factories lining the river have closed, others continue to operate to capacity.

In 1787, the area was a stop for a group of Moravian missionaries. After camping for a few days with a group of Indians they had converted, the missionaries were forced to leave by the Delaware Indians. Twenty years later, a trading post was established here. In 1810, a settler named John Reid had established a post office, justice office and a tavern. By 1819, the shipbuilding industry had taken hold.

Lorain was originally known as Black River. In 1836, it was incorporated as Charleston. During this period, Charleston grew in anticipation of being chosen as the terminus for the new Ohio & Erie Canal. The village also held hopes of being on the route of the railroad. Both aspirations were not realized, as nearby Elyria got the railroad and the canal met Lake Erie at Cleveland. Charleston quickly declined, losing its charter.

The small village came back to life in 1872 with the coming of the Cleveland, Lorain & Wheeling Railroad. The town was reincorporated in 1876 as Lorain because the former name Charleston had since been awarded to another town in Ohio. By the 1880s, another railroad, the Nickel Plate, was built through the town and a brass company brought 800 jobs. In 1894, Tom L. Johnson established a steel plant along the river in South Lorain. Johnson, who later was mayor of Cleveland, paid higher wages, bringing a flood of workers to his plant. The purchase and expansion of the plant by U.S. Steel created demand for more labor. Foreign-born workers filled the need as Italians, Hungarians, Slovaks and Poles moved to Lorain, and the population soared from 1,595 in 1880 to 28,883 by 1910.

TOP LEFT: The Lorain Steel Plant in 1910. Today, U.S. Steel and Republic Steel operate mills stretching for nearly three miles on Lorain's south side.

TOP RIGHT: A 1905 view of Lorain, Ohio.

BOTTOM: The American Shipbuilding Company's main yard was located at Lorain. Many ships, including five 1,000-foot-long Great Lakes ore carriers, were built here before the yard closed in 1984. The land has been redeveloped for housing.

In June of 1924, the city was devastated by a tornado, which killed several people in Sandusky before taking 79 lives here. More than 1,000 people were injured and the twister caused $25 million in damage to homes and businesses. Lorain recovered quickly as industrial growth continued at U.S. Steel's National Tube Division, the American Shipbuilding Company and Thew Shovel Company.

By the 1950s, more than 2,000,000 tons of coal were shipped annually from the Port of Lorain, the Ford Motor Company had built its largest automobile assembly plant, U.S. Steel's Lorain-Cuyahoga works expanded and National Gypsum built a plant here. In the late 20th century, some of Lorain's factories and mills closed but other industries flourished. American Shipbuilding launched the 858-foot-long *Roger Blough* as the largest vessel ever built on the Great Lakes, later eclipsing that feat with the launching of the 1,000-foot *James R. Barker*. Huge oil storage tanks were built along the bank of the Black River near the High Level Bridge. The city's population peaked at more than 80,000. Fluctuations in the auto industry have varied the employment levels at Lorain's massive Ford assembly plant.

Lorain is an international port with a growing focus on tourism and recreation. Attractions include the restored Lorain Palace Civic Center (1928), the Black River Historical Society and the 1,000-foot-long boardwalk at Lakeview Park Beach. The Black River runs through the city to Lake Erie after making its way through Elyria, Lorain's neighboring city to the south.

TOP LEFT: Looking south along Lorain's main thoroughfare, Broadway Avenue in the 1940s.

TOP RIGHT: A tornado roared through Sandusky and Lorain in 1924, killing 85. Seventy-nine of the victims were killed in Lorain.

BOTTOM: Looking north from the Erie Avenue Bridge toward Lake Erie at Lorain.

Broad St., looking West, Elyria, Ohio

West Falls, Elyria, O.

Broad Street by Night, Elyria, Ohio.

ELYRIA

ELYRIA, Ohio (population 55,953) is an industrial and residential city, seven miles southeast of Lorain on the Black River.

Heman Ely, a native of West Springfield, Massachusetts, founded Elyria. Ely was a land developer and merchant who invested in the Western Reserve lands of the Connecticut Land Company. In 1816, Ely's agent built a dam and established a gristmill and sawmill. Ely and others arrived to settle in 1817. Ely dedicated a park (now Ely Park) at the center of the planned village in 1822.

A brick courthouse was completed in 1828 and Elyria was incorporated in 1833. A quarry on the east branch of the Black River provided stone for the town's sidewalks. A forge operated on the river's west side until 1832, when the Lorain Iron Company was established.

Today, Elyria's industries include the production of medical equipment, heating systems, plumbing and supplies.

TOP: Elyria, Ohio, circa 1905.

MIDDLE: A 1905 view of falls on the west branch of the Black River at Elyria, Ohio. The bridge, built in 1894, stands today.

BOTTOM: Downtown Elyria in the early 1900s.

134

VERMILION

VERMILION, Ohio (population 10,927) sits at the end of the winding Vermilion River, 10 miles west of Lorain, on one of Lake Erie's finest natural harbors. Vermilion's appearance is much like that of a New England fishing village. The Vermilion Lagoons, canal-like branches of the Vermilion River, are lined with docks for pleasure craft and surrounded by upscale housing.

The Ottawa Indians were attracted to the area because of local clay, which could be used to make red paint. The settlement formed in 1808 and the thriving harbor town grew quickly, incorporating in 1837.

Thomas Alva Bradley built his first ship, the *South America*, here in 1841. Every year, he built more ships and Vermilion became known as a shipbuilding center. Iron furnaces were built and the village also developed through the fishing and lumber businesses.

By the middle of the 20th century, many of Vermilion's industries had declined and the downtown area had become abandoned and decayed. In 1967, the historic business district, known as Harbor Town 1837, was restored. The district includes homes and shops, the town hall, 1883 Opera House and the Old School House.

Vermilion is now a popular resort area with small businesses, shops, restaurants, marinas and the Inland Seas Maritime Museum of the Great Lakes Historical Society.

TOP: Vermilion, Ohio's harbor, circa 1905. Vermilion's peak commercial fishing period took place between 1890 and 1945. Vermilion was home to several commercial fish companies and their tugs.

MIDDLE: A 1908 view of Vermilion's Liberty Street.

BOTTOM: The Vermilion Lighthouse sits on the grounds of the Inland Seas Maritime Museum. It was built in 1991 as a replica of the lighthouse that served here between 1877 and 1929.

135

TOP LEFT: Downtown Huron's business district as it appeared, circa 1910. The business district was razed in the early 1970s as part of an urban renewal plan.

TOP RIGHT: The 72-foot lighthouse on the western pier at the mouth of the Huron River was built in 1936. A similar light was also erected at Conneaut, Ohio that same year.

BOTTOM: Looking west at Huron, Ohio. The fireboat in the foreground was acquired through funding from the Department of Homeland Security.

HURON

HURON, Ohio (population 7,758) is situated around the mouth of the Huron River, eight miles east of Sandusky. It is the Great Lakes' southernmost port. The natural harbor is protected by a long pier that juts into the lake from the western bank of the Huron River.

Huron is a quiet place with most of the activity occurring near the harbor and the marinas. The city is a transshipping port for ore, grain and stone.

The French built a trading post here in 1749. In 1805, an American trader arrived and settlement rapidly followed. The town of over 2,000 fell on hard times as a cholera epidemic killed many residents in 1834. Improvements to the harbor helped develop shipping and shipbuilding as the key industries. The *Great Western*, a steamer with both paddles and sails, was built in here in 1838. One of the most famous ships on the lake, the steamer boasted

luxurious cabins above the main deck for the well-to-do, while immigrants heading west to settle occupied quarters below the deck.

By 1839, the Huron-Milan Canal had moved the shipping and shipbuilding industry a few miles inland to Milan. This led to a decline in Huron's importance as ships bypassed it, heading instead to Milan to receive grain and wheat from the interior for shipment.

Shipping of coal and iron ore along with the fishing industry helped to revive Huron around the turn of the century. In the early 20th century, the Wheeling & Lake Erie Railroad Docks were expanded to receive ore brought from the upper Great Lakes. The docks boasted the largest coal dumper on the lakes in 1937, which could unload 50 coal cars into the holds of a ship in an hour.

Urban renewal projects changed the face of Huron's downtown business district and the waterfront. The late 19th and early 20th century era business district is gone. Today, in addition to shipping, Huron's biggest industries include automotive plastics, paint manufacturing and tourism. Huron is home to upscale subdivisions, a new marina, two public beaches, the James H. McBride Arboretum and the Huron Historical & Cultural Center. Thomas Edison's birthplace of Milan is a few miles south of Huron.

ABOVE: Thomas Alva Edison (1847-1931) was born in Milan, Ohio, not far from Huron. Edison's hundreds of inventions included the light bulb, the phonograph and the stock ticker. (Library of Congress, Prints & Photographs Division LC-USZ61-1976)

TOP: A view to the east, across the marina at Huron, Ohio. The grain elevator and buildings were closed in 2006, and the land was purchased by the Ohio Department of Natural Resources for future development.

BOTTOM: The Huron River, looking south at Huron, Ohio.

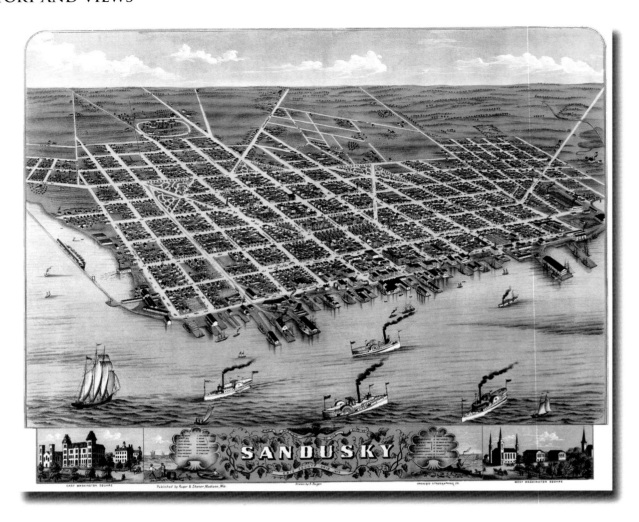

SANDUSKY

SANDUSKY, Ohio (population 27,844) is located along the southeastern shoreline of Sandusky Bay, 50 miles west of Cleveland, protected from the lake by Cedar Point and the Marblehead Peninsula. The 18-mile-long Sandusky Bay gives the city one of the finest natural harbors on Lake Erie. Its location between Cleveland and Toledo brings tourists from both cities and acts as gateway to the area's resorts, islands, beaches, cottages and fishing spots.

The town is relatively narrow, extending two to three miles north to south and five to six miles east to west along the lakeshore. The business district is very attractive, with numerous brick and locally quarried limestone buildings dating to the late 19th century. Washington Park acts as Sandusky's center.

The area around Sandusky was visited in 1679 by French explorers, when La Salle sailed across Lake Erie. The name "Sandusky" came from the Wyandot Indian phrase *san-doos-tee* which meant "at the cold water." The name was applied to the bay because of cool springs in the area. In 1816, the area was settled by New Englanders and called Portland, while another part of the tract was called Sandusky City. The settlements joined in 1824 to become Sandusky. Sandusky became a stopping place for passenger boats from Buffalo, as thousands of immigrants were dropped off here on their way to the interior.

Sandusky also became one of the largest grain markets, with wagons full of corn, wheat and produce being brought to the docks for shipping to Canada and the East.

Sandusky had been passed over in favor of Cleveland as terminus of the Ohio & Erie Canal, but in the early 1830s construction began on the Mad River Railroad, helping to

TOP: A panoramic view of Sandusky, Ohio from 1870. (Geography and Map Division, Library of Congress)

138

CEDAR POINT AMUSEMENT PARK
YESTERDAY & TODAY

Cedar Point was named for the grove of cedar trees that lined the peninsula. In 1870, a bathing beach was opened with small attractions. Today, over three million people visit the park. Cedar Point Amusement Park features 16 roller coasters and many other rides.

CLOCKWISE: The 650-room Hotel Breakers opened in 1905. The hotel's original lobby, decorated with stained-glass windows and a four-story rotunda, remains today. A modern view of the amusement park at Cedar Point. (Cedar Point, Cedar Fair, L.P.) The Lagoons, circa 1910. The *G. A. Boeckling* ferried passengers from Sandusky to Cedar Point from 1909 until 1951.

TOP: An early 1900s view of the foot of Columbus Avenue.

MIDDLE: Looking north along Columbus Avenue in Sandusky, circa 1908.

BOTTOM: The Pennsylvania Coal Loader #3 at Sandusky went into operation in 1939 and could handle 60 rail cars in an hour.

rapidly grow the town. By the late 1840s, the population had grown to more than 4,000 as large numbers of Irish and German immigrants came to the area. A cholera epidemic in 1849 killed 400 residents. The disease was spread as the dead bodies of victims on ocean-going vessels from Europe were dropped into Lake Erie's nearby waters. Unsuspecting residents became infected as they buried the bodies that had washed ashore. The ensuing panic caused half the population to flee the community. People returned to Sandusky in the 1850s along with a large influx of German immigrants. A Civil War prison on nearby Johnson's Island in Sandusky Bay was established in 1862 and held an estimated 12,000 Confederate prisoners.

Through the latter part of the 19th century, fish houses, wineries, breweries and other industries sprang up. Cedar Point opened as a resort in 1870. Ice harvesting was big business here since the bay was the only place along Lake Erie where ice was sure to form every winter. Trains carried tons of ice from Sandusky well into the 20th century. The trans-shipment of coal also increased at this time. The wineries and breweries closed during Prohibition but the wineries rebounded with the repeal.

In the 1940s, Sandusky's population had reached nearly 25,000 as industries produced a variety of products. In addition to fishing, wineries and shipping, factories pumped out paper, crayons, chalk, washing machines, castings, chains, boats, rubber products, radios, farm equipment and fertilizer.

By the 1950s, the Cedar Point resort had fallen on hard times and was sold, slated for demolition and development as a residential area. With the success of Disneyland in mind, its new owners decided to invest millions of dollars restoring the park. Over the years, the most advanced roller coasters and rides have been built and the park remains one of the area's biggest sources of revenue.

Sandusky, despite its industrial base, has the look of a town catering to tourists and recreation buffs. It is home to Battery Park, Cedar Point, the Follett House Museum, the Merry-Go-Round Museum and several wineries.

TOP: An aerial view of Sandusky, looking west. (Ken Winters, U.S. Army Corps of Engineers, Buffalo District)

141

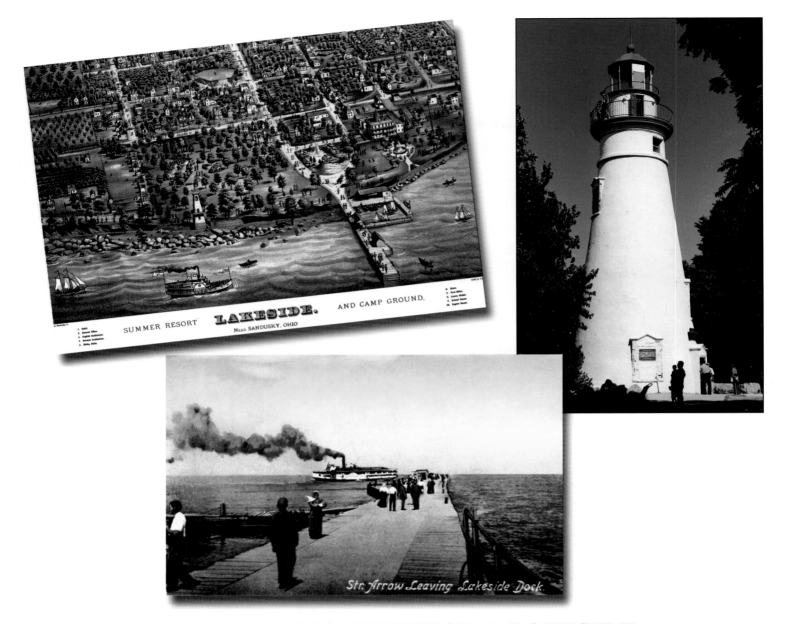

SUMMER RESORT **LAKESIDE.** AND CAMP GROUND.
Near SANDUSKY, OHIO

Str. Arrow Leaving Lakeside Dock.

MARBLEHEAD & LAKESIDE

MARBLEHEAD, Ohio (population 762) is located at the tip of the Marblehead Peninsula, which forms the northern shore of Sandusky Bay. It is the site of one of the oldest and best-known lighthouses on Lake Erie. Constructed in 1821, the Marblehead Lighthouse is the oldest continuously operating lighthouse on the Great Lakes.

The village of Marblehead has a distinctive look, since most of the churches, the schoolhouse and other buildings were constructed using the local limestone. A large quarry has operated here for more than 100 years.

The 20-mile drive around the peninsula affords views of Sandusky Bay, Lake Erie and numerous peach and apple orchards. A ferry bound for Kelleys Island departs from here.

LAKESIDE, Ohio is a small community located on the north shore of the Marblehead Peninsula. Founded in 1873 by the Methodist Church, it is one of the few remaining Chautauquas, providing summer conference facilities and a center for culture, religion, the arts, education and recreation. The resort community features numerous Victorian-era buildings including cottages, bungalows and the Hotel Lakeside, which was completed in 1875.

TOP LEFT: An 1884 panoramic view of the Lakeside resort. (Geography and Map Division, Library of Congress)

TOP RIGHT: Marblehead Lighthouse, the oldest lighthouse in continuous operation on the Great Lakes, began service in 1822.

BOTTOM: The *Arrow*, a passenger steamer made frequent trips between Sandusky, the islands and Lakeside during the early 20th century.

Ballast Island, Put in Bay, O.

LAKE ERIE'S AMERICAN ISLANDS

Just north of the Marblehead Peninsula in Lake Erie, lies a group of islands. The islands on the American side of the border include Kelleys, Green, Rattlesnake, Ballast, Sugar, Starve, Gibraltar, Mouse and the three Bass islands. The 82-acre West Sister Island, part of the Lake Erie archipelago, is located between the main group of islands and Toledo.

Indians inhabited the islands for centuries before the white man settled on them. Gabriel Segard, a French missionary, is said to have discovered the islands in the early 1600s. Other French explorers also viewed them during this period.

France ceded the islands to Great Britain in 1765, with the group of islands mentioned above being ceded to the United States in 1783. The American islands were part of the Firelands, land set aside by Connecticut as compensation for those whose homes were burned during the Revolutionary War.

The islands have been known over the years for their limestone quarries, vineyards, winemaking, fishing and tourism. They are accessible by boat and some may be reached by plane as well.

TOP LEFT: Ballast Island is one-quarter mile northeast of South Bass Island. It is believed to have been named for the rocks Oliver Hazard Perry used to ballast his fleet in the Battle of Lake Erie.

TOP RIGHT: The lighthouse on South Bass Island was in service from 1897 until 1962, when it was replaced by a light on a steel tower. Ohio State University now owns the lighthouse and quarters. (Dave Wobster)

BOTTOM: The view of Put-in-Bay from the Perry's Monument on South Bass Island.

KELLEYS ISLAND

KELLEYS ISLAND, Ohio (population 367) is an island of more than 2,800 acres, three miles north of the Marblehead Peninsula. Seven miles across at its widest point, the island has 18 miles of rocky shores.

In the early 1800s, the place was known as Cunningham's Island for a trader who lived here. Brothers Irad and Datus Kelley acquired the island in 1833. By 1851, vineyards were planted and a wine cellar was in place. The island became known for peaches, grapes and wine. In the 1850s, the quarrying of limestone began here with immigrants from all over Europe coming to work the stone. Most of quarrying ended by 1940, but Lafarge North America continues to operate Kellstone Quarry on the island.

Along the south shore of the island is Inscription Rock, a limestone ledge displaying petroglyphs that were presumably inscribed by either the Eriez Indians or the Mound Build-ers sometime during the early 1600s. The drawings represent the history of the tribe. On the northern side of the island is Glacial Grooves State Park, where the limestone rock contains a number of smooth fluted grooves that originally ran across the island and into the lake. The Ohio Historical Society now protects now protects the 396 feet of the grooves, which remained after quarrying.

The downtown area is lined with shops, restaurants and Victorian homes. The entire island is classified as a National Historic District. Regular ferry service brings visitors from the mainland.

TOP: The Glacial Grooves on Kelleys Island were scoured into the limestone bedrock approximately 18,000 years ago. The rock contains marine fossils that are 350 to 400 million years old.

MIDDLE: A peaceful view Kelleys Island ferry.

BOTTOM: Datus Kelley (1788-1866) and his brother Irad Kelley (1791-1875) be-gan buying parcels of land on Cunningham Island in Lake Erie. It was renamed Kel-leys Island. (Kelleys Island Historical Association)

SOUTH BASS ISLAND

SOUTH BASS ISLAND, Ohio (Put-in-Bay Village permanent population 128) is located three miles north of Catawba Island, which is joined to the Marblehead Peninsula.

It is the largest of the Bass islands, four miles long with a broad harbor on its northern side. Put-in-Bay Village is the center of activity on the island, which caters to tourists in search of entertainment, attractions, shops, saloons, restaurants and wineries.

South Bass Island's history is similar to the others in the area, with its vineyards and wineries. Around 1900, the island was a place of grand hotels for the well-to-do. After several of the hotels burned, the island began to cater to the working class.

The Perry's Victory and International Peace Memorial is located on the narrow neck that connects the wider portions of the island. This giant column is the third tallest memorial in the United States (behind the Gateway Arch in St. Louis and the Washington Monument) and was built to commemorate Commodore Oliver Hazard Perry's victory over the British fleet in the Battle of Lake Erie during the War of 1812. Built at a cost of $480,374, it was dedicated in 1913 at the centennial celebration of the victory and declared a national monument in 1936. The monument is made of pink granite from Milford, Massachusetts and is capped with an 11-ton bronze urn. The remains of three American and three British officers killed in the battle are interred beneath the rotunda floor. An elevator takes visitors to an open-air observation platform for a panoramic view from the top of the monument.

The island has beaches and is honeycombed with caves, including Mammoth, Crystal and Perry's caves. Other attractions include the Lake Erie Islands Historical Museum, the Stonehenge historical home, Aquatic Visitors Center and State Fish Hatchery. Fishermen visit the area for its plentiful population of walleye, bass, perch and other fish. The island is accessible from the mainland by several air and ferry services.

TOP LEFT: An 1872 wood engraving of Put-in-Bay.

RIGHT: Perry's Monument is 352 feet tall. It was built to honor those who fought in the Battle of Lake Erie during the War of 1812 and to commemorate the long-lasting peace between Great Britain, Canada and the United States.

BOTTOM LEFT: The Round House in Put-in-Bay was opened as a restaurant in 1873.

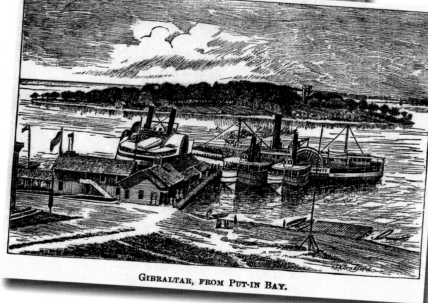

GIBRALTAR, FROM PUT-IN BAY.

GIBRALTAR ISLAND

TOP LEFT: The Needle's Eye on Gibraltar Island was formed by wave action on the limestone cliffs.

TOP RIGHT: Construction began on Cooke Castle in 1864. The mansion and the island now belong to Ohio State University.

MIDDLE: An 1870s engraving of Gibraltar Island.

BOTTOM: Jay Cooke (1821-1905), called the "Financier of the Civil War," owned Gibraltar Island.

GIBRALTAR ISLAND, Ohio is a six-acre island that rises sharply above the water at the western part of Put-in-Bay harbor. Also known as the "Gem of Lake Erie," the island was named Gibraltar because it resembles the famous fortress at the entrance to the Mediterranean Sea. It is composed of dolomite and limestone.

In 1807, title to the island was transferred from the state of Connecticut to Pierpont Edwards. In 1854, it was sold to Jose DeRivera, a New York capitalist. Financier Jay Cooke bought the island for $3,001 in 1864 and lived there during the summers for 40 years in a 15-room Victorian castle-like home. Cooke's daughters sold the island in 1925 to Julius Stone of Columbus, who immediately turned the property over to Ohio State University's Board of Trustees to become the Theodore Stone Laboratory for students of biology. The island is not open to the public.

MIDDLE BASS ISLAND

MIDDLE BASS ISLAND, Ohio (permanent population 40) lies between North Bass and South Bass islands. It is three miles long and one mile wide.

Known to the French as the *Ile de Fleurs* or Island of Flowers, it is believed La Salle's exploration team on the *Griffin* stopped here in 1680 and Father Louis Hennepin said Mass.

This island was part of the Connecticut Western Reserve and owned by Pierpont Edwards. In 1812, laborers sent by Edwards to clear the land and plant wheat were driven off the island by British soldiers.

Jose DeRivera gained possession of all three Bass islands and other area islands in 1854. He persuaded German winemakers to move here and he established a growing winemaking industry. The island also became a retreat for the wealthy and prominent. U.S. presidents Hayes, Cleveland, Harrison and Taft, and industrialist Mark Hanna entertained at the private Middle Bass Club.

The Lonz Winery was established here in 1884 and operated in the stone and brick castle-like building until it closed in 2000 following the tragic collapse of a patio deck. The buildings and surrounding land were turned over to the State of Ohio to become a park.

Ballast Island is located a mile to the east of here, where just before his naval encounter with the British in 1813, Oliver Hazard Perry is said to have picked up limestone rocks to ballast his ships.

TOP: The Middle Bass School operated between the 1860s and 1982.

BOTTOM: The Lonz Winery was built in 1884. The building and grounds are being developed to become part of an Ohio State Park.

On the Cliff, Catawba Island, O.

NORTH BASS ISLAND & CATAWBA ISLAND

NORTH BASS ISLAND, Ohio lies one mile south of the Canadian border and is roughly a mile across at its widest point. The vineyard-covered private island is closed to all except residents and their guests.

A squatter inhabited the island in the 1820s and other settlers did not arrive until the 1840s. As was the case with the other Bass islands, vineyards were planted and winemaking grew here, starting in the 1850s.

The area around North Bass Island was especially good for commercial fishing until the early 20th century. Nets with flagged buoys attached extended for miles, reaching nearly 60 feet below the lake's surface for catches of whitefish and herring. Overfishing and pollution destroyed the industry.

Prohibition ended the winemaking business here for several years while some vineyards survived by producing grape juice. During this period, rum runners darted cross the narrow channel between here and Canada's Pelee Island. Repeal of Prohibition brought about a rebound in the winemaking business and the vineyards on North Bass Island were again in full production.

Along the island's south shore a protected basin is a gathering place for boaters and swimmers who snorkel in the clear water. The area's waters also attract sport fishermen.

CATAWBA ISLAND, Ohio (Catawba Village population 312) lies just north of the Marblehead Peninsula.

While not technically an island as the name implies, Catawba Island is part of an ancient reef structure that makes up the chain of islands stretching from this point across the lake to Point Pelee in Ontario. The island is agricultural and supports a limestone quarry. It is also dotted with cottages and permanent residences.

Ferries depart from the northern tip of the island for Put-in-Bay. Catawba Island is accessible by a road on its western side and by a causeway.

ABOVE LEFT: A 1940s view of the Put-in-Bay auto ferry dock on Catawba Island.

TOP RIGHT: An early-1900s view of Catawba Island.

PORT CLINTON

PORT CLINTON, Ohio (population 6,391) lies at the mouth of the wide Portage River, 65 miles west of Cleveland and 35 miles east of Toledo. The community is the Ottawa County seat. The attractive main street of the business district ends at the waterfront where a fish house still operates. State Route 163 passes through town and over a drawbridge across the Portage River.

The town was platted in 1828 by General William Lytle of Cincinnati, the Surveyor-General of the Northwest Territory, along with Ezekiel and Elias Haines, O.M. Spencer and others. Port Clinton was named for Dewitt Clinton, the New York governor and Erie Canal builder who, in 1824, proposed the building of the Sandusky-Scioto Canal from the mouth of the Portage River to the Ohio River. The canal was never built because of an insufficient water supply. Instead, canals heading to the Ohio River were built from Cleveland and Toledo. Port Clinton's fishing industry developed during the late 19th and early 20th centuries and the area's numerous fruit orchards supported the economy.

Today, the area continues to support many vineyards, orchards and vegetable farms. Local deposits have triggered the development of plants handling gypsum and various

TOP LEFT: Unloading fish at Port Clinton, circa 1910.

TOP RIGHT: Fish packing houses lined the Portage River at Port Clinton in the early 20th century.

BOTTOM: An aerial view of Port Clinton's harbor. (Ken Winters, U.S. Army Corps of Engineers, Buffalo District)

ABOVE: Rutherford B. Hayes (1822–1893) served as 19th President of the United States from 1877-1881. Hayes made his home in Fremont, Ohio, just a few miles from Port Clinton. (Library of Congress, Prints & Photographs Division LC-BH82601-400)

TOP: Port Clinton, looking north, circa 1909.

MIDDLE: A 1930s view of Camp Perry, west of Port Clinton. The camp hosts rifle matches and provides training facilities for units of the Ohio National Guard.

BOTTOM: A 1940s view of Madison Street in Port Clinton, looking north toward the Portage River.

minerals. Port Clinton's economy is also tied to fishing, boating, beaches and tourism, with the city serving as the gateway to the resort islands of Lake Erie. Port Clinton is known as the "Walleye Capital of the World."

Camp Perry, located west of Port Clinton, hosts national rifle and pistol matches and provides training facilities for units of the Ohio National Guard as well as lodging facilities for visitors to Ohio's northern shore. A downtown revitalization program began in 1999 to add landscaped boulevards, trees and pavilions. A ferry departs from here, bound for Put-in-Bay. The Davis-Besse nuclear power plant, located between Port Clinton and Toledo at Oak Harbor, went on-line in 1978. Fremont, the home of President Rutherford B. Hayes, is located along the Sandusky River, a few miles to the southwest of Port Clinton.

TOLEDO

TOLEDO, Ohio (city population: 313,619, metro population: 656,696) is a major industrial center at the very western end of Lake Erie, running for several miles along both banks of the Maumee River. The Maumee is the largest tributary flowing into the Great Lakes system. Toledo is the third busiest port on the Great Lakes, with a natural harbor frontage of 35 miles.

Most of the city lies on the western side of the river, with several bridges connecting both sides of the city. The central business district is eight miles south of Maumee Bay and actually does not have a view of Lake Erie.

Etienne Brulé, a French-Canadian guide, visited the site of the present-day Toledo in 1615. He found the Eriez Indians living at the mouth of the Maumee River. The area was opened to settlement after the Battle of Fallen Timbers in 1794, when General "Mad" Anthony Wayne defeated the Indians.

ABOVE: Toledo's 27-story art deco Ohio Savings and Trust Building was completed in 1932. It now is known as the National City Bank Building.

Toledo: The Glass City

ABOVE: A panoramic view of Toledo, Ohio on the Maumee River. The tallest buildings from left to right: Fiberglass Tower, Riverfront Apartments, National City Bank and One SeaGate. The Cherry Street/Martin Luther King Bridge is at right.

MIDDLE: The *Willis B. Boyer* was launched in 1911 and worked on the Great Lakes until 1980. In 1987, it became a museum ship on the Toledo waterfront.

BOTTOM: The Toledo Museum of Art building was opened in 1912. The museum contains collections of glass, European and American art. It also includes Renaissance, Roman, Greek and Japanese collections.

MIDDLE: The Toledo Harbor Lighthouse went into operation in 1904. It continues to guard the entrance to the shipping channel. (Dave Wobster)

BOTTOM: Fifth Third Field, the current home of the Toledo Mud Hens baseball team, was opened in 2002.

Fort Meigs, a log-and-earth fortification, is located up the Maumee River in nearby Perrysburg. The fort held off the British and Canadian troops and Tecumseh's warriors in their efforts during the Northwest Campaign in 1813.

Fort Industry was located at the mouth of Swan Creek where downtown Toledo stands today. Following the War of 1812, the area was settled. A treaty in 1817 formally gave Indian land in the area to the U.S. government. In 1833, two settlements, Port Lawrence and Vistula, joined to become Toledo, which was incorporated in 1837. The reason the city is called Toledo is not officially known, but many different stories have circulated over the years. The most widely held belief is that the city was named for Toledo, Spain.

Toledo's early years were challenging for residents as a cholera epidemic plagued the area in 1832 and 1833, severe drought hit in 1838 and a financial panic slowed business for two years. The Toledo War between Ohio and Michigan from 1835 to 1836, added further strain. Early maps of the area were erroneous, placing the tip of Lake Erie too far south and Lake Michigan too far north. Ohio's decision to use the Maumee River in its canal system created a fierce dispute, pitting Ohio against Michigan over the state boundary line. Residents mobilized to transfer control of the area to Ohio. Michigan's 21-year-old acting governor, Stevens T. Mason, sent troops to stop the uprising. Ohio Governor Robert Lucas responded by sending the militia, and the Ohio State Legislature organized the area in question, naming it Lucas County. Before there was any bloodshed, President Andrew Jackson settled the dispute, awarding the land to Ohio. A year later, the U.S. Congress compensated the Michigan Territory by awarding it the Upper Peninsula and granting Michigan statehood.

In the fury to build canals, Toledo became the terminus of Wabash & Erie Canal and the Miami & Erie Canal. Both canals merged at Defiance, Ohio, extending along the Maumee River to the lake. The Erie & Kalamazoo Railroad, completed in 1836, was the first railroad to be built west of the Allegheny Mountains. Mills, factories, foundries and shipping facilities were built, spurred by the discovery of local deposits of gas and oil in 1844. By 1860, Toledo's population had grown to more than 13,000. Toledo became a key player in the abolitionist movement during the Civil War period as an important stop on the Underground Railroad.

By the 1870s, Toledo was connected by more railroads, accelerating its industrial and population growth. By 1880, 50,000 people lived here and the city became the nation's third largest rail center. The abundance of natural gas in the Maumee Valley helped fuel the glassmaking industry, brought to Toledo by Edward Libbey and Michael Owens. At the same time, the shipping of coal and ore was being handled along the waterfront. Lumber, furniture, iron and steel production grew at a frenzied pace. The drilling of oil wells, particularly on the eastern side of Toledo, helped build the refining industry. Cultural advances were

TOP: William Henry Harrison built Fort Meigs on the Maumee River in 1813 to protect northwest Ohio and Indiana from the British. Today's reconstructed fort includes a 10-acre log enclosure, seven blockhouses and five emplacements.

sale to settlers at $1 per acre for up to 300 acres.

Judah Colt, a native of Lyme, Connecticut, arrived in the area in 1795. He offered the Pennsylvania Population Company $1 an acre for a large section of land in the Triangle. The request was denied, but impressed with Colt, the company appointed him as a land agent for Erie County in 1797. Headquarters were set up at Colt's Station, nine miles south of the lakeshore, near French Creek. Soon, Colt built a road from Freeport on Lake Erie (near North East) across the summit to French Creek. In 1804, Colt surmised that land along the

lakeshore was preferable to his settlement in the hills, so he moved to Erie where he died in 1832.

In 1796, another company, the Harrisburg and Presque Isle Company, was formed to settle, improve and populate the land near and along Lake Erie. Additional portions of land were also reserved. The Commonwealth donated land to General William Irvine as a reward for his services during the Revolution. He selected his land while laying out the town of Erie. Another piece of land, a 24-square-mile section around Erie's harbor, became the Erie State Reserve.

The first portion of the Buffalo Road from Erie toward the New York State line was laid out in 1805 and completed in 1812. Once opened, communities began to spring up along the road, which later became U.S. Route 20.

THE CONNECTICUT WESTERN RESERVE IN OHIO

Before the American Revolution, Connecticut laid claim to all of the land from its western border to the Mississippi River. This strip of land included parts of New York and Pennsylvania. Once the U.S. government was set up, Connecticut relinquished claims to these lands with the exception of a 120-mile strip in Ohio. Profits from the sale of Connecticut Western Reserve lands (map on page 33) were to be used to fund public schools in Connecticut. The western portion of this land, currently Ohio's Huron and Erie counties, was used to compensate those Connecticut residents whose property had been burned or destroyed by the British during the American Revolution. These lands were called the "Firelands."

Connecticut sold the rest of the land, about three million acres, to the Connecticut Land Company for about 40 cents an acre. General Moses Cleaveland was hired as the land agent to survey and sell the land. After signing a treaty with the Indians in June of 1796, Cleaveland and a small party made their way to the Reserve, arriving at Conneaut, Ohio on July 4, 1796 (see Chapter 9 profiles of Conneaut, Ashtabula and Cleveland).

The surveying party broke into two groups. Cleaveland took one group and continued down the lakeshore to the mouth of the Cuyahoga River. The other group headed south along Pennsylvania's western border. The teams laid out townships on a grid of ranges in five-mile squares. Before returning to Connecticut, Cleaveland stayed just long enough to survey the land and map out a plan for what later became the city of Cleveland.

MAP: A late 18th century map, which includes the western portion of Pennsylvania before the purchase of the Erie Triangle. *(History of the Mission of the United Brethren among the Indians of North America.* Library of Congress, Geography and Map Division)

LEFT: Judah Colt (1761-1832) was the general agent for the Pennsylvania Population Company, which held the warrants for all the land in the Erie Triangle. (Pennsylvania Historical and Museum Commission)

BOTTOM: General Moses Cleaveland (1754-1806), a director of the Connecticut Land Company, was sent to survey lands within the Western Reserve. In 1796, he established the settlement of Cleaveland (Cleveland) on the banks of Lake Erie at the mouth of the Cuyahoga River. (Western Reserve Historical Society, Cleveland, Ohio)

Within two years, settlers began to arrive in New Connecticut. Families traveled 600 miles to this new land to set up towns and villages. The distinctively New England look can still be seen today. Unlike other villages in the Lake Erie region, these communities, like those in Connecticut, were set up around village squares. Often, these towns were named after the Connecticut towns from which the settlers arrived.

By 1820, the population of the Western Reserve amounted to more than 55,000. Within five years, the opening of the Erie Canal brought an even larger stream of settlers to the area.

THE NORTHWEST TERRITORY OF OHIO AND MICHIGAN

The Michigan Territory was opened to settlement after the British finally gave up control of Detroit and Indians had been forcibly removed from the area. To prevent the United States from developing the Great Lakes area, the British supplied Indians with arms. U.S. military efforts to subdue the Indians were unsuccessful before General "Mad" Anthony Wayne defeated the Indians near Toledo at the Battle of Fallen Timbers in 1794. This military action forced the British to abandon the northwestern forts, and in 1805, the Michigan Territory was organized. The region still was not ready for significant settlement. In 1813, a British force of 1,300 soldiers and Indians attacked the American army at Monroe in the Battle of the River Raisin. Later that year, U.S. forces returned to drive the British from Michigan's soil.

After the war, Michigan's growth was slow until the Erie Canal was opened in 1825. As was the case with the Western Reserve in Ohio, the canal brought a steady stream of immigrants, mostly from New York and New England. In 1837, Michigan became the nation's 26th state.

ABOVE: General "Mad" Anthony Wayne (1745-1796) defeated the Indians at the Battle of Fallen Timbers. The Northwest Territory was then opened to white settlement. (Independence National Historical Park)

TOP: General Moses Cleaveland's party traveled along the shoreline of the Lake Erie while surveying the lands of Connecticut's Western Reserve. The shoreline pictured is near North Perry, Ohio.

BOTTOM: "Charge of the Dragoons at Fallen Timbers" painted by R.F. Zogbaum. (The Ohio Historical Society)

Libbey Cut Glass Works, Toledo O.

THE LIBBEY GLASS

COPR. DETROIT PUBLISHING CO.

also great during the late 19th century, as opera houses and theaters were built. The Toledo Museum of Art and Toledo Zoo were founded during this period.

When Toledo's population reached 131,000 in 1900, it became the 26th largest city in the country. The city became the leader in production of low-priced glass bottles and light bulbs. In 1908, John Willys moved his Overland automobile factory from Indianapolis to Toledo. The glass and automobile industries complimented one another. Soon, other related industries located in Toledo, producing gears, spark plugs and other auto parts.

With 290,000 inhabitants in 1930, growth came to an abrupt halt during the Great Depression. A bitter and violent strike in 1934 brought national attention to Toledo and signaled the start of unionization of the auto industry. During the 1940s, Toledo's workers were kept busy, supporting the war effort and producing numerous goods, including Jeeps.

The complexion of the Toledo area changed during the second half of the 20th century. Toledo's suburbs grew after World War II, but unlike the other large cities around Lake Erie, Toledo's population loss did not begin until after 1970, when it peaked at 383,818.

TOP: Toledo, Ohio on the Maumee River, depicted in an 1876 panoramic map. (Geography and Map Division, Library of Congress)

MIDDLE LEFT: The Libbey Cut Glass Works at Toledo, circa 1910.

BOTTOM: An early 1900s view of the Maumee River and the old Cherry Street Bridge, Toledo, Ohio.

ABOVE: John N. Willys (1873-1935) moved his Overland car company from Indianapolis to Toledo in 1908. In 1912, he built the company's seven-story head-quarters. (Library of Congress, Prints & Photographs Division LC-USZ62-50781)

TOP TO BOTTOM: Pre-1920s views of the Willys-Overland plant. Advertisements show the Willys vehicles' uses in the military and in civilian life.

During the late 1980s and 1990s, the downtown area gradually came back to life as old buildings were renovated and new development began to take place on both sides of the Maumee River.

Today, Toledo's downtown area and waterfront continue to be revitalized. New buildings include the striking headquarters for the Owens-Corning Corporation. The city's appealing downtown area sits across the Maumee River from restaurants and clubs that have been built on formerly industrial land.

Toledo's manufacturing base consists of glass production, plastics, petroleum, machinery, scales, furnaces and primary metal products, as well as automotive assembly (notably Jeeps) and parts production. The city is home to the University of Toledo, established in 1872, the Toledo Botanical Gardens, Toledo Museum of Art, Toledo Zoo, Toledo Science Center and the Willis B. Boyer Museum Ship. The Toledo Mud Hens (International League) baseball team plays at Fifth Third Field, a 10,300-seat downtown facility that opened in 2002. The Toledo Walleye hockey team (ECHL) began play in the new 9,000 seat Lucas County Sports Arena in 2009. A dramatic cable-stayed bridge carrying Interstate 280 across the Maumee River was completed in 2007. Historic Fort Meigs is located in nearby Perrysburg. Three of the original six locks that connected the Maumee River to the Miami & Erie Canal are located in nearby Maumee.

ABOVE: The Veterans' Glass City Skyway was opened in 2007, replacing the bascule lift bridge in the background. (Ohio Department of Transportation)

10 Michigan Shoreline

Michigan's share of Lake Erie's shoreline may be smaller than that of neighboring states and Ontario, but this stretch of lakefront is indeed very beautiful and historically significant. This was the site of fierce battles for an expanding nation, an area where thousands of immigrants came to work and also a place where the natural beauty of the lake remains.

Michigan's shoreline extends from a point just above the Maumee River estuary, north of Toledo, to the mouth of the Detroit River. As with the Niagara River, the Detroit River is included because of its geological, historical and commercial ties with Lake Erie. Like the Niagara River, the Detroit River is actually a strait with no major tributaries.

North of Toledo, Lake Erie's Michigan shoreline extends generally northward toward the Detroit area. It is dotted with summer communities, beaches, marshlands, preserves and creeks. Halfway between Toledo and the mouth of the Detroit River, the Raisin River enters western Lake Erie. For miles along the western shore of the lake, the smokestacks of Detroit Edison's plant at Monroe and the cooling towers of the company's Fermi 2 nuclear power station can be seen on the horizon.

The mouth of the 29-mile-long Detroit River is at the northwestern part of Lake Erie. This strait brings the water of three other Great Lakes to Lake Erie. Like the other main Great Lakes connecting channels, the water in the Detroit River is generally clear, since the lakes act as giant settling basins.

The residential Grosse Ile sits just north of Lake Erie in the Detroit River. The smaller industrial Downriver cities line the lower portion of the river, while the city of Detroit occupies most of the remainder of the western bank to the north.

The suspension Ambassador Bridge carries auto traffic 152 feet above the Detroit River, linking the Motor City with Windsor, Ontario. This is North America's busiest border crossing. A bend in the river creates a strange twist of fate, as much of Detroit is actually located immediately north of the neighboring Canadian city of Windsor.

Just to the east of the parklands of Belle Isle, the water from the upper Great Lakes exits Lake St. Clair into the Detroit River, which in turn transports it to Lake Erie.

TOP: An aerial view of a portion of Michigan's shoreline on the western end of Lake Erie. The Fermi 2 nuclear power plant is in the foreground. Railroads, Interstate 75 and U.S. Route 24 cross the upper left portion of the image. The Huron River is at the upper right.

BOTTOM: The resort community of Luna Pier is similar in apperance to other small settlements along Michigan's portion of Lake Erie.

PAGE 159: A rowing crew practices on the Detroit River. The view is from Belle Isle.

LUNA PIER, TOLEDO BEACH, BOLLES HARBOR

LUNA PIER, Michigan (population 1,483) is six miles north of the Ohio border on Lake Erie. A long crescent-shaped pier protects this small resort community. Luna Pier was developed as a resort community during the early 20th century. A post office was opened in 1929 and Luna Pier was incorporated in 1963. The town includes a mix of cottages and year-round homes. It is also a bedroom community for Toledo.

TOLEDO BEACH, Michigan is a small resort community seven miles north of the Ohio border. An amusement park opened at Toledo Beach in 1906, closed during the Depression, and reopened after World War II. The Toledo Railway & Light Company operated an interurban line to Toledo Beach. Cars departed every two minutes for Toledo Beach during its heyday. The park included a dance hall, picnic grounds and amusements along the sandy beach. Toledo Beach amusement park closed in 1970. Today, Toledo Beach is known for its marinas.

BOLLES HARBOR, Michigan (population 4,651) is four miles south of Monroe, at the southern side of the mouth of LaPlaisance Creek on LaPlaisance Bay. At the beginning of the War of 1812, there were 14 homes in the LaPlaisance Bay settlement. Today, known as Bolles Harbor, this growing resort community is known for fishing and boating.

TOP: Looking west along LaPlaisance Creek at Bolles Harbor, Michigan.

BOTTOM RIGHT: Toledo Beach, Michigan circa 1910. The postcard image was taken from "The Chutes," an amusement slide.

BOTTOM LEFT: Behind the cottages of the resort community of Luna Pier, Michigan, boats are kept safe in a canal-like slip.

MONROE

MONROE, Michigan (population 22,076) is located on the Raisin River, four miles west of where it empties into Lake Erie, at the midway point along Lake Erie's western shore, sitting 20 miles north of Toledo and 40 miles south of Detroit.

The eye-catching downtown area includes numerous two-story brick buildings from the late 19th and early 20th centuries. The business district is surrounded by established neighborhoods.

French missionaries visited the area as early as 1634, naming the river *riviere aux raisin* for the abundance of wild grapes in the area. A trading post and fort were established here in 1778, and two years later the first white settler arrived. The settlement was originally called Frenchtown for the French families who moved here from Detroit and Canada, but was later renamed Monroe in anticipation of a visit from the President of the United States.

The Battle of River Raisin took place here during the War of 1812, as Indians in support of the British massacred hundreds of white prisoners. Following the War of 1812, Monroe County was established in 1817 with the organization of the Michigan Territory and the settlement became the county seat.

The bloodless Toledo War was centered at Monroe in 1835 (see Chapter 9 profile of Toledo). The dispute arose between Michigan and Ohio over possession and the location of Michigan's southern boundary. Two years after Ohio's admission to the Union in 1803, surveyors drew a line between the southern end of Lake Michigan and Lake Erie, defining the border, but the line was in error, giving Michigan a portion of land in northern Ohio. In 1817, Congress resurveyed the strip, placing it wholly in Ohio. The Michigan Territory continued to exercise jurisdiction over the area. By 1835, Ohio Governor Robert Lucas proclaimed authority and attempted to validate Ohio's control through a court session. The Monroe County sheriff organized posses to raid Toledo, while Ohioans held a secret late night court session to validate Ohio's claim. The issue was finally settled when Congress refused to give Michigan statehood unless it gave up all claims to the disputed land. To heal

TOP: An 1866 panoramic map of Monroe, Michigan. The Raisin River empties into Lake Erie, which is in the distance. (Geography and Map Division, Library of Congress)

MONROE. MICH.
Bathing Beach Monroe Piers

View on Government Canal at Monroe Piers, Monroe, Mich.

MONROE STREET. LOOKING NORTH. MONROE. MICH.

wounded egos, Congress awarded the Upper Peninsula, a part of the Northwest Territory, to Michigan and granted it statehood. The state later realized the value of this consolation prize when its natural resources were developed.

The glass industry started in Monroe in 1836 because of the area's siliceous sand and sandstone deposits. For years, Monroe's factories produced most of the glass in the Midwest. By the 1850s, nurseries were established to grow trees, shrubs and flowers, earning Monroe the nickname the "Floral City."

General George A. Custer lived here for many years. Custer was killed in 1876 when Sitting Bull's warriors defeated his troops in the Battle of the Little Big Horn.

In the early 20th century, Monroe continued to grow, adding steel and paper mills, manufacturing plants, quarries and fishing to its economic base. The paper industry was the top employer by 1920. Today's industry is very diverse, ranging from agriculture to the manufacture of reclining chairs. A 3,100-megawatt coal-powered generating plant operates on Monroe's Lake Erie's shoreline. Nearby, the River Raisin Battlefield Visitors Center highlights the area's role in the War of 1812.

TOP LEFT: A 1905 image, looking north along Lake Erie's shoreline at Monroe Piers, Michigan.

TOP RIGHT: Looking east toward Lake Erie on the Government Canal (the mouth of the Raisin River) at Monroe Michigan, circa 1910.

MIDDLE: Monroe Street, looking north at Monroe, Michigan.

BOTTOM: George Armstrong Custer (1839-1876) spent much of his childhood living with his half-sister and his brother-in-law in Monroe. A statue of Custer on his horse stands near downtown Monroe. (Library of Congress, Prints & Photographs Division LC-USZ62-48894)

ESTRAL BEACH & GIBRALTAR

ESTRAL BEACH, Michigan (population 486) is a small summer resort community, eight miles northeast of Monroe on Lake Erie. The community is located on the northern side of Swan Creek across the creek from Detroit Edison's Fermi 2 power plant. Estral Beach was developed as a resort area in the early 1900s and was incorporated as a village in 1925. Cottages and homes line marshy inlets.

GIBRALTAR, Michigan (population 4,264) is primarily a residential community 22 miles south of downtown Detroit at the mouth of the Detroit River, adjacent to the southern tip of Grosse Ile. At Gibraltar, the "Venice of Michigan," the Detroit River finishes its work, carrying the flow of the upper Great Lakes into Lake Erie.

One of Michigan's smallest cities, Gibraltar is made up of a portion of the mainland and four islands: Main, Hall, Edmund and Horse. The islands are formed by canals running through the community and connected by bridges.

Gibraltar has had several names since the area was first explored and settled. The French used a variety of names to describe this place, including *chenal de la presque ile, la roche debout, point auroche, gros* or *grosse roches*. The Wyandot Indian village located here was referred to as Brownstown. When the area was under British control, the name was changed to Gibralter. The spelling was changed from Gibralter to Gibraltar in 1900.

River Road (West Jefferson), which runs through Gibraltar, was a trail ceded to the United States by the Indians to be used as a supply route for the garrison at Detroit. Jefferson Avenue runs along the entire length of the Detroit River.

Settlement began in the 1830s. In 1836, the Gibralter-Flat Rock Land & Canal Company was organized to build a canal between Gibralter and Muskegon on Lake Michigan. The plan attracted settlers, yet never came to fruition. Later in the 19th century, farming and a shipyard were the primary businesses in the settlement. Gibraltar was formed as a village in 1954, and in 1961, it was incorporated as the second smallest city in Michigan.

The Bob-Lo Island Amusement Park's ferry dock was moved here from downtown Detroit and operated for a short time in the early 1990s. The McLouth Steel Corporation opened a cold steel roll mill in 1955. It operated in Gibraltar until 1996.

TOP: One of several marinas at Gibraltar, Michigan.

BOTTOM: Detroit Edison's Fermi 2 nuclear power plant cooling towers loom over wheat fields and Lake Erie's shoreline near Estral Beach at Newport, Michigan.

GROSSE ILE

GROSSE ILE, Michigan (population 10,894) sits in the middle of the Detroit River, six miles north of the Detroit River Light, which marks the entrance to Lake Erie. The township actually consists of several islands, including Elba, Upper Hickory (Meso), Hickory and Swan along with the uninhabited islands of Calf, Celeron (Tawas), Fox, Stony, Sugar, Round and Dynamite. Grosse Ile is the name of the main island, actually two islands divided by the Thorofare Canal. The main island is seven miles long and one and a half miles wide.

The island was included in Father Hennepin's description of the river, and Detroit founder Sieur Antoine de la Mothe Cadillac considered the place for his Fort Pontchartrain, eventually settling on a point upriver. The early French explorers called the island *la grosse ile*, meaning "the large island."

On July 6, 1776, the Potawatomi Indians ignored the rights of the Ottawa and Wyandot Indians and deeded the land to Detroit merchants William and Alexander Macomb. Eventually, President James Madison confirmed the Macomb's title to the island. After the War of 1812, the U.S. government removed Indians who were threatening Macomb's tenants.

By the late 1800s, Sugar Island had become an amusement park with a dance pavilion and bathing beach, attracting people from Detroit on steam-powered paddle wheelers. For several years, the railroad carried passengers and cargo from the mainland to Grosse Ile and over another bridge to Stony Island. From there, the cars were put on a ferry bound for Ontario, then put back on track to continue on to Buffalo. The railroad eventually discontinued this route, but commuter rail service to Detroit continued until the mid-1920s when automobile travel became fashionable.

Some of Detroit's famous automotive families had summer homes here. Ransom E. Olds built a summer estate on Elba Island in 1916. Charles and William Fisher (Fisher Body)

TOP: Looking south along the Trenton Channel of the Detroit River from Grosse Ile, Michigan. The County Bridge and Detroit Edison's Trenton Channel Power Plant are in the background.

BOTTOM: An aerial view of Grosse Ile, looking north along the Detroit River. (Grosse Ile Airport)

TOP LEFT: The Michigan Central Railroad depot on Grosse Ile was built in 1904. It was abandoned in 1925 and later used as a school, a library and township offices. The Grosse Ile Historical Society now uses the depot and the adjacent 1871 U.S. Customs House as a museum. (Grosse Ile Historical Society)

TOP RIGHT: The Victorian Wedding Cake House on the east side of Grosse Ile is a private residence, which was built in 1861.

BOTTOM: Looking east from Grosse Ile toward Stony Island. A rail ran from the mainland, across Grosse Ile to Stony Island. From there, a ferry carried the rail cars to and from the Canadian side of the Detroit River. (Grosse Ile Historical Society)

built mansion-type summer homes. William S. Knudsen (General Motors) spent summers in a home near the County Bridge. Henry Ford bought land here in the 1920s, but never built a home. He sold pieces of the property to key Ford employees.

Grosse Ile Municipal Airport is located at the south end of the main island. Curtiss-Wright operated a flying school here and the first all-metal dirigible was built here for the Navy. In the 1920s, a Navy seaplane base was built and the Navy developed the site for military flight training during World War II. During the war, the U.S. Naval Air Station expanded to train large numbers of American and British fliers. The Navy continued operations here until the base was closed in 1969. A year later it was deeded to the township.

The Grosse Ile Lighthouse at the north end of the island was built in 1894 and rebuilt in 1906 to guide ships on the river between Grosse Ile and the Canadian shore. It ceased operations in the 1940s but remains in place today. Two bridges connect with the mainland. To the north, the privately owned Grosse Ile Toll Bridge was built in 1913. The free Wayne County Bridge, opened to vehicular traffic in the 1930s, is located to the south.

Exclusive subdivisions began to be built in the 1920s and today new upscale home construction continues. Historic sites abound on the island and include the home of descendants of the Macomb brothers who purchased Grosse Ile in the 1700s. The Great Flowing Well was an attraction on the lower end of the island. Its building is now shuttered and inconspicuous amongst homes in a quiet subdivision. Westcroft Gardens is a Michigan Centennial Farm operated by Macomb descendants, which includes botanical gardens and a nursery known for azaleas and rhododendrons.

TRENTON

TRENTON, Michigan (population 19,584) is 20 miles south of Detroit on the Detroit River, adjacent to Grosse Ile. It is one of the four downriver cities, which also include Wyandotte, Ecorse and River Rouge.

Abraham C. Truax, a member of the Territorial Militia and present when General Hull surrendered Detroit to the British in 1812, founded the settlement as Truaxton in 1827. The settlement consisted of several log cabins and a few houses. Limestone from a quarry, opened here in the early 1800s, was used for the fort and other buildings in Detroit.

Because of its location and a plentiful supply of oak in the area, the settlement developed through shipbuilding in the 1840s. This industry flourished until wooden ships became obsolete. Many residents left the town when one of the shipyards moved to Toledo in the late 1880s, but shipbuilding lived on here until the mid-1960s. The commercial fishing industry also developed here during this period.

After the opening of the Erie Canal, demand for limestone for buildings in Detroit, Toledo and other cities increased. This led to the development of a quarry near here and the name of the village was changed to Trenton in 1875 for the Trenton Series of limestone in the area.

The Church family later purchased the quarry and the limestone was used to produce baking soda for the family business, Arm & Hammer Baking Soda. The automotive industry in Trenton started in 1912 with a short-lived electric car manufacturer, but the industry continues to be part of today's economy. The quarrying of limestone, which started in the early 1800s, continues here as well. Trenton was incorporated as a city in 1957. Trenton's waterfront is showcased by Elizabeth Park on Slocum's Island, donated by heirs of Elizabeth Slocum, a direct descendent of Major Truax.

While some factories have closed, others continue to operate, including the Chrysler Engine Plant on the edge of town.

TOP LEFT: Downtown Trenton, Michigan.

MAP: A 1915 map of Trenton, the Detroit River and Grosse Ile.

BOTTOM: Elizabeth Park, the oldest in the Wayne County Park System, is located on the Detroit River, linked to Trenton by bridges. The 162-acre park was originally known as "Slocum's Island."

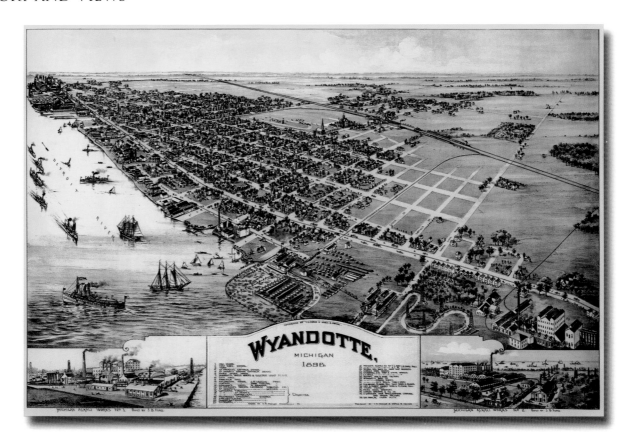

WYANDOTTE & ECORSE

WYANDOTTE, Michigan (population 28,006) is located 12 miles south of Detroit's core. This industrialized city is surrounded by older homes on streets lined with mature trees.

Wyandotte is named for the Wendot or Wyandot Indians, a remaining tribe of the Hurons who lived in this region. Their range included the area around Georgian Bay, south along lakes Huron and Erie and east to the Niagara Frontier in present-day New York State. In the early 1730s, the Wyandot village of Mongnagon was located here on the banks of the Detroit River. The village consisted of dwellings made from bent wood poles covered with tree bark. In 1818, the Wyandot Indians signed a treaty with the United States government relinquishing land in this area. The group moved to an area near Flat Rock, Michigan, then to Ohio, Kansas and finally Oklahoma.

In 1818, Major John Biddle purchased 2,200 acres, including the Indian village, and built a large farm and his home, naming his spread "The Wyandotte" after the Indians who had lived here. The middle of the 19th century saw the arrival of industry as the Eureka Iron Company bought Biddle's estate in 1854. The company planned streets and sold land for homes and businesses. In 1860, Wyandotte's population was 1,700; in 1867, Wyandotte became a city. The iron works used ore from the Upper Peninsula of Michigan and timber from forests in the area for fuel, producing the first steel using the Bessemer process. Falling iron prices and a dwindling wood supply finally resulted in the closing of the works in 1892.

While drilling in search of a cheaper source for fuel for the iron works, salt beds were discovered. Captain J.B. Ford, an industrialist known for his involvement in the manufacture of plate glass in the United States, took advantage of this resource for its use to make soda ash. The Michigan Alkali Company started producing a number of chemicals here in the 1890s. In the 1940s, the name was changed to the Wyandotte Chemical Company. Today known as

TOP: An 1896 panoramic map of Wyandotte, Michigan. (Geography and Map Division, Library of Congress)

RIGHT: The Wyandotte Museum is located in the Ford-MacNichol Home, an 1896 restored Queen Anne Victorian structure.

BASF, the company produces soaps, detergents and other products. Other industries sprouted during the late 1800s, including shipbuilding and the manufacture of stoves and trunks. More than 200 ships, including tugs, steamers and ferries, were built here at the American Shipbuilding Company's Wyandotte yards. Hulls constructed in Wyandotte were then taken upriver to Detroit to be outfitted.

During Prohibition, Wyandotte was infamous for rum running. Police dumped confiscated illegal shipments into the Detroit River. Later, divers would search the river bottom for the contraband. In recent years, some homeowners have discovered secret rooms and passageways that led to the river during the Prohibition era.

Wyandotte's population peaked at more than 40,000 in 1960. Today, Wyandotte continues as an industrial and residential city. It is a community rich in Hungarian and Polish ethnic traditions. It has its own cable company and electric and water plants. Recreational opportunities include 13 parks, an arena and golf course. Henry Ford Wyandotte Hospital and BASF are Wyandotte's largest employers.

ECORSE, Michigan (population 11,229) is located on the Detroit River between Wyandotte and River Rouge at the mouth of the Ecorse River. Ecorse is the oldest of the downriver communities. The Ecorse River or *riviere aux ecorses* was named for the bark along the shore, which the Indians used to build canoes. After the War of 1812, the settlement built on Wyandot Indian lands was called Grandport.

During Prohibition, Ecorse became the nation's largest port of entry for illegal Canadian liquor as speedboats eluded authorities, whipping in and out of bulletproof boat wells on the American side. The liquor was loaded into cars, which sped to clubs, roadhouses and homes in Michigan, Ohio and other states. A high board fence cut off the waterfront. With the repeal of Prohibition, the rum running ended abruptly and the fence came down. Over the years, industry in Ecorse has included the manufacture of steel.

TOP LEFT: Biddle Avenue, Wyandotte's main thoroughfare, circa 1910.

TOP RIGHT: In 1893, Captain John Baptiste Ford (1811-1903) established the Michigan Alkali Company. The layer of salt beneath the area was used with limestone to produce a variety of sodium-based industrial and consumer products.

BOTTOM: A view to the south along the Detroit River at Ecorse.

169

RIVER ROUGE

RIVER ROUGE, Michigan (population 9,917) is located where the meandering Rouge River meets the Detroit River. Of the four industrial downriver cities, River Rouge is closest to Detroit, which borders to the north.

The Woodland Indians were the first to settle here, followed by the French, the British and Americans. The Rouge was an early lifeline for food, water and transportation. From the late 19th century to the middle of the 20th century, industrial development, immigration and urban growth were fast and furious. River Rouge became a village in 1899 and a city in 1921, partly as a result of the building of Ford's industrial complex in nearby Dearborn.

In 1915, Henry Ford purchased land in Dearborn to build the River Rouge Complex, one of the industrial wonders of the world. He built his estate, Fair Lane, four miles upstream. In 1927, Ford's final assembly line was shifted from Highland Park to the 2,000-acre Rouge site to build the Model A. By the late 1930s, Ford had constructed more than 25 buildings, designed by Albert Kahn. The complex was especially notable because Ford had realized self-sufficiency. The process was a continuous flow that began here with the iron ore and other raw materials and concluded here with finished automobiles rolling off the assembly line. The development had docks, blast furnaces, steel mills, foundries, a rolling mill, metal stamping facilities, an engine plant, a glass manufacturing shop, tire plant, and its own power house for steam and electricity. Ford's River Rouge Complex saw a peak employment of 120,000 during World War II and is listed as a National Historic Landmark.

The city of River Rouge has been home to many industries over the years. The Great Lakes Engineering Works produced hundreds of boats, including the *William G. Mather* in 1925 and the *Edmund Fitzgerald* in 1958. Steel mills, refineries, petroleum storage, a gypsum plant and other factories have also operated here.

The heavily used Rouge River became one of the nation's most polluted waterways. Sewers and septic tanks overflowed into the river, pollution churned from smokestacks and parts of the river were channeled in concrete to control flooding. Although pollution increased in the 20th century, efforts were made to restore the river. In 1940, the Detroit Wastewater Treatment Plant was built and more than 50 miles of land adjacent to the river was acquired for public use. The Rouge River system totals more than 126 miles with four separate branches, the Main, Upper, Middle and Lower.

ABOVE: Along the Rouge River at Detroit, Michigan.

The great-grandson of Henry Ford, chairman of the Ford Motor Company, is looking to redesign the company's automobile manufacturing complex for the 21st century, making the river the focal point. In the meantime, the Rouge Partnership, an environmental concern, is proposing plans for walkways, bike paths and green space. The plans also include boat tours up and down the Rouge and returning the oxbow-shaped bends to the river. A new bend in the river would be located at Greenfield Village, where fish would be able to swim upstream to a dam at the Ford estate. There, a fish ladder will allow them to migrate further up the recovering river.

TOP: River Rouge, Michigan, circa 1910.

MIDDLE: Ford's massive River Rouge Plant at Dearborn, Michigan.

BOTTOM: U. S. Steel's Great Lakes Works on Zug Island looms behind the Rouge River.

171

Detroit: The Motor City

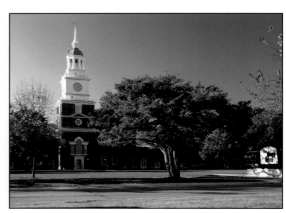

CLOCKWISE: Ford Field in downtown Detroit is the home of the Detroit Lions. The Henry Ford Museum at nearby Dearborn. The Renaissance Center is the headquarters of General Motors. Detroit's 36-story art deco Guardian Building was completed in 1929.

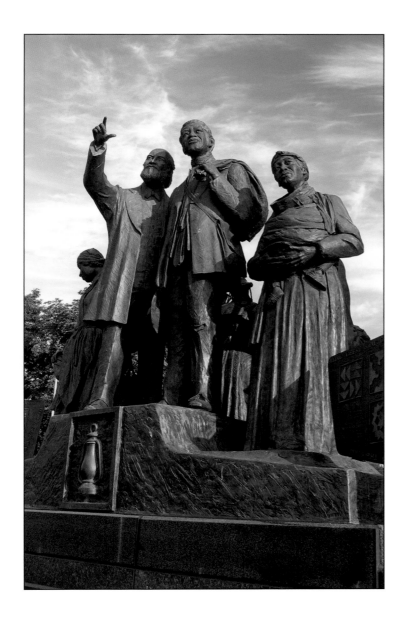

CLOCKWISE: A sculpture on Detroit's riverfront commemorates the Underground Railroad and a point of embarkation to Canada. The Penobscot Building was opened in 1928. The Automotive Hall of Fame is located at Dearborn.

173

DETROIT

DETROIT, Michigan (city population: 951,270, metro population: 4,043,467) is directly north of Windsor, Ontario on the Detroit River, the 29-mile strait that delivers the waters of the upper Great Lakes to Lake Erie. The core of Michigan's largest city is 20 miles up the Detroit River from the point where it empties into Lake Erie. This major city covers 139 square miles of southeastern Michigan.

Detroit was founded in 1701 by Sieur Antoine de la Mothe Cadillac, who was in the service of King Louis XIV of France. To protect the area from the British, who were seeking control of the area, and from Indians, who were urged to rise against the French, Cadillac was authorized to establish a fortified settlement at *d'etroit* or "the strait," referring to the Detroit River. The settlement was an important trading post and was named Fort Pontchartrain after the Minister of the Marine. Cadillac was later moved to Louisiana to become governor in 1710.

ABOVE: Sieur Antoine de la Mothe Cadillac (1658–1730) was a French explorer and colonial administrator who founded Detroit in 1701. He was governor of Louisiana from 1710–1716.

TOP: A 19th century engraving of Detroit, from the Canadian side of the Detroit River. (*Picturesque America* 1872)

MAPS: The Detroit River and vicinity in 1869 and Fort Detroit in 1812. (*The Pictorial Field-Book of the War of 1812*/F775, box MU 2102, Archives of Ontario)

By 1750, Detroit had 650 inhabitants. Following France's surrender to the British and the end of the French and Indian War in 1760, the British gained control of Detroit. The Indians' resentment of the British resulted in the alliance of several tribes led by Chief Pontiac of the Ottawa Confederacy. After several unsuccessful attempts to attack and take over the fort, Pontiac finally gave up.

The British remained in control of Detroit for several years following the Revolutionary War. In 1796, after General Anthony Wayne pressured the

174

ORIGINAL PLAN PERFECTED AFTER FIRE OF 1805

Used through the kindness of the Imperial Life Ins. Co.

BIRDS EYE VIEW — SHOWING ABOUT THREE MILES SQUARE — OF THE CENTRAL PORTION OF THE CITY OF DETROIT, MICHIGAN.

British, a treaty was signed releasing the Northwest Territory, and the Stars and Stripes were raised over Detroit. In 1802, both men and women had voting privileges and what is believed to have been the first town meeting in the Midwest was held here. In 1805, Congress organized the Michigan Territory, which included Detroit. That same year, a devastating fire swept through Detroit, destroying all 200 of its buildings except a stone warehouse. After the fire, Judge Augustus B. Woodward developed a new city plan with wider streets and room for growth. The War of 1812 caused hardship for the recovering settlement as Loyalists left, many buildings were burned, and 700 soldiers and many civilians died, victims of diseases.

Growth resumed and Detroit was incorporated as a city in 1815. Following the arrival of the steamer *Walk-in-the-Water* from Buffalo in 1818 and the completion of the Erie Canal through New York State in 1825, Detroit's growth was exponential. Sale of public land through an office in Detroit began in 1820. Eighty-acre parcels of land were sold for $1.25 an acre. In 1837, Michigan became the 26th state, and Detroit's population had reached nearly 10,000. During the 1800s there were four cholera epidemics. The worst in 1834 killed 122 people, representing seven percent of the city's population.

William Austin Burt patented the typewriter here in 1829. Between the 1830s and 1850s, railroads were rapidly built, breweries and factories sprang up, libraries and schools were established and three daily newspapers were printed. The population doubled every decade from 1830 to 1860. Detroit's population in 1860 had soared to 45,619. The manufacture of stoves was Detroit's leading industry during this period.

Detroit's location across the river from Canada made it a key terminus on the Underground Railroad. The Detroit Anti-Slavery Society was organized in 1837. In 1863, the First Michigan Colored Infantry gathered in Detroit as nearly 1,400 black soldiers enlisted in the Union Army.

During the Civil War era and afterward, Detroit's industries continued to grow with the smelting of copper and iron, the manufacture of steel, railroad cars, stoves, shoes and furniture. Perhaps most important to the later development of Detroit was the production of carriages and bicycles. These businesses laid the foundation for the automobile industry.

Detroit was the first city in the nation to assign individual telephone numbers in 1879, and the late 1800s brought the first horseless carriage. The Brush Electric Company began to power streetlights in 1882 and electricity was available for use in homes by 1893. Detroit's population reached 205,876 in 1890. The Detroit International Fair & Exposition was held

TOP LEFT: An 1807 plan of Detroit after an 1805 fire, which destroyed nearly all of the settlement's buildings. (American State Papers, Public Lands Series)

TOP RIGHT: An 1899 panoramic view of Detroit, Michigan. (Geography and Map Division, Library of Congress)

just downriver from downtown Detroit between 1889 and 1892. Sparked by the interest of city businesses to bolster commerce in Detroit, the world's first convention bureau was established 1896. The city began to attract visitors for summer vacationing and was a magnet for various industrial businesses, no doubt fueled by the automotive industry.

Detroit's history was to be forever marked by Henry Ford. Ford was born in nearby Dearborn in 1863 and became interested in combustion engines in 1885. In 1893, a year after the historic arrival of the Duryea machine, Ford had built his first motorcar. In 1899, he became the chief engineer and manager of the Detroit Automobile Company, and in 1903, at the age of 40, he organized the Ford Motor Company. By 1907, the company was producing nearly 15,000 vehicles, and before long, investors were realizing 10,000 to 300,000 percent profits on their investments. In 1909, Ford moved his operations from Detroit to Highland Park, introducing the assembly line in 1913, which revolutionized the automobile industry. By 1915, the millionth car had driven off his assembly line.

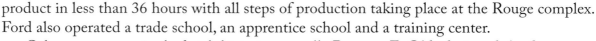

In 1917, Ford began the development of his massive complex on the River Rouge in Dearborn (see River Rouge). Operations were shifted to this self-sufficient facility and production of the Model T was shifted to the Model A in 1929 and to the V-8 in 1932. The more than 140-mile-long conveyor system made it possible for each worker to perform a single continuous function. Iron ore was converted into the finished product in less than 36 hours with all steps of production taking place at the Rouge complex. Ford also operated a trade school, an apprentice school and a training center.

Other car companies had rich histories as well. Ransom E. Olds designed the first popular economy car. The "Oldsmobile" was a two-seater with a one-cylinder engine. Sales for this car grew dramatically between 1901 and 1905.

William C. Durant bought the Buick Motor Company in 1904 and merged Buick with Cadillac, Oldsmobile and Oakland (Pontiac) in 1908 to form the General Motors Corporation (GM). In 1916, the Chevrolet Motor Company introduced a four-cylinder model, which eventually passed Ford as the best selling car in the U.S. GM bought the operating assets of Chevrolet in 1918.

ABOVE 1: William C. Durant (1861-1947) formed the General Motors Corporation.

ABOVE 2: Ransom E. Olds (1864-1950) founded the Olds Motor Vehicle Company in 1897. He left the company in 1904 and formed the REO Motor Company. General Motors discontinued the Oldsmobile brand in 2004. (Library of Congress, Prints & Photographs Division LC-USZ62-93715)

ABOVE RIGHT: Henry Ford (1863-1947) founded the Ford Motor Company in 1903. Ford used the assembly line for mass production of automobiles. (Library of Congress, Prints & Photographs Division LC-USZ62-98129)

BOTTOM: An early traffic light on Woodward Avenue in Detroit. (Burton Historical Collection, Detroit Public Library)

John and Horace Dodge had built a strong company that was making 1,000 cars a day by 1924. In 1928, the Dodge brothers' company was sold to Walter P. Chrysler for $175,000,000. The Chrysler Corporation began selling Dodges, DeSotos, Plymouths and Chryslers. Several other manufacturers also produced cars in Detroit.

America's love affair with the automobile left an early mark on Detroit. One of the nation's first concrete paved roads, Woodward Avenue, was built here just after the turn of the century, and Detroit installed the nation's first traffic lights at the corner of Woodward and Michigan avenues in 1915. The "Great Migration" of African-Americans from the South began during World War I. Recruiting agents brought trainloads of families to Detroit work in the factories. By 1920, the city's population was multiplying rapidly and reached 993,678 residents, becoming the nation's fourth largest city. In the late 1920s, tunnel and bridge access to Canada began with the opening of the Detroit-Windsor Tunnel and the Ambassador Bridge. Detroit's population hit 1,568,662 in 1930.

The Great Depression put a temporary halt to Detroit's growth during the 1930s, a decade marked by fluctuations in

Within the means of millions

Automobile parking grounds adjacent to factories may be seen today in every American industrial center. They offer a striking proof of the better standard of living that workers in this country enjoy.

Here Ford cars usually outnumber all others. Their low cost and operating economy bring them within the means of millions; and in families where the cost of living is high even in proportion to income, the purchase of a car is possible with little sacrifice through the Ford Weekly Purchase Plan.

Runabout . $260	Tudor . . $580
Touring . . $290	Fordor . . $660
Coupe . . $520	All Prices F. O. B. Detroit

On Open Cars Starter and Demountable Rims $85 Extra. Full-Size Balloon Tires Optional at an Extra Cost of $25.

Ford

THE UNIVERSAL CAR

FORD MOTOR COMPANY ∴ DETROIT, MICH.

MAKE SAFETY YOUR RESPONSIBILITY

ABOVE 1: John F. Dodge (1864-1920) and Horace E. Dodge (1868-1920) supplied parts to the automobile industry. By 1917, the brothers were manufacturing their own line of cars and trucks.

ABOVE 2: Walter P. Chrysler (1875-1940) formed the Chrysler Corporation in 1925. (Library of Congress, Prints & Photographs Division LC-USZ62-38486)

CLOCKWISE: Advertisements for the Ford Motor Company, the Chrysler Corporation and the Chevrolet Motor Division.

Cadillac Square, looking West.

Ford Motor Company, Detroit, Mich.

Harbor, Detroit, Mich.

TOP TO BOTTOM: A 1920s-era view of Cadillac Square, which was named for the founder of Detroit, Antoine de la Mothe Cadillac. The Dodge Brothers Automobile Plant, circa 1916. A 1915 view of Ford Motor Company's Highland Park Plant. A circa-1915 view of Detroit's harbor.

the automotive and other industries. Prohibition sparked crimes, Mafia battles erupted and rum running was notorious on Detroit's riverfront. Detroiters looked to sports to forget their troubles as the Tigers captured the World Series title, the Lions were National Football League champions, the Red Wings won the Stanley Cup twice and "The Brown Bomber," Joe Louis Barrow, won the world's heavyweight boxing championship, all in the 1930s.

As was the case with other Great Lakes cities, Detroiters went back to work during World War II and the city became known as the nation's "Arsenal of Democracy." By the 1940s, Detroit was known as a national leader in many industrial fields, including salt products, electric refrigeration, seeds, adding machines, stoves, farm equipment, engines and, of course, automobiles.

Similar to Cleveland and Buffalo, Detroit's population peaked in 1950. The city boasted 1,849,568 residents before war veterans started their families in the suburbs. Detroit began to construct its massive system of freeways as the city's population shifted throughout the growing metropolitan area. One of the nation's first shopping malls opened in Southfield, signaling a shift from the city to a suburban lifestyle.

The 1960s were marked by racial tension as the city was brought into the spotlight through rioting and violence. This tension highlighted the need to improve relations as the Rev. Martin Luther King Jr. debuted his "I Have a Dream" speech in Detroit before its

famous delivery in Washington, D.C. "New Detroit" was founded as the nation's first urban coalition, organized to improve education, employment, housing and economic development following the city's major civil disturbance. During this decade, the unmistakable Motown sound founded by Berry Gordy Jr. put Detroit in a positive light as groups such as the Supremes, Four Tops, Temptations, Martha Reeves and the Vandellas and Smokey Robinson and the Miracles hit top spots on music charts.

Detroit's rebirth began in the 1970s as Coleman Young took office as Detroit's first African-American mayor. A group of business leaders created Detroit Renaissance, Inc. to construct the Renaissance Center. It was the largest privately financed project in the world and was completed in 1977.

Detroit's hosting of the 32nd Republican National Convention at Joe Louis Arena, the first Detroit Grand Prix held on city streets, the opening of the Detroit People Mover and the completion of the expansion of the Cobo Conference/Exhibition Center highlighted the 1980s.

While the population of the city continued to decline in the 1990s, plans for more buildings were unveiled and the city renewed its commitment to the downtown area with plans for sports arenas and other forms of entertainment.

Detroit's population represents nearly every ethnic group. The metropolitan area includes Greektown and the predominantly Polish city of Hamtramck. Nearby Dearborn is home to the largest Arabic community in the world outside of the Middle East. Many of Italian descent immigrated to the city's east side. Mexicantown in the southwest area is home to a growing number of Latino residents and suburban Oakland County is home to many

TOP: Rum runners at Detroit's riverfront in 1929. (Dossin Great Lakes Museum)

LEFT: "Hitsville U.S.A." was the headquarters of Motown Records until 1968. Located on Detroit's West Grand Boulevard, the building is now site of the Motown Historical Museum.

DETROIT'S BELLE ISLE

Detroit's Belle Isle greets Lake St. Clair's waters as they squeeze into the Detroit River for the trip to Lake Erie. Indians first knew the two-and-a-half-mile-long island as *wah-nah-be-zee* (White Swan). The French called it *ile St. Claire* and also referred to it as *ile de cochons* (Island of the Hogs) for the wild pigs, which had been placed there by settlers.

Possession of the island changed hands several times before Belle Isle was sold to the City of Detroit in 1879. The first bridge connecting Belle Isle with mainland was built in 1889. It was destroyed by fire in 1915. A temporary steel bridge was used was used until the present bridge was completed in 1923.

In 1883, renowned landscape architect Frederick Law Olmstead was hired to create a master plan for the island's development. Olmstead also designed Buffalo's park system, New York's Central Park, Chicago's South Park and the Capitol grounds in Washington, D.C.

The park included a zoo, which closed in 2002. Today, the island park is home to fishing piers, a lighthouse, nature center, music shell, the Scott Fountain, conservatory, greenhouse, athletic complex, beach, carillon tower casino building, Coast Guard Station, Detroit Boat Club, Detroit Yacht Club, golf course and the Dossin Great Lakes Museum. Opened in 1904, the Belle Isle Aquarium was the oldest continuously operating public aquarium in North America before closing in 2005.

CLOCKWISE: The aquarium on Belle Isle was opened in 1904. The bridge to Belle Isle was built in 1889 and destroyed by fire in 1915. Canoeing was the top recreational activity at Belle Isle in the early 1900s.

Russian-Jewish immigrants. Newly arrived Japanese have settled to the south near the airport. African-Americans make up the majority of the city of Detroit's population, comprising 82 percent.

Today, Detroit is internationally known for automobile manufacturing and trade. Metropolitan Detroit is the world headquarters for General Motors Corp., Ford Motor Co., Chrysler and Volkswagen of America. Industry in the area includes the production of paints, non-electrical machinery, automation equipment, pharmaceuticals, rubber products, synthetic resins and garden seed. National and international corporations headquartered here include ThyssenKrupp Budd, Delphi Automotive and Federal Mogul. Detroit's industries also include the manufacture of machine tool accessories, internal combustion engines, iron and steel forged products, plumbing fittings, metal cutting tools, flower-bedding, distilled liquor and potato chips.

Detroit is one of the five largest ports in the country, with nearly 30 million tons of cargo passing through each year. It is such a busy place for shipping that it has a floating post office, the *J.W. Westcott II*, which serves passing ships.

Nine universities, several colleges and a number of trade schools are in the Greater Detroit area along with a large medical community. Other Detroit assets include Belle Isle Park with its beach, golf course, aquarium and zoo; Dossin Great Lakes Museum; and Detroit Boat Club. The city celebrates music annually with the Montreux Detroit Jazz Festival.

Most of Detroit's professional sports teams now play within the city limits in new venues. The Detroit Tigers (AL) baseball team plays in the 41,782-seat Comerica Park, completed in 2001. The Lions (NFL) began play at the 65,000-seat indoor Ford Field in 2002. The Red Wings (NHL) hockey team calls Joe Louis Arena home. Opened in 1979, replacing the legendary Olympia, it has a capacity of 20,066. The Pistons (NBA) basketball team plays at the suburban 22,076-seat Palace of Auburn Hills, which opened in 1988.

Detroit opened its Riverfront Promenade at Hart Plaza in July, 2001, as part of the city's 300th birthday celebration. This development includes a 3,000-foot-long landscaped walkway between Hart Plaza and Joe Louis Arena. The International Underground Railroad Monument, symbolizing Detroit's role in the movement, was dedicated in 2001. A companion monument stands on the Windsor, Ontario side of the Detroit River. With more than four million people, Greater Detroit is the sixth largest metropolitan area in the U.S. and the nation's ninth largest city.

ABOVE: An early evening view of the Detroit skyline from Windsor, Ontario.

11 Ontario Shoreline

Canada's most populous province is steward to Lake Erie's entire northern shoreline. The Dominion's southernmost border extends from the lake's main source, the Detroit River to the west, to its eastern outlet, the Niagara River.

Quiet and generally unspoiled, the views along Canada's portion of the Lake Erie shoreline include a mixture of beaches, woods and marshes. Small resort communities, farms and fishing villages are sprinkled down the lakeshore along with several provincial parks.

The Detroit River carries the flow of the three upper Great Lakes and Lake St. Clair past the city of Windsor, with a view of its American neighbor, Detroit. The river then turns south, passing Fighting Island and the residential Bob-Lo Island before reaching Lake Erie. The northern shoreline of Lake Erie begins a few miles south of Amherstburg and runs generally to the east and northeast.

A road built by Colonel Thomas Talbot, sent by the Crown to manage settlement of the region in the early 1800s, follows Lake Erie's northern shoreline. Natives originally used the ridge on which the road was built as a trail. It continues to connect towns in the area. Today, Highway 401 handles most of the heavy east-west traffic several miles north of Talbot's road.

Between the Detroit River and Point Pelee, the shoreline is dotted with small communities whose livelihood is based heavily on agriculture. Low cliffs sit back from white sandy beaches.

Along the lake's central basin, the northern shoreline arcs gently toward Long Point, broken only by the Rondeau Peninsula. Small fishing villages sit quietly at the bottom of ravines, which cut through cliffs on this portion of the lakeshore. Picturesque farms hug the shoreline and numerous oil and gas wells quietly do their work.

TOP: A view of Kettle Creek at Port Stanley, Ontario at dusk.

BOTTOM: The blue of Lake Erie provides a backdrop to Ontario's rich farmland along Lake Erie's central basin.

PAGE 182: Along Ontario's Lake Erie shoreline, water breaks at the tip of Point Pelee. In the distance, the underwater portion of this unique and ever-changing geological feature can be seen just below the lake's surface.

Long Point marks the beginning of the eastern section of Canadian shoreline. A mix of tiny resort communities and fishing villages lines this portion of the lakeshore. Most of the area is agricultural, with tobacco farms being the most distinctive feature. The only signifi-

cant heavy industry along this section of shoreline is at Nanticoke and at Port Colborne where the Welland Canal meets the lake. Exposed flat bedrock and some sandy beaches make up this portion of the shoreline. Between the mouth of the Grand River and Fort Erie, the land along the shoreline is generally lower without cliffs. The lakeshore ends abruptly at Fort Erie where the Niagara River heads north, carrying the outflow of Lake Erie.

The land along the gently winding upper portion of the Niagara River is followed by a treed parkway. Farms and homes are set well back from the scenic route between Fort Erie and Niagara Falls. After the water plunges over Niagara Falls, the river and parkway continue to make their way down to Lake Ontario. Similar in character to the American side, the area around the lower portion of the Niagara River is agricultural, featuring quaint villages and historic sites.

TOP: Looking west on Lake Erie's Long Point Bay at Port Rowan, Ontario. The neck of the Long Point peninsula is in the background.

MIDDLE: Views of flue-cured tobacco drying kilns are a familiar sight along Lake Erie's northern shoreline.

BOTTOM: An aerial view of Windsor, Ontario on the Detroit River. (Convention & Visitors Bureau of Windsor, Essex County & Pelee Island)

Windsor: City of Roses

CLOCKWISE: A panoramic image of Windsor, Ontario from Detroit's riverfront. Dieppe Gardens, dedicated in 1959, fronts Windsor's downtown area. Conceptually linked with a sculpture on the American side of the Detroit River, Windsor's waterfront features a sculpture representing the freedom of Canada, the final stop on the Underground Railroad.

CLOCKWISE: Windsor's waterfront on the Detroit River. The Peace Fountain at Coventry Gardens. Fireworks over Windsor on the Detroit River. (Convention & Visitors Bureau of Windsor, Essex County & Pelee Island)

WINDSOR

WINDSOR, Ontario (city population: 216,473, metro population: 323,342) is directly south of Detroit, Michigan, across the Detroit River.

The early history of Windsor is intertwined with Detroit. In 1701, the first European settlement occurred in the area as Sieur Antoine de la Mothe Cadillac and a group of 100 civilian and military personnel founded Fort Pontchartrain across the river from here.

Initially, most settlement occurred on the Detroit side of the river. In 1748, a Jesuit mission to the Huron Indians was established here. By 1760, a French settlement devoted to agriculture had grown along both sides of the river. Fort Pontchartrain on the Detroit side of the river was surrendered to the British, and in 1783, the Detroit side was surrendered to the United States. Despite these events, both sides of the river effectively remained under British control until 1796 when United States' forces assumed the occupation of Detroit.

During this period, the French were the dominant group remaining in the settlement. The division of land and some of the street patterns from the French period exist today, including the long narrow farms that front the river. In 1797, the village of Sandwich was established for settlers of both French and British origin from the U.S. side who chose to live under British rule after the United States took occupation of Detroit. This brought English-speaking people to the settlement.

Michigan Central Tunnel, Windsor, Ont., Canada.

LAGOON PARK, WINDSOR, CANADA.

Sandwich St. Windsor, Canada.

TOP TO BOTTOM: The Ford Motor Company's plant at Windsor along the banks of the Detroit River. The Michigan Central Railroad Tunnel under the Detroit River was opened in 1910 and remains in use today by the Canadian Pacific Railway. A 1905 view of Lagoon Park, an amusement park in Windsor. A pre-1910 view of Sandwich Street in Windsor.

189

In the early 1830s, a site for a settlement was laid out and in 1836, the place was named after Windsor, England.

Windsor began to overtake Sandwich in population and as the chief port-of-entry to the region across the river from Detroit. In 1854, the Great Western Railway chose Windsor as its termination point, igniting significant industrial growth. That same year, Windsor was incorporated as a village.

In 1857, Hiram Walker built a distillery east of the present downtown area where the new railroad met the river, and he laid out the town of Walkerville. The town plans included provisions for agriculture, industry and residences. Through the second half of the 19th century, residences were built, ranging from row houses for industrial workers to large estates for the well-to-do. Several of these Victorian Era residences remain. Windsor became a town in 1858 and a city in 1892.

To take advantage of Imperial trade preferences, the Ford Motor Company was also established on the Canadian side of the river in 1904. By the 1920s, "Ford City," a huge industrial complex, was in place in East Windsor. The present Chrysler and GM plants were also built here during this period.

In the early 1930s, the separate cities of Windsor, East Windsor or Ford City, Walkerville and Sandwich merged to become the city of Windsor with a population of more than 100,000. Windsor continued to absorb suburban areas through the latter part of the 20th century.

Today, Windsor is home to numerous parks and gardens and is known as the "City of Roses." Windsor is an industrial city with factories and suppliers for "The Big Three" automakers. Attractions include a large casino, the Art Gallery of Windsor and Jackson Park, with its Queen Elizabeth Garden. The François Baby House, Windsor's Community Museum, is housed in the 1811 structure used as the headquarters for generals William Hull and Isaac Brock during the War of 1812. In 2001, the first international memorial to the Underground Railroad was dedicated. Designed by Ed Dwight, it includes monuments on both the Detroit and Windsor sides of the river, linked conceptually. Detroit's monument is located in Hart Plaza, while Windsor's is on the Civic Esplanade.

TOP: The international Ambassador Bridge. Windsor is in the foreground. Detroit, Michigan is to the left and in the background.

BOTTOM: Dieppe Gardens was built on the former site of the Windsor-Detroit ferry landing.

AMHERSTBURG

AMHERSTBURG, Ontario (population: 13,410, town population: 21,748) is 18 miles south of Windsor on the east bank of the Detroit River, where the river empties into Lake Erie.

Amherstburg is one of the oldest towns in Ontario. It was named for Lord Jeffrey Amherst, who was commander of the British forces, which controlled this part of Canada. Amherstburg is one of the oldest settlements in southwestern Ontario. Originally settled by the French, it came under British control in 1760. The *H.M.S. Detroit*, the flagship of the British fleet in the Battle of Lake Erie during the War of 1812, was built here.

The town's origin is tied to Fort Malden (originally Fort Amherstburg), which was built at the mouth of the Detroit River in 1796. Loyalists laid out Amherstburg after the British evacuated Detroit. The fort was a center for British operations during the War of 1812 and a rallying point for their capture of Detroit. The British burned the fort as they retreated to the east in 1813. The United States occupied the ruins of the fort until July of 1815 and worked to rebuild it.

Old Fort Malden, Amherstburg, Ont.

The British assumed control of the site once again in the summer of 1815. Buildings were added to the fort during the 1820s. Basic maintenance and minor repairs were also completed but not much was done to upgrade the earthworks. The last British troops were withdrawn in 1836 as tensions between Britain and the United States lessened. By then, the fort had fallen into disrepair.

From 1837 to 1839, the Upper Canada Rebellion was taking place and that meant Fort Malden was needed once again. British troops were sent back to the fort to repel the rebels and their sympathizers from the United States. The fort was almost completely rebuilt between 1838 and 1840. Two barracks for 400 soldiers, officers' quarters, guardhouse, a jail and numerous other buildings were erected. Cannons armed the newly repaired earthworks.

TOP: A scene on Lake Erie near the mouth of the Detroit River at Amherstburg, Ontario.

BOTTOM: An early 1900s view of Fort Malden at Amherstburg.

The end of the rebellion and improved relations with the United States once again meant less need for a large military presence in the Detroit River area. In 1851, regulars were pulled out of Fort Malden, leaving retired soldiers to maintain the fort and farm the land.

Between 1859 and 1870, the fort and grounds were used as an insane asylum and later as a lumberyard and planing mill. In the early 20th century, the site was subdivided for private residences.

In 1921, the Historic Sites and Monuments Board of Canada recognized Fort Malden as having national historic significance. The Canadian government acquired land for the park in 1937 and has since expanded it.

In the period leading up to the Civil War in the United States, Amherstburg was a key destination for escaping slaves who made their way here via the Underground Railroad. During the years between 1800 and 1860, it is believed that 60,000 to 75,000 fugitive slaves made the pilgrimage to freedom. Many slaves crossed the Detroit River at Amherstburg because it is narrower at this point. This made Amherstburg one of the largest Underground Railroad destinations in Canada.

During the era of Prohibition, a thriving rum running business operated across the Detroit River, depending on Amherstburg as an export center.

More recently the area has been known for its salt and limestone deposits, which supply the soda ash industry. Other businesses include a tomato processing plant, metal stamping plant and a bakery.

Today's largest industries include a distillery and chemical plants. Honeywell and Church and Dwight are large employers here. King's Navy Yard, the shipyard where the *H.M.S Detroit* was built, is now a waterfront park with floral gardens. Other attractions include the Gordon House (1798), the oldest building originally built in Amherstburg, and the Park House (1796), a French frame log structure. The Park House was moved to Amherstburg in 1799 when its Loyalist owner decided to float it across the river in pieces from River Rouge, near Detroit. Amherstburg is also home to the North American Black Historical Museum and Cultural Centre.

TOP: Fort Malden on the Detroit River at Amherstburg, Ontario.

BOTTOM: A re-enactment at Fort Malden. (Convention & Visitors Bureau of Windsor, Essex County & Pelee Island)

TOP: Amherstburg's Navy Yard in 1813. The brig *Detroit*, a British war vessel, is on the stocks. Commodore Oliver Hazard Perry captured the ship at the Battle of Lake Erie. (Parks Canada, Fort Malden Historical Site)

MIDDLE: The Park House was built in the 1790s at the mouth of the Rouge River in Detroit. When Detroit was ceded to the United States, the owners floated it down the Detroit River to Amherstburg.

BOTTOM: The North American Black Historical Museum at Amherstburg features exhibits on Africa, slavery and the Underground Railroad.

BOIS BLANC ISLAND

BOIS BLANC (BOB-LO) ISLAND, Ontario is situated in the Detroit River across from Amherstburg, 18 miles downriver from Windsor. A part of the town of Amherstburg, the island is approximately three miles long and one-half mile wide.

The French called the island *bois blanc*, believed to mean "island of the white wood," for the birch and beech trees that covered the island. Indians inhabited the island after the French had established a mission here in the early 1700s, later using it as a base for fur trade with the British. It was headquarters for Tecumseh, the Shawnee leader, who in aid to the British used it as a base during the War of 1812.

The lighthouse was built in 1837 and the island was an important stop on the Underground Railroad for escaping slaves en route to the Canadian shore.

The island, minus the acreage at the lighthouse, changed hands several times. In 1898, it came into the possession of the Detroit, Belle Isle & Windsor Ferry Company. This marked the beginning of the Bob-Lo Excursion Line that brought visitors to the island. In 1902 and 1910 the steamers *Columbia* and *Ste. Claire* were built with a capacity of more than 2,500 passengers each. They brought nearly 800,000 visitors to the island annually. Attractions on the island included picnic grounds, a carousel and Henry Ford's dance hall, built and designed in 1903 by Albert Kahn.

During World War I, with the exception of this Canadian island, American men of draft age were not allowed to leave the U.S. Later, business slowed during the Depression when excursions were temporarily ceased.

In 1949, the island's name became known officially as Bob-Lo. The Browning family of Grosse Pointe, Michigan, owners of a steamship company, purchased the island and the excursion boats that same year. The family built an amusement park with rides, roller coasters, a funhouse, Ferris wheel, dance hall, zoo, antique car exhibit and miniature railroad. Big band sounds echoed from the excursion boats and the dance pavilion during the early 1950s.

In the 1960s and 1970s, the dock and rides were upgraded. The Thunderbolt, a steel roller coaster, was built along with a log flume and the 1878 carousel with 48 horses was restored. The Brownings sold the island in 1979 and it changed hands again several times.

During the 1980s rowdiness on the boats and the island discouraged families, and crowds became sparse. The carousel's animals were auctioned off piece by piece in 1990 and replaced

ABOVE: An aerial image of the Bob-Lo Island Amusement Park, which operated between 1898 and 1993.

with plastic replicas. In 1991, the boarding dock in downtown Detroit was moved to Gibraltar, Michigan, just across the channel from the island. In 1994, the rides were sold, and in January 1996, the *Columbia* and the *Ste. Claire* were auctioned off, ending an era on the island. Today, the island is being developed as an exclusive residential area.

TOP TO BOTTOM: An early 1900s view of the Bob-Lo Island Lighthouse, which was built in 1836. The *Ste. Claire* served as a Bob-Lo Island excursion steamer from 1910 until 1991. The Pavilion Dance Hall opened 1913 and housed the largest dance floor in North America until the Crystal Ballroom opened at Crystal Beach on Lake Erie. Early 1900s visitors make their way up the embankment at Bob-Lo Island.

195

The McLean Beach, Colchester, Ont.

COLCHESTER & KINGSVILLE

COLCHESTER, Ontario (population 900) is 10 miles west of Kingsville and roughly the same distance east of the entrance to the Detroit River. Colchester is a small settlement in the Town of Essex with a mixture of homes and cottages, surrounded by agricultural land. Colchester Reef Light was built in 1885 to mark a dangerous reef just under Lake Erie's surface, four miles offshore.

KINGSVILLE, Ontario (population: 6,173, town population: 20,908) is 22 miles east of the mouth of the Detroit River on the north shore of Lake Erie. The settlement formed around a grain mill in the late 1700s and was occupied by British soldiers and Loyalists who moved here from Pennsylvania. Kingsville was incorporated in 1852 and was named for Colonel James King, a veteran of the Upper Canada Rebellion.

During the 19th century, Kingsville became an important port on Lake Erie for the shipment of potash, lumber and grain. The town also developed as a fishing center. Further growth followed the railroad's arrival in 1889. In the 1890s, Kingsville grew as a summer resort for the well-to-do when distiller Hiram Walker built a luxurious hotel not far from the dock.

Just north of town is the Jack Miner Bird Sanctuary. Its founder, John Thomas Miner, was born near Cleveland, Ohio at Dover Center in 1865, moving here in 1878. Miner was an avid hunter who discovered on his outings that geese recognized him as an enemy. However, he noticed that they were not threatened by the presence of nearby farm workers. So Miner decided to become a friend.

TOP LEFT: A circa-1910 view to the west at the quiet resort community of Colchester, Ontario.

TOP RIGHT: Division Street, looking south during the early 1900s at Kingsville, Ontario.

Harbor, Kingsville, Canada

Miner established his sanctuary by digging a pond in 1904. After a few years, the geese began to arrive in great numbers. In 1909, Miner began banding the migratory geese and ducks to determine their movements. Each bird's band included Miner's name and a verse from the Bible. During his life, Miner spoke extensively on wildlife conservation throughout North America. In the 1930s, to perpetuate his work, the Jack Miner Migratory Bird Foundation was established in the United States and Canada. Miner, known as the "Father of Conservation," died in 1944 after having banded and tracked more than 50,000 ducks and 30,000 geese. The sanctuary attracts many visitors and is a "stop over" where migratory waterfowl are given food, water and protection. It has no admission fee.

Today, Kingsville is home to numerous attractions including beaches, a winery and the Southwestern Ontario Heritage Village, in addition to Jack Miner's Bird Sanctuary. Ferries depart from here to Pelee Island and Sandusky, Ohio.

TOP RIGHT: An early view of the busy harbor at Kingsville.

MIDDLE: Jack Miner (1865-1944), the "Father of Conservation." (Jack Miner Bird Sanctuary)

BOTTOM: The *M/V Jiimaan* was built in 1992 with the capacity to transport 400 passengers and 34 vehicles. The *Jiimaan* makes trips between Kingsville, Leamington and Pelee Island, Ontario and Sandusky, Ohio.

TOP: The beach and dock at Leamington, Ontario. Boats operating from the dock ferry passengers to Pelee Island, Sandusky, Ohio and Lake Erie's islands in the U.S.

MIDDLE: A 1950s view of Talbot Street in Leamington, Ontario.

BOTTOM: Leamington is the "Tomato Capital of Canada." The community hosts a tomato festival on the third weekend each August. Leamington's unique summer tourist information booth was built in 1961.

LEAMINGTON

LEAMINGTON, Ontario (population: 17,086, town population: 28,833) is 32 miles south-east of Windsor and eight miles east of Kingsville. This area was inhabited by Indians and explored by the French in the late 1600s, but it wasn't until the mid-1800s that its first settler, Alex Wilkinson, arrived. The settlement had three names: Wilkinson Corners; Gainesborough for William Gaines, a prominent townsman; and ultimately Leamington, after Gaines' hometown in England.

Tomato Season, Heinz Factory, Leamington. Ont., Canada

A dock was built here to handle large freighters. In 1907, the H.J. Heinz Company opened a plant here to process tomatoes and other vegetables. Leamington became well known as the "Tomato Capital of Canada." Other industries including fishing developed along the waterfront.

The area surrounding Leamington is mainly agricultural. About 1,000 acres of cucumbers, tomatoes and flowers are grown in greenhouses. Area farms also grow asparagus, beans, corn, onions, lettuce, carrots, celery, zucchini, peppers, melon, squash and potatoes. Fruits, including peaches, grapes, apples and strawberries, are grown here. The canning business is also an important part of Leamington's economy.

Local fishing boats still work the lake, bringing daily catches of perch and other fish. Leamington is the gateway to Point Pelee National Park, attracting those interested in the migration of birds and butterflies. Ferries from Leamington connect Pelee Island, Lake Erie's U.S. islands and Sandusky, Ohio. Leamington's southern location along the 42nd parallel means the town is as far south on the globe as Rome, Italy and northern California.

TOP LEFT: Roadside stands selling fruits and vegetables are common at Leamington. The area boasts the largest concentration of greenhouse-grown vegetables in North America. The area is known as the "Sun Parlor of Canada" for its southern location in the country.

TOP RIGHT: In 1909, the H.J. Heinz Company expanded to Canada and set up manufacturing operations at Leamington, Ontario.

BOTTOM: Leamington's Heinz factory first started processing pickles, vinegar and beans in 1907. In 1910, it began producing ketchup. Later, cooked spaghetti, soups, juices and baby foods were produced.

PELEE ISLAND

PELEE ISLAND, Ontario (2001 population: 287, summer population: 1,000) is Lake Erie's largest island and is in the lake's western basin, nine miles southwest of Point Pelee, 16 miles south of Leamington and 23 miles north of Sandusky, Ohio. Pelee Island, together with nearby Middle Island, is the southernmost point in Canada. The 10,000-acre island is nine miles long and three and a half miles wide and includes 55 miles of roads.

Ottawa and Ojibwa Indians were living here when Europeans first visited. Thomas McKee leased the island in 1788. It was sold for $500 in 1823 to William McCormick, who moved here in 1834 with his wife and 11 children. The island's 4,000 acres of marshland were so full of wildlife that McCormick took 6,000 muskrat pelts per year. McCormick attracted tenant families who arrived to work in the island's sawmill. Commercial fishing in the area included catches of whitefish, lake herring, black bass and sturgeon.

In 1868, Pelee Island was incorporated as a township. In the 1880s, sections of the island were sold and canals drained much of the marshland to create farmland for grape vineyards, apples, peaches and potatoes. By 1900, the island had nearly 800 residents, four schools, churches and three general stores.

The island rests on a limestone bed, which continues to be quarried today. This limestone has been used to build the lock walls of the Welland Canal and pave the streets of Toronto and other cities. The limestone Pelee Island Lighthouse, second oldest on the Canadian side of Lake Erie, was established in 1833, abandoned in 1909 and restored in 2000.

This resort island is home to marinas, a winery and the Pheasant Farm, which raises 25,000 birds for hunting. West Dock is the island's downtown district, which includes shops, restaurants and the Heritage Centre Island Museum. East, Middle, Hen and Chicken islands are in nearby Canadian waters.

TOP: The Pelee Island Lighthouse was built in 1833 to guide ships through the treacherous Pelee Passage. It is the second oldest Canadian lighthouse on Lake Erie. Its exterior was restored in 2000.

PELEE POINT, THE MOST SOUTHERLY POINT IN CANADA

2803 Published for J. Leonard, Leamington

LEAMINGTON, ONT.

POINT PELEE

POINT PELEE, Ontario is a triangular peninsula jutting out into Lake Erie from the
northern shoreline in Leamington Township. It is the southernmost mainland point in
Canada and is located six miles southeast of Leamington. Five miles of the peninsula, from
the tip, is designated as Point Pelee National Park. Geological studies indicate the point,
made of sand, used to extend much further into the lake.

French explorers named the peninsula *pointe pelée*, which means "bald" or "bare" point.
Archaeologists have discovered that Point Pelee was inhabited for hundreds of years before
the Europeans arrived. Early native settlements near the marsh have been documented. The
largest of these known sites was occupied between 700 AD and 900 AD. Archaeologists also
believe the point was not as heavily populated from 1100 to the 1600s, because it may have
been used as a buffer zone between warring Indian tribes.

TOP: The old entrance booth
to Point Pelee National Park.

MIDDLE: The tip of Pelee
Point, circa 1907.

BOTTOM: A modern view of
Pelee Point.

In 1670, French Sulpician priests François Dollier de Casson and René de Brehaut de Galinée camped here during their exploration of the region. In 1763, during the Pontiac Wars, a group of Royal Americans and Queen's Rangers camped on the eastern side of the peninsula on their way to Detroit. A group of Wyandot Indians attacked, killing 54 of the Europeans.

In 1799, the southernmost portion of the Pelee Peninsula was declared a naval reserve. Forests along the northwestern shore of Lake Erie had timber perfect for the masts of the British fleet. The reserve was in place to protect the tall, straight pines and oak trees from being cut by settlers. More than 100 years later, the naval reserve's boundaries defined the border of Point Pelee National Park.

In 1812, General Sir Isaac Brock's troops landed here just before their capture of Detroit. Also during the early 1800s, there was a settlement with approximately 100 Chippewa Indians on the peninsula. They taught the Europeans about the "carrying place," a portage route through the marsh to avoid dangerous waters encountered when rounding the tip of the peninsula. Indians continued to inhabit the peninsula during the 1800s, but their numbers were dwindling. By 1871, they were gone.

In the early 1830s, squatters were the first white settlers within the Point Pelee Naval Reserve. In the 1880s, the government allowed squatters to purchase land on which they lived. The squatters initially fished for their own needs and later fished commercially. Commercial fishing peaked in 1891 with 22 fisheries operating from the reserve. Over-fishing of lake trout, whitefish and herring closed most of these fisheries within 10 years. The squatters also planted vineyards and farmed the land for asparagus, peaches and apples. They also permitted their livestock to roam freely.

Bear, deer, muskrat, beaver, wild turkey, pigeon and ruffed grouse were hunted. Much of the wildlife was gone by the late 1800s, including the entire population of deer, which was reintroduced in the 1940s. Muskrat hunting was also important to the squatters. Before Point Pelee was made a national park, nearly 10,000 pelts were taken from the marsh every year.

Percy Taverner, Canada's first Dominion Ornithologist, proposed to the Federal Commission of Conservation that Point Pelee be declared a national park. Taverner enlisted the support of bird enthusiast Jack Miner, known for his Canadian Geese sanctuary in Kingsville, Ontario; some prominent Leamington residents; and two Essex County Wildlife Protection

Associations. Miner appeared before the Prime Minister of Canada to make the request. In 1918, a government order created Point Pelee National Park.

The creation of the park actually caused more stress on the ecosystem. Campers used the park heavily and private cottages still existed. In 1922, roadways and infrastructure were added. By the mid-1930s, 250,000 visited the park annually. Grounds and hotels on the peninsula were filled to capacity, and in the 1940s and 1950s, expansion projects further increased park use. Roads were paved and parking lots were added at the tip. By the mid-1950s, 600,000 visited the park yearly. What was the smallest national park in Canada was also the busiest. The number of visitors peaked in 1963 at 781,000. In addition to the visitors, muskrat trapping continued in the park until the late 1950s and commercial fisheries operated here until the late 1960s.

In 1972, a plan was introduced to continue a buyback program, eliminating private ownership of property within the park. Campsites were removed from the park and campers began using privately owned campgrounds nearby. The Point Pelee transit system greatly reduced automobile traffic and the need for parking lots. Duck hunting ended in 1989.

Outside of the park, much of the northern portion of the peninsula is farmland. Two thirds of the park is marshland. The upland portion of the park consists of sand dunes and forests with many types of trees. Pigeon Bay is located to the west of the point. Point Pelee is a stop on the Atlantic and Mississippi flyways and more than 345 species of birds have been spotted here. Monarch butterflies begin their migration from Point Pelee to Mexico in September.

TOP: The wooded drive on Point Pelee.

BOTTOM: Mainland Canada's southernmost point of land slips quietly under Lake Erie's waters at Point Pelee, Ontario.

203

WHEATLEY

WHEATLEY, Ontario (population 1,686) is eight miles east of Leamington, north of the eastern shoulder of Point Pelee. It is part of the city of Chatham-Kent and home of the largest commercial fishing fleet on the Great Lakes.

The construction of the southwestern portion of Colonel Thomas Talbot's road finally began after the War of 1812 had delayed the project. By 1818, the road extended through here, running along the northern shoreline of Lake Erie.

Once the Talbot Road was completed, settlers began to trickle into this part of Canada. The village is named for Richard Wheatley, who arrived here from England in 1832.

Within 25 years, a commercial fishery was built, along with a wooden dock and storage facility for grain. The settlement was named Wheatley when a post office was established in the 1860s. By 1869, Wheatley had 150 residents and two hotels. A general store, school, churches and a handful of other businesses soon followed. By 1890, more than 200 were living here when a fire destroyed most of the business district.

Before the dawn of the 20th century, a natural gas well was drilled and village residents anxiously awaited the building of the Two Creeks Canal. The proposed plan envisioned the canal beginning at the mouth of Two Creeks just east of Wheatley, connecting Lake Erie to Lake St. Clair. The 14-mile cut would allow ships to avoid the dangerous Pelee Passage and navigational hazards in the Detroit River. It would also shorten the trip by 75 miles. But the dream of building a canal this late in history would never be realized since railroads had already become well established.

Former passenger steamers, the *City of Dresden* and the *Louise*, gathered fish from area commercial fishing boats. They took catches to other nearby ports since Wheatley's port lacked docking facilities for vessels of their size.

In the early 20th century, the population of Wheatley reached approximately 500 and Wheatley was incorporated as a village in 1914. In 1927, a new eight-mile section of pavement was in place on the road between Wheatley and Leamington.

The commercial fishing operations in the Wheatley area grew as catches of yellow and blue pickerel, perch, white bass, herring, whitefish and sturgeon were caught in pound nets. The fish were shipped primarily to the United States. In 1940, a freezing plant was built here so that fish packed upon arrival at the dock could be quickly deep-frozen.

Further improvements to the harbor in the 1950s helped business, tourism and recreation. Point Pelee is nearby to the south and Wheatley Provincial Park is to the east.

TOP: Part of the fishing fleet at Wheatley, Ontario's harbor.

BOTTOM: An early 1900s view of the intersection of Talbot and Erie streets in Wheatley.

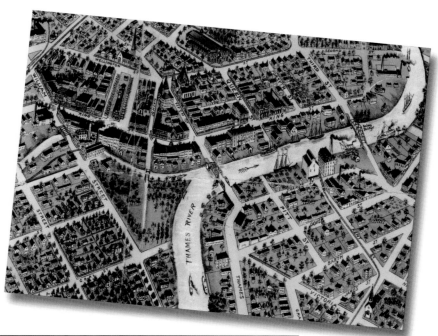

CHATHAM

CHATHAM, Ontario (population: 43,690, municipality: 108,177) is 10 miles north of Lake Erie and 45 miles east of Windsor on the banks of the Thames River. The Thames River empties into Lake St. Clair, 15 miles west of Chatham.

With beginnings as a military outpost, Chatham was one of the earliest settlements in western Ontario when it was laid out in 1795. The settlement was named to honor William Pitt, the Earl of Chatham. The village was incorporated in 1851 and became a city in 1895.

The area was a terminus on the Underground Railroad before the American Civil War. A third of Chatham's population was comprised of people of African descent. Some of the community's residents were slaves who had escaped.

Today, the area is the center of a rich agricultural area. Much of the industry is food-related. In 1998, Chatham's city government merged with Kent County to become the City of Chatham-Kent.

Chatham's Tecumseh Park opened in 1880 as a memorial to Shawnee Indian Chief Tecumseh who died supporting the British at the Battle of the Thames. The Chatham-Kent Museum, Lake St. Clair and Lake Erie's shores are popular destinations in the area.

TOP LEFT: A view to the east on the Thames River.

TOP RIGHT: An 1870 panoramic map of downtown Chatham, Ontario. (Geography and Map Division, Library of Congress)

BOTTOM: Looking east along King Street at Chatham.

THE BATHING BEACH

Lake View Hotel, Erieau, Ont.

ERIE BEACH & ERIEAU

ERIE BEACH, Ontario (population 223) is 15 miles east of Port Alma and two miles west of Erieau. It is a small, treed settlement with well-maintained cottages and substantial permanent homes.

ERIEAU, Ontario (population 442) is on the western peninsula that separates Rondeau Bay from Lake Erie. This resort community lies across Rondeau Harbor from the Rondeau Peninsula and Rondeau Provincial Park.

Erieau was developed as a shipping port. Trains came here to receive coal and other materials. Other rail traffic brought passengers who visited resorts and stayed at cottages. Erieau continues to support more than a dozen commercial fishing vessels, which bring in catches of yellow perch and pickerel. Sailboats and boats used for sport fishing line the docks at Erieau's marinas. Anglers also use a breakwater extending from the harbor entrance into Lake Erie.

TOP: An early 1900s view of Erieau, Ontario.

MIDDLE: Hotels and beach resorts sprang up at Erieau after the railroad arrived in 1889.

BOTTOM: The well-protected harbor at the village of Erieau is on Rondeau Bay.

RONDEAU PENINSULA

RONDEAU, Ontario is a peninsula that arcs into Lake Erie, midway between Point Pelee and Port Stanley in Harwich Township. Extending nearly five miles southwest into the lake, it is across the harbor from Erieau. Most of the peninsula is part of Rondeau Provincial Park, created in 1894 as Ontario's second oldest provincial park.

The peninsula was formed when melting glacial ice caused Lake Erie's water level to rise, eroding cliffs in the area. The erosion and deposition of sand created sandbars. As water levels varied over time, parallel sandbars formed on the floor of the lake. As the lake neared its present level, the sandbars were exposed to form the peninsula. Nutrients from the lake initially supported grasses, which in turn added to the soil's fertility. Trees took root and the once sterile sandbar supported a forest of white pine, black walnut, oak, sugar maple and beech trees. This lush forest sustained Indians.

The peninsula was later visited by French explorers who camped here, naming this place *ronde eau* meaning "round water." In 1795, under British possession, the area was declared ordnance land and reserved for the Navy. As was the case at Point Pelee, tall pine trees were used for ship masts and wood from oak trees was cut to repair decks and hulls.

In the late 1800s, the commercial fishing industry grew here, with several fisheries landing catches of whitefish and sturgeon.

Today, the park includes campsites, several miles of beach, trails and a visitors' center. The peninsula contains the largest southern hardwood forest in Ontario with vegetation resembling that in areas much further south. The lake's moderating effect on the climate creates a "Carolinian" environment, characterized by a longer growing season and plenty of rain. The park is home to southern species of plants and animals including the tulip tree, sassafras, opossum, yellow-breasted chat and an endangered species of warbler.

The peninsula attracts birds migrating across the lake, beginning with Tundra Swans in March and continuing through May with flocks of warblers.

TOP: An aerial view of the Rondeau Peninsula and bay. The outlines of beach ridges can be seen by the lines of vegetation growing on the peninsula. Erieau's harbor is to the left and Blenheim, Ontario is at the upper left.

BOTTOM: A commercial fishing boat at Rondeau. The harbor features a 30-berth commercial fishing center and a 200-berth recreational marina.

BLENHEIM

BLENHEIM, Ontario (population 4,780) is four miles north of Erieau and the Rondeau Peninsula on the Talbot Trail. It is believed that prior to 1796, Lieutenant-Governor John Graves Simcoe may have named the town for Blenheim Palace, which is near Oxford, England.

The settlement grew on the ridge where Talbot's road was built during the early 19th century. Lumbering was Blenheim's first industry and agriculture took over as the land was cleared. Blenheim was incorporated in 1885.

Today, the village is a quiet place with shops and is a center for the surrounding agricultural areas. Blenheim hosts the annual Cherry Festival, which features a pit-spitting contest.

TOP: The autumn harvest near Blenheim, Ontario.

MIDDLE: A 1940s view of Talbot Street looking east at Blenheim.

BOTTOM: Blenheim, Ontario.

River Thames, London, Canada

LONDON

LONDON, Ontario (city population: 352,395, metro population: 457,720) is 20 miles north of Lake Erie, midway between Hamilton and Sarnia on the Thames River.

In 1793, London was chosen by Lieutenant-Governor John Graves Simcoe to be the site of the capital of Upper Canada. By the time the city was founded in 1826, the capital had already been located at Toronto. However, a place was still needed as an administrative center for the vast London District. The location on the Thames River was chosen to be Head of the District in 1826.

London was incorporated as a town in 1840. That same year, a road was built from London into the district's territory. Tanneries and iron-related businesses sprang up.

Following devastating fires in London's core, the town was rebuilt quickly, and by 1850 had a population of more than 4,500. The town experienced a boom following the arrival of the railroad in 1853, and London became a city in 1855. Located in a rich agricultural belt, London and surrounding communities shipped wheat to supply the Union Army during the American Civil War. London's prosperity in the 1870s is reflected in mansions along Queens and Grand avenues.

Huron College was established in 1863 and the University of Western Ontario in 1878. The London Street Railway began operations in 1873. Areas around London were annexed, and by 1915, the population reached nearly 55,000.

TOP: The Thames River flows west 169 miles through southwestern Ontario, through London. In 1793, Lieutenant-Governor John Graves Simcoe named the waterway after the River Thames in Britain. Early Indians called the river *askunessippi* (antlered river).

BOTTOM: The skyline of London, Ontario.

TOP LEFT: The John Labatt Centre arena in London, Ontario. (Craig Glover/John Labatt Centre)

TOP RIGHT: Dundas Street in London, Ontario, circa 1910.

BOTTOM: The Skyline of London, Ontario. The building in the background at left is One London Place. Completed in 1992, the 24-story building is the tallest in the city, and the tallest office tower in Ontario outside of Toronto.

In 1881, the ferry *SS Victoria* capsized in the Thames River, drowning 200 passengers. Two years later, the first of two of the most devastating floods in London's history killed 17 people.

Areas around London were annexed, and by 1915, the population reached nearly 55,000. The second major flood struck London in 1937. The water quickly rose by 15 feet in just a few hours. One resident was killed and hundreds were left homeless.

London continued to grow through annexation, bringing the population to nearly 250,000 by the early 1960s. London's core was changed greatly during the 1970s as buildings were razed and replaced by modern structures.

The John Labatt Centre, home to hockey's London Knights (OHL), was opened in 2002. The facility seats 9,000 for hockey and 10,000 for other events. In addition to education, London's economy is diverse.

ST. THOMAS

ST. THOMAS, Ontario (population 36,110) is eight miles north of Lake Erie's shore on Kettle Creek, midway between Windsor and Fort Erie on the Talbot Trail.

St. Thomas is named for Colonel Thomas Talbot who received a land grant for settlement in 1803. Both Port Talbot on Lake Erie and St. Thomas were burned several times during the War of 1812.

A plank road was built between Port Stanley and London, through St. Thomas in 1844. St. Thomas was incorporated as a village in 1852. In 1854, London was the winner in a bid to have the Great Western Railway pass through town. St. Thomas responded by backing the London & Port Stanley Railway, which would run between London and Lake Erie's shore. Instead, this further hurt trade in St. Thomas.

St. Thomas was incorporated as a town in 1861. Growth resumed in St. Thomas when the Canada Southern Railway was built through the town on a route between Amherstburg and Fort Erie. By 1880, St. Thomas' population had grown to 8,367. In 1881, Alma College opened as a private school for girls.

TOP: An 1896 panoramic map of St. Thomas, Ontario. Kettle Creek flows through St. Thomas before reaching Lake Erie at Port Stanley.

BOTTOM: St. Thomas, Ontario, circa 1907. (Geography and Map Division, Library of Congress)

TOP LEFT: Jumbo (1861-1885), an African elephant, was purchased from the London Zoo by the Barnum & Bailey Circus. In 1885, the nearly 11-foot-tall animal died at St. Thomas after being hit by a train. A statue commemorates the tragedy.

TOP RIGHT: Talbot Street is the main thoroughfare in St. Thomas.

MIDDLE: Historic St. Thomas Church, built in 1824, is located on the eastern side of the city bearing the same name.

BOTTOM: One of several murals painted on buildings in downtown St. Thomas, "Magic Carpet: A View From Above," was created in 2000. The painting depicts many significant features of St. Thomas, including the city hall, the Jumbo monument, the street railway and the old St. Thomas Church.

St. Thomas became a large rail town as other railroads were built in the area. The city was electrified earlier than others in the area. Electricity arrived in 1911 from Niagara Falls' hydroelectric plants. However this convenience eventually caused problems. St. Thomas was hit harder than other towns since the 25-cycle power it was receiving was not compatible with modern industry's 60-cycle requirements.

By 1940, the population was 16,500 and climbed to 20,000 by the end of the decade. A number of industrial complexes were built during the middle of the 20th century.

St. Thomas is part of the London Metropolitan Area.

AYLMER

AYLMER, Ontario (population 7,069) is nine miles north of Port Bruce. In the early 19th century, the settlement was called Hodgkinson's Corners. Since many residents had moved to the area from Troy, New York, Troy was a popular choice to rename the settlement. Instead, the name Aylmer, for the Governor of Canada, was chosen because of tensions between the British and Americans at the time.

Transportation between Port Burwell, Port Bruce and Aylmer helped fuel the community's growth. Factories were built and area farmland supported several cheese factories. Railroads established through Aylmer helped further grow the settlement, and the area became incorporated in 1872. Industries like carriage making, canning, organ building, and dairy and pork production became key businesses.

Aylmer experienced a spike in population during World War II, influenced by the R.C.A.F. Technical Training School. The school later became the Ontario Police College to supply recruits for police forces across Ontario. A tobacco company was also established here during the 1940s.

Aylmer boasts a fine parks system and the Aylmer Wildlife Management Area, a resting spot for thousands of swans along their migration route.

TOP LEFT: The Aylmer Post Office was built in 1913. It now serves as the town's municipal office.

TOP RIGHT: Talbot Street, Aylmer's main thoroughfare, pictured during the early 20th century.

BOTTOM: Another view of Aylmer, circa 1910.

PORT STANLEY

PORT STANLEY, Ontario (population 2,385) is 20 miles south of London, Ontario, in a valley at the mouth of Kettle Creek. It serves as the Lake Erie port for London and nearby St. Thomas. Port Stanley has a big beach and the largest natural harbor on Lake Erie's north shore.

The Iroquois called Kettle Creek *kanagio*, the Ojibwas called it *akiksibi* and the French referred to it as *riviere tonti*. The village, named for Lord Stanley, was incorporated in 1874. The Neutral Indians occupied the area until 1653, when the Iroquois displaced them. French explorer Joliet, followed by Dollier and Galinée, passed through here in the late 1600s. During the 1700s, other explorers and travelers made their way through this area.

Colonel Thomas Talbot, who managed land settlement for the Crown, passed through here in 1801, and John Bostwick became the first settler in 1804. General Sir Isaac Brock's expedition camped on the beach here in the summer of 1812 en route to attack Detroit.

Ferry service between Port Stanley and Buffalo commenced in 1832. The protected harbor helped grow the village as a port for shipping and fishing. The Port Stanley Terminal Rail trains now run on the tracks of the London & Port Stanley (L&PS) Railway. The rail line, built in 1856, upgraded transportation between Port Stanley and London. The route, previously served by a plank road, was built just after the Great Western Railway had reached London. The railroad originally had a five-foot gauge, later changing to the standard gauge of four feet, eight and a half inches. Trains carried passengers and freight between London and Port Stanley. The 23-mile railroad carried shipments of coal, lumber and other products that arrived at Port Stanley.

In 1913, Sir Adam Beck, the mayor of London, Ontario, and a promoter of hydroelectric power at Niagara Falls, rebuilt the line for high-speed electric trains. The smokeless trains

brought thousands of people here to visit the L&PS-owned amusement park, beach, dining hall and dance pavilion. The pavilion, later known as the Stork Club, opened in 1926. Through the early 1950s, the club attracted top-name performers of the day including Louis Armstrong, Benny Goodman and nearby London's Guy Lombardo. Port Stanley became known the "Coney Island of the Great Lakes."

ABOVE: Sir Adam Beck (1857-1925), a politician and founder of the Hydro-Electric Power Commission of Ontario rebuilt the London & Port Stanley Railway for electric trains. (Courtesy of Ontario Power Generation)

RIGHT: The King George VI Lift Bridge at Port Stanley was built in 1939. This Kettle Creek crossing was named for the ruling British Monarch of the day.

BOTTOM: The commercial fishing fleet at Port Stanley's large protected harbor. Transport Canada operates the harbor.

PANORAMIC VIEW OF PORT STANLEY, ONT.

Bridge Street, Port Stanley

STANLEY BEACH CASINO

Stanley Beach Casino

At its peak in 1943, 1.1 million passengers used the L&PS train, but automobile travel finally ended passenger service by 1957. The line was completely abandoned in 1982 after washouts destroyed sections of track.

Port Stanley Terminal Rail purchased the line and began to restore it for passenger use in 1983. It has grown since then and future plans include the extension of the operation into downtown St. Thomas, where a railway museum is located.

Today, working commercial fishing boats still line the docks. Port Stanley is one of the few remaining working ports on Lake Erie's north shore. The King George VI Lift Bridge rises at regular intervals to allow pleasure boaters to head down the creek. Tourism is a booming industry in the attractive town.

TOP: The view looking south during the early 1900s at Port Stanley, Ontario. Kettle Creek runs through the village and the tracks of the London & Port Stanley Railway can be seen to the left. Lake Erie is in the background.

MIDDLE LEFT: A steam-powered incline railway was installed in the 1870s to transport people between "Picnic Hill" (also known as "Fraser Heights") and Stanley Beach. The incline was later operated by electricity. It was removed in the 1960s.

MIDDLE RIGHT: The view along Port Stanley's Bridge Street, circa 1905.

BOTTOM: The Stanley Beach Casino (Hopkins Casino) was opened in 1909. The building was destroyed by fire in 1932.

PORT BRUCE

PORT BRUCE, Ontario (population 268) is 12 miles east of Port Stanley on Lake Erie's northern shore in Malahide Township. The small village of homes and cottages is nestled in the valley where Catfish Creek winds its way to the lake.

Originally Catfish Harbour, the village is named for James Bruce, the Earl of Elgin and a governor-general of Canada in the 1840s. It was co-founded in 1851 by grain merchants Lindley Moore and his brother-in-law, Amasa Lewis. Warehouses and a pier were constructed, and the village became popular as a summer resort during the latter half of the 19th century. Commercial fishing developed here during this period and continues today. Sport fishing and Port Bruce Provincial Park also attract visitors to this village.

TOP: Catfish Creek at Port Bruce, Ontario.

ABOVE LEFT: Port Bruce, Ontario, circa 1910.

RIGHT: The small settlement of Port Bruce in the 1940s.

BOTTOM: The pier at Port Bruce is a popular place to fish for Lake Erie perch.

PORT BURWELL & VIENNA

PORT BURWELL, Ontario (population 864) is 22 miles west of Long Point, at the mouth of Big Otter Creek on Lake Erie's north shore. Its harbor is cut into the sand-hill shoreline. The small village has many large historic homes and several churches. Cherry orchards, fields of wheat and tobacco farms surround the area.

The village is named after Lieutenant-Colonel Mahlon Burwell, the land surveyor for Colonel Thomas Talbot. Talbot was sent by the Crown in 1803 to manage the land between the Detroit River and Long Point. For Burwell's efforts as surveyor, Talbot awarded him a land grant that included the site of this village, which Burwell surveyed in 1830. Other settlers moved to the area, and by 1836, there were 200 residents.

Port Burwell grew around the shipbuilding industry, fed by a good supply of hardwoods from nearby stands. Timber was also shipped from here after being floated three miles down Big Otter Creek from the sawmills in Vienna. In 1840, the lighthouse was built, fueled by an oil lamp behind a lens imported from France. The lighthouse operated from 1840 until 1963, was restored in 1986, and remains today as Canada's oldest wooden lighthouse. Fishing also became an important commercial industry during the 19th century.

ABOVE: Mahlon Burwell (1783-1846) was a surveyor and political figure who laid out the settlement of Port Burwell, his namesake, in 1830. (The London and Middlesex Historical Society)

TOP: Looking eastward along the beach at Port Burwell, Ontario.

LOWER LEFT: Port Burwell's historic eight-sided wooden lighthouse was built in 1840. Fifty-five steps take visitors to the top of the 65-foot-tall structure.

LOWER RIGHT: Port Burwell's harbor was known for its commercial fishing fleet and shipyard. This early 1900s photo shows Big Otter Creek. The historic lighthouse can be seen in the upper left.

In 1900, the arrival of a spur line on the Canadian Pacific Railway helped grow Port Burwell as a receiving point for coal shipped from across the lake. The rail car ferry *Ashtabula* made the trip daily from Ashtabula, Ohio from 1907 until 1958, when it sank in Ashtabula Harbor.

Today, some commercial fishing continues from Port Burwell, while sport fishing, beaches, tourism and recreation make up the economic base. The Port Burwell Historic Lighthouse and Marine Museum are located in the village.

The village is also home to the Trinity Anglican Church. This colonial-gothic structure was built in 1836 with funds and on land donated by Colonel Burwell. Port Burwell Provincial Park is located on the western edge of town, and Sand Hill Park, which features a 450-foot-high sand dune, is located seven miles east of here. At one time, equipment on the top of the hill was used to relay nautical information across the lake to Pennsylvania.

VIENNA, Ontario (population 490) is a small village, four miles north of Port Burwell on Big Otter Creek. Colonel Mahlon Burwell divided the area for settlement and named it Shrewsbury. Residents wished for another name and asked Captain Samuel Edison (Thomas Edison's grandfather) to suggest a name. Edison suggested Vienna because the area reminded him of Austria.

The lumber industry flourished along Otter Creek, and by the 1850s, Vienna's population had grown to 1,200.

The village was not able to recover from several devastating fires and a flood during the mid-1800s. The population dropped to 900 by 1870. Another fire in 1912 and a flood in 1937 challenged Vienna's citizens. The quiet village is nestled in the hills on the road between Port Burwell and Tillsonburg.

ABOVE: Thomas Alva Edison (1847-1931) had family connections to Vienna, Ontario. His ancestors lived here. The famous inventor was born on the other side of Lake Erie at Milan, Ohio, but often visited family in Vienna. (Library of Congress, Prints & Photographs Division LC-USZ62-92228)

TOP RIGHT: The Edison Museum of Vienna, in the hometown of Thomas Alva Edison's parents, is located in an 1853 home on land once owned by the Edison family.

BOTTOM: Big Otter Creek winds its way through Vienna, Ontario on the way to Lake Erie.

TILLSONBURG

TILLSONBURG, Ontario (population 14,822) is 12 miles north of Port Burwell. George Tillson, and others from Massachusetts, settled the area in 1825. Originally known as Dereham Forge, the village was renamed Tillsonburg in honor of its founder, Tillson.

Since Tillsonburg was a logging center, the main street, Broadway, was laid out 100 feet wide so wagons could make turns. The original plan benefits Tillsonburg today as there is plenty of parking space along the wide thoroughfare.

Tillsonburg was incorporated as a town in 1872, with E.D. Tillson as its first mayor. Early industries included a sawmill, planing mill, gristmill, spinning mill, a pottery and tannery. Later, milk production, manufacture of shoes, textiles and tobacco production became Tillsonburg's predominant businesses.

TOP: Tillsonburg's wide main thoroughfare is known as Broadway Street.

BOTTOM: Tillsonburg's first mayor, E.D. Tillson, built the Annandale House during the 1880s. It is now a museum.

DELHI

TOP: A 1960s-era postcard of tobacco being readied for flue curing at Delhi. Views of flue-cured tobacco sheds are common in this part of Ontario.

BOTTOM: An autumn view of Big Creek at Delhi, Ontario. The creek joins Lake Erie near Port Rowan on the eastern side of Long Point.

DELHI, Ontario (population 5,000) is located midway between Tillsonburg and Simcoe, Ontario along Highway 3. The village in Norfolk County is surrounded by tobacco fields and is known as the "Tobacco Capital of Ontario." The multicultural community includes residents of Belgian, German, Polish, Dutch, Portuguese, Greek, Ukrainian, Lithuanian and British descent.

Delhi is home to the Ontario Tobacco Museum and Heritage Centre. It houses a large agricultural collection, which includes exhibits on tobacco, ginseng and alternate crops as well as a large multicultural display maintained in partnership with the Multicultural Heritage Association of Norfolk and the multicultural halls in Delhi. The community hosts Harvestfest annually in September.

LONG POINT

LONG POINT, Ontario (population 360) is a giant sandbar whose arm juts 20 miles into Lake Erie along on the north shore of the lake's eastern basin. The water around the point is remarkably clear and blue.

Wind and water continue to shape the shoreline of Lake Erie. At few points is this process more apparent than at Long Point. This shifting peninsula creates a large bay sheltering Port Rowan, Port Ryerse, Port Dover and several other villages. The continually growing arm stretches nearly halfway across the lake.

For early travelers along the north shore of Lake Erie, a portage crossing the isthmus joining Long Point to the mainland helped avoid the open waters and the longer trip around the point. Indians had been using the portage for many years by the time it had been noted by Sulpician missionaries, Dollier and Galinée, in 1670. Traffic increased over the portage as the French expansion to the southwest took place. Settlement occurred when the area was purchased from the Mississauga Indians.

Approximately 30 squatters had settled here by 1791. Some of the squatters remained after surveying was completed and Lieutenant-Governor John Graves Simcoe had visited in 1795. Land grants were also awarded to approved applicants, including many Loyalists. During the War of 1812, Major-General Sir Isaac Brock organized volunteers here for the attack on Detroit. The settlement's farms and mills supplied the British army until they were burned by U.S. troops in 1814. Not long after the War of 1812, the settlement was again prosperous. In 1837, the settlement became part of the new Talbot District.

The southern side of Long Point was notorious during the 1800s for rough settlements of lumbermen and shacks where outlaws lived. Stories of the plundering of ships, poaching, gambling, prostitution and sunken treasures were legendary. In 1866, complaints about these activities and their effects on the ecology prompted the Canadian government to sell the point to a group of citizens known as the Long Point Company, a private hunting club, whose interest was conservation. In the years since, this portion of Long Point has returned to a state similar to that seen by the first explorers. The club continues to own this parcel of land.

TOP: Looking west at the tip of Long Point from the air. (Fred Mudge/Rose-Le Studio, Ltd.)

Long Point became an island when a natural channel was cut through the peninsula during the 1833 storm. The Old Long Point Light, originally called the Cut Light, was built in 1879 to mark the channel. A 1906 storm filled in the cut and the light was no longer necessary. The lighthouse was decommissioned in 1916 and today is a private residence.

For many years, patrolmen on Long Point were assigned the grim task of scanning the beach following storms, for shipwrecks and the bodies of sailors. Because of the more than 200 shipwrecks, the area around the point is known as the "Graveyard of the Great Lakes."

In 1852, 250 lost their lives when the steamer *Atlantic* sank after colliding with another steamer, the *Ogdensburgh*. The 250-foot *Wocken* sank with 17 aboard and only three survivors in 1893 during an autumn gale in which two other ships capsized and a total of 41 people were lost. In 1897, the steamer *Idaho* sank in Long Point Bay with only two crewmen surviving by climbing into the crow's nest, which remained at water level. When they were finally rescued, their arms were frozen to the mast. In 1899, the steamer *Niagara* was lost eight miles east of the point, killing 16 men. The passenger steamer-turned-cargo ship *City of Dresden* wrecked here in 1922.

The Highway 59 causeway, built in 1927, links the mainland with the base of Long Point. The area near the causeway includes Big Creek National Wildlife Area, home to muskrats, birds, fish, turtles and water plants.

Hundreds of species of birds have been recorded, with roughly 150 species nesting here. The marshland is also home to numerous reptiles including turtles, which lay their eggs in the sand dunes every June.

TOP: The quiet beach at Long Point Provincial Park. The hills of Pennsylvania can be seen across the lake on this clear day.

BOTTOM: The Old Cut Light was built in 1879 and is still standing just outside the boundary of the Long Point Provincial Park. It was taken out of use in 1906 after storms filled the cut in Long Point. Today, the lighthouse serves as a private residence.

The upper part of the peninsula near the village of Long Point is scattered with cottages, campsites and stores. Beyond this area is a park, the private grounds of the Long Point Company, and further out the point is the Long Point National Wildlife Area, which extends to the tip. Most of Long Point is inaccessible to the public, with a few areas accessible only by boat. The peninsula has the distinction of being a World Biosphere Reserve, as designated by the United Nations.

The Long Point Provincial Park, Long Point National Wildlife Area and the Long Point Bird Observatory are located here.

PORT ROWAN

PORT ROWAN, Ontario (population 846) is situated on the shore of Inner Bay on the eastern side of the base of Long Point, protected by the sheltering arm of the peninsula. The small village is located north of the mouth of Big Creek. Boathouses and a marina are situated on the bay and the business district sits on the hill.

In 1798, Yorkshire, England native John Backhouse built a gristmill just north of this place. Returning after service during the War of 1812, he found his mill had escaped the fate of most of the other buildings in the area, which had been burned by the Americans. The three-story structure remains today and is said to be the oldest continuously running mill in Ontario. The Backus family (Backhouse's descendents shortened the family name) sold the mill in 1955 to become part of the Backus Heritage Village.

In 1854, Port Rowan resident Abigail Becker became known as the "Heroine of Long Point." With her husband away, she repeatedly ventured into the cold November waters of the lake to rescue eight sailors aboard the wrecked schooner *Conductor*. They were fed and housed in her cabin until they had recovered from the effects of their ordeal.

The Long Point Bird Observatory, run by Bird Studies Canada, is headquartered nearby. This unique habitat near Port Rowan suits the large variety of birds that pass through on their migration or stay to breed.

Port Rowan's industries include fishing, farming and tourism. The area is home to the Backus Heritage Conservation Area, including John Backhouse's gristmill, and the adjacent Backus Woods. The woods are Canada's largest remaining example of a "Carolinian" forest (see Rondeau). Nearby St. Williams is a quiet community with historic homes.

TOP LEFT: The John C. Backhouse Mill was built with hand-hewn beams in 1798. It was one of the few mills to escape fire during the War of 1812. The mill, part of the Backus Heritage Village, continues to grind wheat today.

TOP RIGHT: A 1960s-era aerial postcard view of Port Rowan, Ontario.

BOTTOM: Boathouses at Port Rowan, Ontario.

TURKEY POINT & NORMANDALE

TURKEY POINT, Ontario is a small resort settlement just west of Normandale. It is part of the city of Norfolk.

The courthouse built in 1803 was used as a barracks for soldiers during the War of 1812. Fort Norfolk, a short-lived project to build a navy yard, included a housing detachment for 50. After a blockhouse was built, the location was deemed unsuitable and abandoned. At the end of the war, the settlement included the courthouse, a jail, a fort and a tavern. The site is now Turkey Point Provincial Park. Today, Turkey Point is a quiet resort area.

NORMANDALE, Ontario is a small settlement on Lake Erie's Long Point Bay just east of Turkey Point and 12 miles west of Port Dover.

In 1818, Samuel Mason settled here and built a foundry where much of the region's ironware was made. Originally known as "Potter's Creek," the settlement was later named after Joseph Van Norman who, with others, purchased the foundry in 1822. The foundry soon employed up to 200 men using the supply of "bog iron," a spongy brown material found in nearby marshes. The furnace needed nine tons of bog iron to produce three tons of iron. During some years, the annual output would reach nearly 800 tons. The foundry operated until 1847, producing household utensils including pots, kettles, irons, pails and cooking stoves.

The village includes several historic homes. The post office and Union Hotel date to the early- to mid-19th century. The country store was built in 1875. The hamlet of Fishers Glen is nearby.

TOP LEFT: Normandale's historic Union Hotel and post office.

TOP RIGHT: Overlooking Turkey Point, Ontario from the bluff during the 1930s.

BOTTOM: The beach and homes of Normandale, Ontario.

FOUR BRAVE GIRLS.
WHO CROSSED FROM PORT RYERSE TO LONG POINT,
DURING STORM OF JULY 20TH.1907.

PORT RYERSE

PORT RYERSE, Ontario (population 184) is a small hamlet at the mouth of Young's Creek, five miles west of Port Dover. The sleepy settlement lines the creek's ravine and includes permanent homes and cottages and a general store.

Port Ryerse is named for Lieutenant-Colonel Samuel Ryerse. Born in 1752, Ryerse was a Loyalist commissioned in the New Jersey Volunteers during the American Revolution. After taking refuge in New Brunswick, he arrived here in 1794. Ryerse received 3,000 acres of land and built the first gristmill here a short time later.

The settlement grew during the early 1800s and was capital of the London District. A courthouse was built here along with a post office and many businesses. During the War of 1812, Port Ryerse did not escape the fate suffered by other towns along the lakeshore in the Long Point region. During a raid, the Americans burned the gristmill built by Ryerse, the courthouse and other buildings. Access to timber was cut off, sending many to settle further inland. Other gristmills were built during the 19th century, and the shipping of lumber and grain was the main industry in Port Ryerse.

Samuel Ryerse, members of his family and other early settlers are buried in a small graveyard behind the Anglican church, just up the hill from the settlement.

TOP: In 1907, four teenage girls were rowing a small boat at Port Ryerse when a sudden storm trapped them on the lake for nearly 10 hours. The girls landed safely on Long Point, 20 miles away.

BOTTOM: Samuel Ryerse, the founder of the settlement, is buried behind the Anglican Church at Port Ryerse.

SIMCOE

TOP LEFT: The Carillon Tower at Simcoe, dedicated in 1925, is 60 feet tall and holds 23 bells weighing over 8,000 pounds.

TOP RIGHT: Peel Street, looking west at Simcoe, Ontario.

BOTTOM: The scenic Lynn River runs through Simcoe on its way to Lake Erie at Port Dover.

SIMCOE, Ontario (population 19,941) is six miles north of Port Ryerse. The quiet city has an attractive business district, park and lake.

The settlement originally known as Theresaville and Birdtown was named Simcoe for Lieutenant-Governor John Graves Simcoe in 1829. A sawmill and gristmill were established in the 1820s. The South Norfolk Railway Company's railroad made its way from Simcoe to Lake Erie at Port Rowan in 1889.

Simcoe's Wellington Park features a carillon tower. The Eva Brook Donly Museum is a furnished Georgian style house depicting life in the 1860s.

Steamer Keystone leaving Port Dover, Canada.

PORT DOVER

PORT DOVER, Ontario (population 5,398) is 50 miles west of Port Colborne, at the mouth of the Lynn River, and is protected by Long Point Bay. The town took its name from Dover, England.

A pier juts into the bay from the mouth of the Lynn River. A mixture of shops and restaurants lines Port Dover's main street, up the hill from the beach.

The area was first visited by white men in the winter of 1669-1670, when Sulpician priests François Dollier de Casson and René de Brehaut de Galinée arrived here and erected a cross, pronouncing possession in the name of the King of France. The priests started their journey at Montreal. Nine canoes carried members of the expedition and their Seneca guides to spread Christianity to the tribes of the southwest. Dollier and Galinée came here by way of the St. Lawrence River, Lake Ontario, the Grand River, and subsequently Lake Erie. Members of their group built a cabin, erected the cross on the lakeshore, and after five months, continued up the lakes to Sault Ste. Marie and finally back to Montreal via the Nipissing route.

In 1763, the Treaty of Paris transferred possession to the British. Settlers, loyal to the Crown, came a few at a time from New York State and New Jersey to work the rich soil. A gristmill was built upstream, followed by a sawmill and a distillery. The settlement was called Dover Mills.

TOP: Looking to the east along Main Street, Port Dover, circa 1910.

BOTTOM: An early 20th century view of the pier at Port Dover. The lighthouse was established in 1846.

BLACK CREEK AND THE BRIDGES, PORT DOVER, CANADA.

During the War of 1812, gristmills on the Canadian side became targets of the Americans, since they supplied flour for British troops. On May 15, 1814, about 800 American regulars and militia under Lieutenant-Colonel John Campbell arrived, looted and burned the settlements, moving on to do the same at Port Ryerse. Houses were destroyed and livestock was slaughtered. Campbell said he was retaliating for raids on Buffalo and the Niagara Frontier by British troops. The U.S. Army subsequently found that Campbell was justified in the burning of the mills but condemned his destruction of private homes. In July, after Campbell's death at the Battle of Chippawa, British retaliation against the Americans escalated to a point where public buildings in Washington, D.C. were burned.

After the war, reconstruction took place closer to the mouth of the creek at the harbor. In 1835, a village plan was recorded for Port Dover. By 1850, the harbor was much improved, making Port Dover a principal Lake Erie port. Shipyards, fisheries, tanneries and a wool mill added to the agricultural base, further growing the economy. Port Dover was incorporated as a village in 1879 with 1,100 residents.

During the 20th century, Port Dover had the largest commercial fishing fleet on the Great Lakes, a distinction held until it was recently overtaken by Wheatley, Ontario. The community also developed as a resort community with entertainment. Trainloads of vacationers came to Port Dover to enjoy the beaches, hotels and restaurants. The Summer Garden, a music and dance pavilion, was opened in 1921, bringing some of the biggest musical acts to the Lake Erie resort town for many summers. The venue burned to the ground in 1979, marking the end of an era.

Today, Port Dover remains home to a commercial fishing fleet, the Harbour Museum is housed in a restored fishing shanty and the village continues to serve as a recreational port featuring the Lighthouse Theatre Festival, yacht clubs, bed and breakfast establishments and other accommodations. The village hosts the annual Fish Fest and Summer Festival. A few miles east of here, near the village of Nanticoke, is an industrial area along the lakeshore. The Lake Erie Steel Company Ltd. (Stelco Inc.), Nanticoke Thermal Generating Station, one of the world's largest coal-fired plants, and the Imperial Oil Refinery are located there. The small village of Selkirk is a few miles east of Nanticoke.

TOP LEFT: Fishing shanties lined Black Creek during the 19th and early 20th centuries at Port Dover.

TOP RIGHT: The Nanticoke coal-fired generating station, one of the world's largest, is located east of Port Dover. The plant produces 3,920 megawatts of power. (Courtesy of Ontario Power Generation)

BRANTFORD

BRANTFORD, Ontario (population 90,192) is 25 miles north of Lake Erie, along the Grand River.

Settlement dates to 1784, when Captain Joseph Brant led the Six Nations Iroquois Indians from New York State to land along the Grand River. Brant was loyal to the British and he fought for them during the American Revolution. After the war, Brant requested land in Canada for his people. In 1785, King George III honored Brant by building a chapel in the village.

Brantford was named for Brant in 1826. A canal along the Grand River was built in the 1840s between Port Maitland on Lake Erie and Brantford. The agricultural lands in the area attracted settlers from the United States, Scotland and Ireland.

Alexander Graham Bell made his home here after arriving from Scotland in 1870. Bell invented the telephone in Brantford in 1874. The town became a city in 1877 as the population rose to nearly 10,000.

Another famous Brantford resident, Wayne Gretzky, became one of the greatest players in the history of the National Hockey League.

Today, Brantford remains an industrial center. The Bell Homestead contains artifacts including original furnishings and household items. Canada's first telephone business office is on the site.

ABOVE: Alexander Graham Bell (1847-1922) is widely considered to be the inventor of the telephone. Bell emigrated from Scotland to Brantford at the age of 23. (Library of Congress, Prints & Photographs Division LC-USZ62-14759)

TOP LEFT: The Bell Homestead at Brantford was the setting for the invention of the telephone in 1874. In 1910, the year this image was taken, the home was opened to the general public.

MIDDLE: An 1875 panoramic map of Brantford, Ontario. (Geography and Map Division, Library of Congress)

BOTTOM: Joseph Brant (1742-1807) was a Mohawk leader and British military officer during the American Revolutionary War. Brant, for whom the city is named, is buried at the Chapel of the Mohawks in Brantford. (Painting by Gilbert Stuart, courtesy New York State Historical Association)

Bridge and Water View, Dunnville, Ont.

Junction of Canal and Lock Streets, Dunnville, Ont.

DUNNVILLE

DUNNVILLE, Ontario (population 12,581) sits 22 miles west of Port Colborne and four miles north of Port Maitland on the Grand River.

Historically, Dunnville has served as a link between Lake Erie and the interior. Named for the Receiver General of Canada, John Henry Dunn, Dunnville was settled in 1829 when the dam and feeder canal for the first Welland Canal were built here. The feeder canal diverted water from the Grand River to the Welland Canal in the years before it was connected directly to Lake Erie at Port Colborne. The canal's original route started at Port Dalhousie on Lake Ontario, then turned east at Allanburg, using Chippawa Creek (Welland River). It then headed south from Chippawa against the strong currents of the Niagara River to Buffalo and Lake Erie. Dunnville's feeder canal, with just a four-foot depth, could only support small scows, so goods first had to be offloaded from steamers, and then transferred before continuing to the Welland Canal.

The entrance to the feeder canal was later moved down the Grand River to Port Maitland, but Dunnville remained an important link as steamboats from Lake Erie continued to arrive here. Smaller boats traveled further upriver through eight locks to Brantford. Dunnville's business grew as sawmills were built and lumber was shipped from here. Gristmills, a tannery, a distillery, a brewery, a customs office and a post office were also built during this period. By the 1850s, the village's population reached 1,000.

The railroad's arrival in the latter part on the 1800s kept the community strong. In 1889, Dunnville became a town and industry continued to develop. Major floods occurred here in 1913, 1916 and during the 1930s. Today, Dunnville continues as the commercial center for agriculture in the area. Tourism and recreation also support the economy.

TOP RIGHT: The Grand River, and the former connection to the Welland Canal in the foreground, at Dunnville, circa 1905.

BOTTOM: An early 1900s view of downtown Dunnville.

The Harbor, Port Maitland, Ont.

PORT MAITLAND

PORT MAITLAND, Ontario (population 100) is 20 miles west of Port Colborne at the mouth of the Grand River, where it flows into Lake Erie. The settlement of Port Maitland is named for Sir Peregrine Maitland, Lieutenant-Governor of Canada West.

The Neutral Indians were early inhabitants of the mouth of the Grand River and also lived in villages further upriver. They were known as Neutrals because they traded with both the Hurons and Iroquois but did not take sides between these warring tribes. Despite their position, the Iroquois eliminated the Neutrals and also destroyed the Huron villages in this area. The Chippewas, also known as the Mississaugas, later inhabited the settlement that was eventually called Port Maitland.

After the American Revolution, the Governor-in-Chief of Canada, Sir Frederick Haldimand, granted land to the Six Nations of the Iroquois, which extended six miles outward from both banks of the Grand River from its source to its mouth at Lake Erie. The land, purchased from the Mississaugas in 1784, rewarded the Iroquois for their aid to the British during the war and also compensated them for the loss of their lands in the Mohawk Valley of New York State. Much of this land was later sold to white settlers, when they began to pressure the Indians to sell some of their prime land along the Grand River. Approximately 350,000 acres were divided for sale, although a reserve still exists upriver from here.

In 1815, the Royal Navy began to construct the Grand River Naval Depot. The base served to support only four ships of the drastically reduced British naval force on Lake Erie, made smaller as a result of the Rush-Bagot Agreement in 1817. The wharf and several buildings washed away in a storm in 1827, and the depot was abandoned in 1834.

Port Maitland was an active part of the Welland Canal system when the feeder canal that was established upriver in Dunnville was connected here. The feeder canal supplied the original Welland Canal with water from the Grand River before it was connected directly to Lake Erie at Port Colborne. When the feeder canal was enlarged and connected at Port Maitland, a lock 200-by-45-foot lock with a nine-foot draft was constructed. The feeder was deepened and was the only route available between 1845 and 1850 while the main canal was being constructed to Port Colborne.

The Port Maitland Light was built in 1848 and sits at the end of the pier that juts into Lake Erie at the mouth of the river. Today, the tiny and quiet settlement is popular with sport fishermen.

ABOVE: Sir Peregrine Maitland (1777-1854), for whom Port Maitland is named, was the Lieutenant-Governor of Upper Canada.

TOP LEFT: An early 1900s view of Port Maitland.

PORT COLBORNE

PORT COLBORNE, Ontario (population 18,599) is on Lake Erie, 19 miles west of Fort Erie at the southern entrance to the Welland Ship Canal. The settlement founded in 1832 was originally known as "Gravelly Bay" and later renamed for Sir John Colborne, a Canadian Governor-General. It became a village in 1870 and a town in 1917.

In 1818, William Hamilton Merritt originally conceived the Welland Canal, which bisects the city, as a way to divert trade from the Erie Canal and New York. It was opened in 1829 to replace the portage around Niagara Falls between Lake Ontario and Lake Erie. The canal did not arrive here until 1833, since it did not initially connect directly with Lake Erie. Instead, two routes were available from Lake Ontario, one by way of the feeder canal to Dunnville and Port Maitland and the other by way of the Welland River to the Niagara River. Eventually, after much discussion and surveying, Port Colborne was chosen as the canal's Lake Erie terminus. When the extension was completed and put into operation in 1833, the canal linked Port Colborne with Port Dalhousie on Lake Ontario. The 326-foot difference in water level was handled by 40 locks, which were 110 feet long, 22 feet wide and eight feet deep (see Chapter 6).

During the middle of the 1800s, several changes were made to the canal and its locks. By 1887, the canal had a 14-foot draft. Construction of the current Welland Ship Canal began

TOP: An early 20th century view of the Welland Canal at Port Colborne.

BOTTOM: The Welland Canal at Port Colborne, Ontario. The old lock chamber is to the left of the lift bridge.

West St. — Port Colborne, Ont.

in 1913, stopping in 1916 during World War I and resuming in 1919. The canal was completed in 1932, 100 years after the founding of Gravelly Bay.

The Welland Ship Canal is now 27 miles long, 310 to 350 feet wide and 30 feet deep. It extends to Port Weller on Lake Ontario, three miles east of Port Dalhousie. Seven lift locks and one guard lock now do the work of the original 40. The current lift locks are 859 feet long, 80 feet wide and 30 feet deep (over the sills) and each has a lift of over 45 feet. Eleven bridges cross above the canal and three tunnels pass beneath it. Port Colborne's Humberstone Lock at 1,381 feet is one the world's longest locks.

Port Colborne is an industrial and shipping port with industries that include an iron smelting plant and a cement works. It is home to the Historical and Marine Museum, which focuses on the history of the city and the Welland Canal in a village setting. The Roselawn Complex is a restored heritage mansion, used for the professional Showboat Festival Theatre. Nickel Beach is located immediately east of the entrance to the Welland Canal and Sherkston Shores is further east. Port Colborne's recreational opportunities include marinas, beaches, scuba diving and fishing. Shipwatching at the canal is also an attraction. Mud Lake Conservation Area, in the northern section of the city, attracts hikers, birdwatchers and cross-country skiers. The Canal Days Festival is an annual event held in August.

ABOVE: Sir John Colborne (1778-1863), for whom Port Colborne was named, served as Lieutenant-Governor of Upper Canada between 1828 and 1836.

TOP LEFT: West Street at Port Colborne. The Welland Canal is at right.

BOTTOM: The view to the south along the Welland Canal at Port Colborne. Lake Erie is in the background.

At Crystal Beach, Steamer "Americana" in distance, near Buffalo, N.Y.

CRYSTAL BEACH

CRYSTAL BEACH, Ontario (population 6,321) is 10 miles west of Fort Erie on the northern shoreline of Lake Erie.

Point Abino, located just west of here, protects the beach. The Point Abino Lighthouse was built in 1917 to warn ships of dangerous rock shelves surrounding the point. It operated until 1996, when the Canadian Coast Guard installed offshore buoys.

Crystal Beach, an amusement park of the same name, operated here from 1888 until 1989. The park began as a Chautauqua religious campground in 1888 with an auditorium, tents and picnic grounds. Soon amusements were added, roller coasters and rides were constructed and hotels were built. Piers were put up for the *Americana* and *Canadiana* steamships, which brought visitors from both the U.S. and Canadian sides of the border.

The village grew around the park with cottages springing up for visitors who stayed throughout the summer season, adding to the village's prosperity. In 1925, the Crystal Ballroom was completed, with a dance floor that could hold up to 3,000 dancers at one time. The park continued to grow in the 1930s and 1940s despite the Depression and World War II.

TOP: A 1914 panoramic view of Crystal Beach, Ontario.

MIDDLE: Crystal Beach in the early 1900s.

BOTTOM: The Comet roller coaster at Crystal Beach.

Well-known roller coasters over the years included the Cyclone and its replacement, the Comet, built in 1948. The Comet was later moved and remains in use today at the Great Escape & Splashwater Kingdom amusement park at Lake George, New York.

By the 1950s, big bands became less popular and the dance hall eventually was turned into a roller skating rink. Park attendance continued to drop and ferry service from Buffalo ended in 1956. Those who came did so by automobile. The 214-foot, 2,000-passenger *Canadiana* steamship sat idle in Buffalo and Port Colborne before it was scrapped in 2004.

Competition from other regional amusement parks in the 1980s made it even more difficult for Crystal Beach's park. Its 1906 Philadelphia Toboggan Company carousel was auctioned off piece-by-piece to raise money. The merry-go-round had two chariots, 23 horses and 21 other animals including a camel, giraffe, lion, wolf and a St. Bernard dog. The park was sold to new owners who attempted to revive business in anticipation of its 100th anniversary in 1988.

The Crystal Beach amusement park finally closed after the 1989 season. Rides and buildings were auctioned off, and what was left, including the ballroom, was demolished. The area is now occupied by a housing development.

TOP : The business district of the resort community of Crystal Beach, Ontario.

BOTTOM: A 1910-era view of the midway at Crystal Beach, Ontario.

235

Ridge St., Ridgeway, Ont., Canada

RIDGEWAY

RIDGEWAY, Ontario is a quiet little village just west of Fort Erie. The name Ridgeway came from its location along a limestone ridge. Ridge Road, which was an old wagon trail, follows this ridge. A farming community, Ridgeway was settled by Loyalists during the late 18th century.

The railroad came through the village in the 1850s and a business district grew. Ridgeway became well known during the Fenian Invasion of 1866. Anglo-Canadian and Irish-American forces fought here in the "Battle of Ridgeway."

In the late 1880s Ridgeway's population had reached 800 and the village boasted a train station, three taverns, 20 shops, three planing mills and a gristmill. It also became the seat of Bertie Township. Today, Ridgeway's attractive business district is lined with shops.

TOP & MIDDLE: The business district of Ridgeway, Ontario during the 1930s.

BOTTOM: The Ridgeway Battlefield Museum is on the site where Irish-American veterans of the U.S. Civil War fought Canadian forces in an attempt to gain Ireland's independence from Britain in June 1866.

FORT ERIE

FORT ERIE, Ontario (population 29,925) is at the easternmost point of Lake Erie's Canadian shoreline, across from Buffalo, New York, at the entrance to the Niagara River. Fort Erie has three distinct business districts. One lies along the river near the Peace Bridge; another, formerly known as Bridgeburg, is just downstream, extending westward from the river on Jarvis Street. To the west, newer development lines Highway 3.

The southern portion of the city was the site of three fortifications. The first, built in 1764, was a wooden structure used by the British, Loyalist troops and Indian allies who supported the Crown during the American Revolution. The fortification was heavily damaged in 1779 by a storm that sent ice crashing into its walls. Repaired in 1783, the fort was abandoned when ice and water again wrecked the structure in 1803. Construction of a second fort began on higher ground in 1805, but the structure was not complete when the War of 1812 began, as the Americans attempted unsuccessfully to gain control of the fort. The following year, the Americans briefly controlled the fort, but only after the British had withdrawn and Canadian troops had burned it. In January of 1814, the British returned and repaired the fort. Then in July of 1814, while only 170 British troops garrisoned the fort, 4,500 Americans captured it once again. The Americans used it as a base for their subsequent battles at Chippawa and Lundy's Lane (near Niagara Falls). The Americans retreated here after they were defeated at Lundy's Lane, surviving a siege by the British in August and September of 1814. In November of that year, the Americans destroyed the fort before returning home. Between 1937 and 1939, the Niagara Parks Commission rebuilt Fort Erie.

From the 1840s through the Civil War period, the Niagara River was a dangerous place as slave hunters prowled the length of the river in search of fugitive slaves trying to make the crossing to the freedom of Canada. A number of safe houses were used to accommodate slaves in Fort Erie including Bertie Hall, built in 1826.

During the Fenian raids, which took place in 1866, a battle took place at nearby Ridgeway. The Fenians were Civil War soldiers who attempted to "liberate" Upper Canada and attain Ireland's freedom from Britain. The unsuccessful invasion may have made Canadians realize they could not depend on Britain for the country's defense, and Confederation followed in 1867.

During the 19th and early 20th centuries, several ferries operated between Fort Erie and Buffalo. While thoughts of building a bridge dated back to 1851, they were not realized for many years because of legislation, opposition from special interests, cost and the Niagara River's swift current.

In 1893, American industrialist Alonzo C. Mather proposed a design for an international harbor on both sides of the river with a bridge to link the two countries by rail, trolley, vehicular and pedestrian traffic. Mather wanted to build a hydroelectric plant under the

TOP: A panoramic view of Fort Erie. In 1939, after laying in ruins for many years, the fort was restored to its appearance during the 1812-1814 period.

237

A modern view of the busy international Peace Bridge, which crosses the Niagara River. Fort Erie, Ontario is to the left. Buffalo, New York is on the right.

MIDDLE: A 1930s view of the Peace Bridge.

BOTTOM: Ferries operated between Fort Erie and Buffalo. Service was discontinued a few years after the Peace Bridge opened in 1927.

bridge, but those with interests in the hydroelectric plants at Niagara Falls opposed him, fearing the competition. Later, the goal of building a bridge was based on a desire to commemorate the 100 years of peace between the two nations since the War of 1812. World War I slowed progress on the plan, but legislation passed and construction finally began. Groundbreaking on the $4.5 million project took place on August 17, 1925. The Peace Bridge opened on August 7, 1927 and was dedicated to 100 years of friendship between the U.S. and Canada. The Prince of Wales (later King Edward VIII) was among the dignitaries who dedicated the bridge.

The opening of the bridge accelerated development during the 20th century, as many from the Buffalo area came across the river for recreation at Erie Beach, the amusement park at Crystal Beach and other places. A large number of Americans bought land and built cottages in the area.

During the 1990s, a team of Canadian archaeologists uncovered one of the largest prehistoric aboriginal sites in northeastern North America near the Peace Bridge. Their work

Grand Stand and Betting Ring, Fort Erie, Ont.

has continued into the 21st century. So far, more than 700,000 artifacts, including vessels, arrowheads, spearheads, drills, scraping tools, knives and burial items have been found. The 60-acre site confirms that the area was a major source of Onondaga flint, a high-quality stone used to make tools. It is believed that the quantity of debris from the manufacture of tools indicates the aboriginal people may have been supplying finished tools throughout a wide area. This discovery also suggests this was a major manufacturing and distribution area dating from nearly 4,000 years ago up to the 17th century. The supply of flint, fish and wildlife, and its location near where the Niagara River was narrow and could be more easily crossed, was the likely basis for this strategic location. The artifacts have become a part of the Fort Erie Historical Museum's collection.

Today, in addition to being an important international trade center, Fort Erie is home to a number of attractions including the Fort Erie Historical Museum, Fort Erie Railroad Museum, Historic Fort Erie, Ridgeway Battlefield Museum and the Mildred M. Mahoney Dolls' House Gallery, housed in Bertie Hall. Fort Erie Racetrack is one of Ontario's oldest, dating from 1897, and is home to the Prince of Wales Stakes, the second jewel of Canada's Triple Crown, held in July. Fort Erie is North America's sixth busiest international border point, with approximately $1 billion in trade crossing weekly and often more than 5,000 commercial vehicles crossing the Peace Bridge daily.

TOP: An early 20th century view of the Niagara River ferries at Fort Erie. (Peace Bridge Authority)

BOTTOM: An early 1900s view of the grandstand at Fort Erie Racetrack.

CHIPPAWA

CHIPPAWA, Ontario is located where the Welland River meets the Niagara River, two miles above the falls. It is a small village, now part of the city of Niagara Falls. The name *chippawa* means "people without moccasins."

The settlement's roots and development are tied to the various forms of transportation that have evolved over the years. Chippawa was the southern terminus of the Niagara Portage Road, which provided a route around Niagara Falls. Designated as the first King's Highway, it was the primary link for travel and commerce, and served as a war supply route between Lake Ontario and Lake Erie. Following the relinquishment of the east bank of the Niagara River to the United States in 1783, the British opened the road between Queenston and Chippawa as the official government route in 1791. Fort Chippawa, also known as Fort Welland, was also built here in the same year to protect the terminus of the portage and serve as a depot for government supplies. It included a blockhouse and was surrounded by a stockade. Later a barracks, storehouse, officers' quarters and earthworks were added to the fort.

During the War of 1812, several bloody engagements occurred in the area. The three-hour Battle of Chippawa occurred on July 5, 1814, when an American army launched its last major invasion of Canada, defeating a British and Canadian force of regulars, militia and Indian warriors. During the battle, about 200 men were killed and 500 wounded. After several months of fighting in the area along the Niagara River, the invading Americans were finally forced back across the river.

Laura Secord, well known for warning the British of an impending surprise attack by the Americans, was a famous resident. One morning in 1813, she awoke to find the Americans had surrounded and taken over Queenston, her home at the time. She got past American lines and made her way through 20 miles of dense forests and swamps to deliver her warning. With 46 soldiers and 70 Caughnawaga and Mohawk Indians, the British force reversed the surprise and captured over 500 Americans. Secord was credited as being greatly responsible for keeping the Niagara Peninsula under British control. She later operated a school at her home in Chippawa.

Transportation again affected the settlement with the completion of the first Welland Canal, briefly putting Chippawa on the route between Lake Ontario and Lake Erie. From 1829 until 1833, Chippawa Creek (the Welland River) from Port Robinson to Chippawa was part of the original Welland Canal. After reaching Chippawa, ships went up the Niagara River to Buffalo. The first railroad in Upper Canada opened in 1841 with horse-drawn carriages running between here and Queenston. In 1849, Chippawa was incorporated as a village, and in 1854 the railroad was converted for steam engines and relocated to serve what

TOP: The small village of Chippawa is now part of the city of Niagara Falls, Ontario.

Old Erie Belle in Harbor
Chippawa, Ontario.

TOP: The *Erie Belle* at Chippawa. The schooner was built in Port Burwell in 1873. The photo was taken in 1907.

BOTTOM LEFT: The Battle of Chippawa was fought in 1814. It was the longest and bloodiest military operation of the War of 1812. The battlefield along the Niagara River is now a park.

BOTTOM RIGHT: A hydro canal between Chippawa and Queenston was built in 1917 to send water to the Sir Adam Beck Generating Stations. The Welland River at Chippawa, which had flowed into the Niagara River, was reversed, taking water from both rivers to the power plants via the swiftly flowing, deep-cut canal.

was to become the town of Niagara Falls. In 1893, the Queenston-Chippawa Railway carried boat passengers from Queenston to Table Rock at the falls and other points along the Niagara River.

The Niagara Portage Road continued to operate, although its importance diminished because of the canal and the arrival of railroads in the 1840s and 1850s. During the 19th century, Chippawa was a thriving community with a tannery, woodworking shop, distillery, sawmill, factories and other businesses.

After a 120-year history as an independent village, Chippawa became part of the city of Niagara Falls in 1970. The Niagara Parks Commission recently acquired 1,000 acres of land to preserve the site of the Chippawa Battlefield, the last untouched War of 1812 battlefield in North America. Niagara Parks also built a 45-hole golf course in the area. With the attractions of Niagara Falls nearby, tourism is the key industry.

Niagara Falls, Ontario:
The Honeymoon Capital of the World

TOP: The growing skyline of Niagara Falls, Ontario. The Rainbow Bridge, which opened in 1941, replaced a bridge that was destroyed by an ice jam in 1938.

BOTTOM: A winter view of the Canadian Horseshoe Falls.

TOP: Niagara Falls, Canada. The mist in the air is from the cataract.

MIDDLE: Clifton Hill in Niagara Falls contains a number of gift shops, wax museums, haunted houses, restaurants, hotels and other attractions.

BOTTOM: The Floral Clock at Niagara Falls was built in 1950 with a face that is 40 feet in diameter. The plantings on the clock are changed twice each season.

243

NIAGARA FALLS

NIAGARA FALLS, Ontario (population 82,184) is on the western bank of the Niagara River across the river from Niagara Falls, New York and 45 miles south of Toronto.

While both Niagara Falls, New York and Niagara Falls, Ontario are famous for the production of hydroelectric power, the Canadian city's roots are more firmly tied to tourism than its industrialized American counterpart. The Niagara Parkway runs the length of the Niagara River, passing through the well-manicured Queen Victoria Park, with its splendid views of both the Canadian (Horseshoe) Falls and the American Falls. In contrast, Clifton Street, extending up Clifton Hill from Queen Victoria Park, has a carnival-like atmosphere. Both sides of the street are lined with arcades, souvenir shops, wax museums and other tourist attractions.

The falls are relatively young by geological standards. They were originally formed seven miles north here some 12,000 years ago (see Chapter 7 profile of Niagara Falls, New York).

It is believed that French explorer Etienne Brulé may have been the first European to see the falls, in 1615. Father Louis Hennepin saw Niagara Falls in 1678 and later published the first engraving of the falls. European settlement of the region was very slow until after the American Revolution.

Niagara Falls was the site of a bloody battle during the War of 1812. On July 25, 1814, after the Americans had been victorious upriver at Chippawa, 2,800 men took on the advancing Americans at Lundy's Lane. After six hours of fighting, both sides had lost more than 800 men. Both sides claimed victory, although the Americans did not displace the British.

Not long after the War of 1812, the tourism industry began to take hold. By the 1820s, attractions began to develop around the falls. A stairway was constructed down the gorge at the brink of the falls and a ferry began shuttling passengers across the lower river. A road was built up the gorge wall from the ferry landing to the rim. Hotels were built, beginning with the Clifton Hotel.

ABOVE: The view from the Skylon Tower at Niagara Falls, Ontario. The Rainbow Bridge connects Canada with Niagara Falls, New York.

Horseshoe Falls From Table Rock House, Can.

Scenic Tunnel under Horseshoe Falls, Canada

Following the arrival of the steam railroad in 1854, the settlement developed rapidly as a tourist destination. The first suspension bridge across the Niagara River was built in 1848 at the narrow Whirlpool Rapids section, where the gorge walls are less than 800 feet apart. John August Roebling, designer of the Brooklyn Bridge, built a second suspension bridge at this part of the gorge in 1855 to carry rail traffic through the area. The first bridge near the falls was built in 1868.

The settlement was named Elgin from 1853 to 1856, then Clifton, and finally Suspension Bridge before it became Niagara Falls in 1881. By the 1870s, the falls were the greatest tourist attraction in North America. As a result, it also attracted those who wished to exploit the tourists. The area near the falls took on a carnival atmosphere as sideshows were set up at nearly every vantage point, peddlers hassled tourists and freak shows displayed human and animal deformities and other oddities. By this time, many were urging the governments of Canada and the United States to step in to create parks (see Niagara Falls, New York).

TOP: A 1920s-era view of the Canadian Horseshoe Falls from above the Table Rock Complex.

MIDDLE: The Horseshoe Falls and Queen Victoria Park entrance, circa 1930.

BOTTOM: The scenic tunnels behind the Horseshoe Falls were built in 1888 and have since been modernized.

On the Canadian side, the Province of Ontario assumed responsibility through the "Niagara Falls Park Act," which was signed in 1885. This act brought about the development of the attractive park grounds that parallels the Canadian side of the river.

Hydroelectric power companies were given rights to build power plants on the park grounds. The building of these plants continued on the Canadian side through the 1950s.

As the park developed along the river, more tourists arrived. They came by coach, rail and boat. By 1896, three boats transported passengers between Toronto and Queenston. In the 1940s, Winston Churchill remarked that the Niagara Parkway, which ran the length of the Niagara River, was "the prettiest Sunday drive in the world." From the time of the building of first bridge, 13 bridges have been built across the gorge to carry motor vehicles, trains and pedestrians. Four of these bridges remain in service today.

In 1902, a railroad was constructed across the Queenston Suspension Bridge. Later, it was extended along the lower gorge on the American side of the river, connecting back into Canada at the Upper Arch Bridge. This transit line, known as the Great Gorge Route, continued in service until the Depression.

The arrival of the automobile and its abundance after World War II helped continue the growth of the tourist industry. Niagara Falls was the backdrop for a movie that further charged this growth. The 1952 motion picture *Niagara*, starring Marilyn Monroe, was filmed here with scenes shot on a motel set built on the grounds of Queen Victoria Park. After the movie's release, tourists tried to call for rooms at the "Rainbow Cabins," only to find they merely existed as a temporary movie set, which had been built in the park.

Niagara Falls has also attracted daredevils. In addition to tightrope walkers who made their way across the gorge, others chose to go over the falls in various contraptions. Annie Edson Taylor, 63, took the plunge in 1901,

ABOVE: A movie poster for the 1953 movie *Niagara*, starring Marilyn Monroe, which was filmed at Niagara Falls. (20th Century Fox)

TOP LEFT: The Sir Adam Beck Generating Station No. 2 went on line in 1954. The Sir Adam Beck Generating Station No. 1 to its right went into service in 1921. The Queenston-Lewiston Bridge can be seen in the upper right.

TOP RIGHT: Stringing power cables during the early 1900s at Niagara Falls. (Niagara Falls Public Library)

MIDDLE: The Sir Adam Beck Generating Plant No. 1.

BOTTOM: Bobby Leach survived a plunge over the Horseshoe Falls in a cylindrical steel barrel on July 25, 1911. (Library of Congress, Prints & Photographs Division LC-USZ62-107150)

surviving the fall. For the next 20 years, she tried to capitalize on her feat, but she died penniless. Bobby Leach was also successful in his attempt to go over the falls in 1911. The Englishman was injured, however, and had to spend six months in the hospital. Others were not as lucky. Red Hill Jr. died in 1951 while trying to go over the falls in a contraption made from inner tubes, held together with netting and straps, called "The Thing." Karel Soucek made a successful attempt using a barrel in 1984, but he died in an accident while performing a stunt a few months later at the Houston Astrodome. Steven Trotter, 22, survived the trip over the falls in 1985. Dave Munday also made two successful trips, first in 1987 and again in 1993. In 1989, Peter DeBernardi and Jeffrey Petkovich made their successful trip strapped together in the same barrel. Jesse Sharp, from Tennessee, tried unsuccessfully to conquer the falls in a kayak in 1990. His body was never recovered. In 1995, Robert Overacker of California attempted the stunt on a jet ski with a parachute. He also perished. Two people are known to have survived the plunge over the Horseshoe Falls without the aid of a safety device (see Chapter 7 profile of Niagara Falls, New York).

The boom period for the further growth of tourism accelerated in the 1990s and continues today. A large casino was built and expanded, several large new hotels have been constructed on the hill overlooking the falls and Clifton Hill has received a facelift.

Today, tourism continues as the leading industry. Others include manufacturing, food products and professional services. Attractions include the Floral Clock, Great Gorge Adventure, Lundy's Lane Historical Museum, Maid of the Mist tour boats, Niagara Falls Botanical Gardens, Niagara Parks Butterfly Conservatory, Niagara Parks Greenhouses, Spanish Aero Car, Queen Victoria Park and the Table Rock Complex.

ABOVE: The 520-foot Skylon Tower overlooks Niagara Falls. Completed in 1965, it stands 775 feet above the base of the falls.

QUEENSTON

QUEENSTON, Ontario is located seven miles north of Niagara Falls, Ontario at the base of the escarpment over which Niagara Falls was created some 12,000 years ago. The small village is positioned above the river opposite Lewiston, New York.

During the War of 1812, the Americans crossed the Niagara River in boats and attacked Queenston. While the British soldiers resisted the attack, Major-General Sir Isaac Brock was killed as he led his forces over Queenston Heights. In 1813, Queenston resident Laura Secord made her famous trek to warn British soldiers of an impending attack (see Chippawa). Secord's homestead is located here.

The King's Highway, the first in Upper Canada, was established through here, and by 1841, the first railroad in Upper Canada ran between Queenston and Chippawa.

Steamship travel between Toronto and Queenston began in the late 1800s. By 1896, three boats were making the trip. The Queenston-Chippawa Railway carried the boat passengers from Queenston to the falls. In 1902, rails were laid across the Queenston-Lewiston Suspension Bridge, eventually connecting with tracks near the bottom of the gorge on the American side of the river. This circular route, known as the "Great Gorge Route," connected back into Canada at the Upper Steel Arch Bridge near the falls.

Sir Isaac Brock's monument, built in 1856, is located at the top of the escarpment in Queenston Heights Park. Visitors can ascend the 210-foot column for views of the park below, Queenston-Lewiston Bridge, Canadian and U.S. power plants, lower Niagara River and the Lake Ontario plain.

ABOVE: Major-General Sir Isaac Brock (1769-1812) was known as "The Hero of Upper Canada." Brock was killed at the Battle of Queenston during the War of 1812. (Government of Ontario Art Collection, 694158)

TOP: An 1840 engraving of the Niagara River, the escarpment and the Brock Monument. (Nathaniel Parker Willis' Canadian Scenery)

MIDDLE: A 1905 view of the lower Niagara River from the Niagara Escarpment. The village of Queenston, Ontario is at the lower left. Steamers from Lake Ontario brought visitors to docks at Queenston and Lewiston, New York.

NIAGARA-ON-THE-LAKE

NIAGARA-ON-THE-LAKE, Ontario (population 14,587) is at the mouth of the Niagara River, downriver from Queenston. It sits opposite Youngstown, New York and Fort Niagara, and is often called "The prettiest town in Canada."

The village is on the site of the Neutral Indian village, which was known as *Onghiara*. Loyalists settled here following the American Revolution. Many of the settlers were part of Butler's Rangers, who previously were stationed across the Niagara River when that area was still under British control. In 1792, the village was established as Newark and was the first capital of the colony of Upper Canada. The Americans burned the village during the War of 1812. After the war, Newark was rebuilt and had an active shipping and shipbuilding industry.

The Fort George National Historic Site is located near the quaint village. The fort was built between 1796 and 1799 to serve as the principal British post in the area. It was captured and occupied by U.S. troops in 1813 and abandoned in the 1820s. Today Niagara-on-the-Lake is home to the Niagara Historical Society, numerous wineries and the Shaw Festival, a series of theatrical performances.

Niagara-on-the-Lake's position at the mouth of the Niagara River marks the end of the Niagara Parkway and *The Circle of Cities and Towns*.

TOP LEFT: The town square of Niagara-on-the-Lake, Ontario, which lies at the end of the Niagara River where Lake Erie's water's are turned over to Lake Ontario.

TOP RIGHT: A Niagara River Line steamer approaches the wharf and rail station at Niagara-on-the-Lake, circa 1905.

MIDDLE: Fort Mississauga at Niagara-on-the-Lake is a brick tower within star-shaped earthworks. It helped the British and Canadians defend the Niagara Frontier against the invading Americans in 1814.

12 Life Aboard a Lakeboat
THE *M/V WALTER J. McCARTHY JR.*

For people who visit the Great Lakes region, the long lakeboats are a very unusual sight. But those who live along the Great Lakes' shores, these vessels are a familiar part of the scenery.

Their simple, functional design is the pride of those who built them and the sailors who navigate them through perilously narrow channels and the vast open inland seas. Under blue skies, with water as smooth as a mill pond, through dangerous fall and winter storms that whip water into a frenzy of waves 20 to 30 feet high, lakeboats quietly do the work of keeping industry supplied, lights burning and food on the table in North America and around the world.

For Great Lakes' enthusiasts, the distinctive silhouettes of these carriers on the water against a setting sun is a most beautiful sight. When watching a lakeboat far offshore on the horizon, it is hard to imagine the activity aboard. A crew of 25 to 30 (mostly men) lives on board for months at a time. With a shipping season that begins in March and extends through late December, work time is compressed. In recent years, through increased mechanization and automation, changes in federal regulations, and agreements between the shipping industry and unions, crews have been reduced in size.

Our trip is aboard the *M/V Walter J. McCarthy Jr.*, a 1,000-foot vessel primarily used to carry coal for Detroit Edison to fuel its power plants. "M/V" stands for motor vessel, a prefix used for ships with fuel-burning engines. The boat is owned and operated by the American Steamship Company, based in Buffalo, New York. The Bay Shipbuilding Company, Sturgeon Bay, Wisconsin, on the Door Peninsula of Lake Michigan, built the *McCarthy* in 1977. Originally christened as the *M/V Belle River*, her name was changed in 1990 to honor the retired CEO of Detroit Edison. Walter J. McCarthy Jr. still makes yearly trips with his family aboard his namesake. Captain Larry Smyth admits that at first he was sorry to see the name *Belle River* changed, but now feels the name change is very appropriate, given Mr. McCarthy's love of the boat and his passion for the lakes.

The *Walter J. McCarthy Jr.* has carried other commodities, but its current job is to transport western (Montana) low-sulfur coal from Superior, Wisconsin to the Detroit Edison power plant on the St. Clair River. This loop of 47 annual trips on average keeps this plant and others in Michigan operating year-round.

On July 2, the *McCarthy* arrives at the St. Clair plant, after having dropped some of its load of coal at Detroit Edison's plant in Monroe, Michigan. Monroe is situated on the western shore of Lake Erie, between Toledo, Ohio and Detroit. Access to the boat is made possible after a check-in at the security guard building at the south end of the plant. From there, a gravel and cinder road winds around industrial lagoons, along a covered coal conveyor to the dock on the St. Clair River bank. There, the size of the *Walter J. McCarthy Jr.* can be appreciated. For perspective, the massive boat dwarfs company trucks sitting on the dock and the boat's crew.

TOP: The *Walter J. McCarthy Jr.* is a 1,000-foot lakeboat. It is too large for the locks on the Welland Canal, so its range is limited to lakes Erie, Huron, Michigan and Superior. (American Steamship Company)

RIGHT: The *McCarthy* moves into position to unload coal at the St. Clair power plant.

PREVIOUS PAGE: The *Walter J. McCarthy Jr.* is underway. The boat transports low-sulfur western coal from Superior, Wisconsin to Detroit Edison's St. Clair and Monroe, Michigan power plants.

While these lake freighters are traditionally referred to as "boats" by those who work on them and by most people from around the Great Lakes, they really are more similar to their ocean-going cousins, "ships."

Depending on the height of the dock and the load on-board, the crew will either gain access to the boat via a gangway on the concrete and steel dock, leading to a doorway in the engine room of the boat, or by a lowered stairway that leads up to the main deck.

The process of unloading coal begins immediately, as any delays can have a domino effect, wasting valuable time. Setbacks can substantially increase costs and reduce the amount of trips made in a shipping season, thus reducing the amount of material transported. At the same time, the process is not rushed in the interest of safety. Regulations, standards and procedures ensure that the work is handled carefully, protecting the crew, plant personnel and the environment.

The *Walter J. McCarthy Jr.* is a "self-unloader," meaning that it has its own apparatus to remove the cargo. Coal on the *McCarthy* is held in seven separate cargo holds, protected by 37 steel plate hatch covers held down by clamps. The hatch covers are lifted and moved away to expose the hold by a large on-board gantry crane straddling the openings and traversing on a parallel set of rails. The steel holds, independent of the hull, each taper toward the bottom to allow the coal to be unloaded on the conveyor belt below. Between the cargo holds and the "skin" of the boat is space for water ballast. This watertight area is divided into several giant tanks that extend along both sides of the cargo holds. When the holds are empty, the ballast tanks are filled with 57,000 tons of fresh water. The water can be pumped out or moved from one tank to another to trim the boat.

During the unloading process, gates are opened and closed at the bottom of the *McCarthy's* cargo holds, dropping the coal to the conveyor belt at the bottom on the boat. The flow from each hold is regulated to ensure even movement of material for offloading. This regulation prevents overloading of the conveyor system and keeps the boat level in the water.

From the conveyor belt, running under the cargo holds, the line of coal moves up and out to the boom level above the main deck, being held together on both sides by a two-belt-loop conveyor system. From there, it moves to yet another conveyor belt on the 250-foot boom taking the coal off the boat. These belts move at a swift 1,200 feet per minute. The coal unloading at the Detroit Edison plant is received in a structure that puts the material on a massive land-based system of conveyors that runs for a mile to huge stockpiles serving the Belle River power station along the St. Clair River.

Looking down through the open hatches during this process is akin to peering down over a giant hourglass, watching black sand sink into a concave abyss. The intense vibration and noise is deafening, sounding like 20 machine guns firing rounds, as air compressors rattle the sides of the hold. This vibration helps liquefy the coal, allowing it to shift more easily to the bottom of the hold where it drops through the open sluice and onto the moving conveyor below. Crewmembers on the deck of the boat assist the flow

ABOVE: The *McCarthy* unloading coal at the St. Clair power plant.

BOTTOM: The cargo holds of the boat are tapered. At the bottom of each hold are gates that open to a conveyor belt that runs along the bottom of the vessel. The coal moves along the conveyor system and is offloaded via the boat's self-unloading boom.

UNLOADING AND LOADING

Hulett Electric Ore Unloader, Conneaut, O.

The Hulet Automatic Bucket in Hold of Boat, Conneaut Harbor, Ohio

Brown Electric Plant, Vessel partially unloaded, Fairport Harbor, Ohio.

Pub. by J. E. Lightner.

...mping Whole Cars of Coal into Hopper to be Poured into Vessel's Hold at the Rate of about 25 Cars per hour, Conneaut, Ohio.

Nearly all the U.S. Great Lakes dry bulk carriers are self-unloading. Historically, early boats were unloaded by hand. In the mid-19th century, following the opening of the locks at Sault Ste. Marie, the first loads of Superior ore made their way down the lakes to the steel mills along Lake Erie. Workman used shovels to lift the cargo to a platform built in the hold of the boat. From there, they shoveled it from the platform to the deck. Then it would be handled again, to take it from the deck to the dock. The process of unloading 130 tons of ore would take four days. Later, a system was devised using a block fastened to the boat. A scoop was loaded by men and pulled out by horses, bringing the cargo out to waiting wheelbarrows. In 1867, J. D. Bothwell and Robert Wallace of Cleveland began using a steam engine to move the scoops and speed unloading. Alexander Brown sought to further improve the process. He was able to eliminate another step by getting the load from the ship directly to freight cars or storage piles.

With the huge demands of the Industrial Revolution, still more speed was needed. Harbors and channels had to be widened and deepened, as did the canal at the Soo (Sault Ste. Marie). At the turn of the century, George H. Hulett devised a clamshell bucket that would go right down into the holds for the cargo, gouging into the iron ore, neatly clamping shut, then lifting the material into freight cars or depositing it onto a stock pile. Hulett's son Frank improved the system in later years. The land-based Hulett unloader could move nearly 15,000 tons of ore in less than three hours. Today, the *McCarthy's* machinery can unload more than 68,000 tons of coal in about 12 hours.

ABOVE: George Hulett (1846-1923), inventor of unloading machinery, was born in Conneaut, Ohio. POSTCARDS: Early 20th century images show various loading and unloading processes.

of coal down though the open gates by pushing it with focused streams of water from powerful hoses.

On this particular day, Captain Larry Smyth and his mates pace back and forth on the bridge of the *McCarthy*, for weather has slowed the unloading process. Heavy rain causes slippage in the power plant's conveyor system, making it unable to keep up with the volume and speed with which the *McCarthy* is able to unload. As a result, the boat must slow its offloading speed and volume. The concern in Smyth's eyes is clear. His impatience is fixed on a rigid schedule that is subject to several types of delays. Mechanical setbacks during loading or unloading, storms, a line of ships waiting in fog for their turn in line to pass through locks at the Soo, and vying for the same dock space to load coal at Superior all may cause serious delays. Less than five minutes after the last hold is filled and all hatch covers are secured, the boat is ready to leave the dock.

Smyth taps his fingers on the bow thruster controls as he watches the crew untie the steel ropes from the docks to be hoisted on board. Smyth looks through binoculars, as the American Steamship Company's co-owned 730-foot *American Mariner* is poised to take the *McCarthy's* spot in the line of boats heading up the St. Clair River. Smyth's ship is ready and will not be delayed any longer. On July 3rd at 11:30 a.m. with a calculating demeanor and the *American Mariner* still at a safe distance, Smyth quietly slips the enormous *Walter J. McCarthy Jr.* into the river channel. Radioing to the *American Mariner*, Smyth jokingly says, "It gives me great pleasure to get in the channel ahead of you." The radio crackles back with a professional response from the *American Mariner's* captain, accompanied by a chuckle. On the bow, a watchman sits on an old faded orange naugahyde chair strapped to a platform to communicate nearly 1,000 feet back to the bridge via two-way radio, notifying the captain if he sees any trouble. On this sunny holiday weekend, pleasure boats jump in and out of the main channel. According to Captain Smyth, many boaters don't realize that a 300-foot blind spot exists immediately ahead of the boat. The watchman can report trouble ahead, but trying to avoid a problem by making a sudden stop or turn is impossible.

Much of the farmland on the banks along the U.S. and Canadian sides of the St. Clair has given way to development. Along the river one sees a mix of power plants, refineries, chemical plants, multi-million dollar homes, docks, cottages, middle class housing, motels, businesses and private retreats. This hodgepodge doesn't seem to bother those who live, work and play along the river.

TOP LEFT: Captain Larry Smyth of the *Walter J. McCarthy Jr.*

BOTTOM: The *Walter J. McCarthy Jr.* passes under the Blue Water Bridges on the St. Clair River before reaching the open waters of Lake Huron.

255

In the early afternoon, the *McCarthy* passes under the twin Blue Water Bridges. These international cantilever spans between Sarnia, Ontario and Port Huron, Michigan are named for the clear bright blue water that moves swiftly in the river below. The first of the two bridges, with an 871-foot main span and 150-foot vertical clearance, was completed in 1938 with its partner opening in 1997. The bridges mark the last international road crossing until the *McCarthy* reaches the long International Bridge at Sault Ste. Marie.

The captain and his mates count off navigational buoys over the VHF radio to Sarnia Traffic Control as the boat moves into Lake Huron. This communication is but one piece of a set of navigational rules and systems. The boat must be able to move through the rivers and the lakes on pleasant summer days and through the near-zero visibility of fog, storms and heavy snow with the aid of a number of navigational systems.

In recent years, Global Positioning Systems (GPS) have become the primary navigational aid used by the boats in the open water. The crews are trained and certified in the use of  other means of navigation, from nautical charts with slide rules, to the gyrocompass, radar and radio beacons. The captain, crew and boat are much safer with these redundancies. Watching the large GPS screens on the bridge allows the crew to monitor the boat's every move toward its navigational target, with precision down to just a few feet. The boat has several headlights and spotlights, green starboard lighting, red port lighting and white lights on the mast. The deck areas are amply lit as well. Even the self-unloading boom is equipped with lighting, and red aircraft beacons make it visible when it is extended for night unloadings. A large plastic owl sits on the end of the boom to keep gulls and other birds away.

The lonely looking boat, traveling an average of 15 miles per hour up the length of Lake Huron, is actually a beehive of activity. Members of the crew scrub and hose coal dust off the deck. Down below, in the engine room, the boat's engineers take turns monitoring its four 3,500-horsepower General Motors diesel engines. They also keep detailed records of the maintenance of the mammoth machinery and other critical systems. While these boats are quiet in the cabins and out on the cargo deck, down below the engineers wear special earplugs to protect them from the deafening roar and screaming of the engines. It is hard not to be impressed with the immensity of the *McCarthy's* engine room. The plant includes reduction equipment that takes the engines' typical 850 revolutions per minute down to the twin propellers' 115 RPM. Pumps keep large quantities of water flowing to toilets, showers, the laundry and the galley. At the same time, the superstructure is a place of activity. Bill Van Vlack, the boat's steward, is coordinating a menu of high-quality cuisine with his galley department. Since the boat does not stop for days at a time, the crew works in rotating shifts of "four hours on, eight hours off."

A mate and a wheelsman stand on duty in the pilothouse to navigate the *McCarthy*. Each pair works through the four-hour watches. Captain Smyth is on the bridge or takes over in dangerous areas or in bad weather, and is frequently in control when the boat is arriving or departing a port or threading the needle in an approach to the locks at the Soo. Because the *McCarthy* is too large for the Welland Canal, its range does not include Lake Ontario or the St. Lawrence River.

ABOVE: An American Steamship Company vessel on Lake Huron heads south toward the entrance to the St. Clair River at Port Huron, Michigan.

The *McCarthy* originally traveled the lakes with a crew of more than 30. Today, through mechanical efficiencies and automation, the crew has been reduced to 25. The crew includes Captain Smyth and his three mates and deckhands, Chief Engineer Al Desmond with his assistants and Steward Bill Van Vlack with his cooks and porters.

THE PILOTHOUSE

The pilothouse on the *McCarthy* is very large and more spacious than similarly sized boats on the Lakes. It is divided with a windowed chart room and office area in the rear and the wheel room forward. The charts are kept in the drawers of a cabinet below the chart table, with the current applicable chart sitting on top of the table. These NOAA charts, produced and regularly updated by the government for more than 150 years, cover all navigable (U.S.) oceans, lakes, rivers, channels and ports in great detail. The pilothouse is fully equipped with the most modern navigational devices and more traditional equipment as well. A full GPS system, Sperry compasses, cruise recorder, auto-pilot system, four sets of binoculars, radios, intercom, safety and rescue associated equipment, public address, two-ways, walkie-talkies, satellite telephone, cell phones and personal computers with e-mail and Internet access are all at the deck crews' fingertips. Various displays indicate engine RPM, any list, angles of rudders, and all critical systems. The old-fashioned-looking engine dial is still a part of these large boats. The engine dial issues directions between the bridge and the engine room and indicates if the engine is being controlled locally in the engine room or by remote operation on the bridge. The dial shows: AHEAD, FULL, HALF, SLOW, DEAD SLOW, STAND BY, STOP, ASTERN, FINISH WITH ENGINE, DEAD SLOW, SLOW, HALF, FULL, BRIDGE CONTROL.

TOP: The pilothouse of the *Walter J. McCarthy Jr.* BOTTOM: An exterior view of the superstructure of the *McCarthy*. Part of the unloading boom is at the lower right.

The cabin areas are a far cry from visions of cramped quarters with stiff metal bunks. The crew's rooms include bathrooms and are equipped with satellite TV, personal VCRs, DVD players, radios and other comforts of home. The crew on the *McCarthy* splits the cost of paying for the satellite TV programming, from a menu of football games, movies, news, weather and network shows. This is a welcome addition for the crews who can spend up to eight months per season aboard the boat. The *McCarthy's* quarters also include two private guestrooms with baths and a luxurious lounge in between.

The meals are very good, with several choices on the menu board for breakfast, lunch and dinner. Bill Van Vlack and his cooks prepare a variety of quality cuisine, from a turkey dinner smoked on a big charcoal grill on deck, to steaks, roast sirloin, pork, chicken, seafood, pasta, salad bar and an array of freshly made desserts, prepared by Ahmed Nasser, the boat's Second Cook.

The crewmembers of the *McCarthy* devote their lives to their ships and the lakes. Some spend most of their lives on these boats. They live in a world that few from the outside know. The crew is tight-knit yet very accommodating, sharing stories of their experiences and explaining the workings of the boat. Most of the *McCarthy's* crew hails from around Great Lakes region and upper Midwest from Toledo, Ohio to various towns in Michigan, Wisconsin and Minnesota. Conversations on board range from their families, movies, books, stories of the lakes and hobbies, to vacations, retirement plans, changes in the latest union contract and the days' responsibilities.

The members of the crew work very efficiently and quietly on a variety of duties. The captain and his mates wear neat jeans, button-down shirts and comfortable shoes. The steward and his galley staff wear white shirts and white pants. The deck staff wears a variety of clothing, depending on what they are doing at the time, often donning coveralls, boots, hard hats, earplugs and safety glasses.

While there are no orders being shouted, there appears to be a clear chain-of-command. This order is more apparent at mealtime as each head of a department sits in a specific seat in the officers' dining room. The captain is seated at the head of the table, the chief engineer at the foot, mates and first engineers sit at the sides; the middle chairs are occupied by any guests. The rest of the crew eats in the mess area across the hallway.

The captain and mates have rooms on the "C" deck; engineering quarters and offices are on the "B" deck; the steward, cook and porter staff live primarily on the "A" deck; the

deckhands room on the main deck level.

The *McCarthy* travels up the length of Lake Huron throughout the night of July 3rd. At 5:00 a.m. on July 4th, the boat leaves the lake through the De Tour Passage, a channel between Drummond Island and Michigan's Upper Peninsula. For the next five hours, the boat negotiates several narrow channels that were blasted through the rock of the Niagara Escarpment as it makes its way toward the locks at Sault Ste. Marie.

RIGHT: After traveling the length of Lake Huron through the night, the sun rises as the *McCarthy* heads through the DeTour passage into the St. Mary's River.

This year, the Great Lakes are at their lowest levels in nearly 40 years. Captain Smyth and his first mate, Bill Stirton, discuss rocks and river bottoms they've never seen exposed before. They point to an area where another laker recently grounded, blocking the down-bound channel for hours. Loads on many of the freighters have had to be lightened

THE SOO LOCKS

Construction on the first set of locks at the Soo began in 1853 to avoid rapids on the St. Mary's River. The purpose was to raise boats 21 feet to the level of Lake Superior. This first set of locks was completed and turned over to the State of Michigan to begin operation on May 31, 1855. In 1881, after the canal was recognized as having national importance, the state turned the locks over to the U.S. government and the Army Corps of Engineers. The Corps removed toll charges at that time and today continues to maintain and operate the locks, free of charge. The lock system has been updated and expanded over the years.

The lock system at the Soo consists of the MacArthur (1943), Poe (1968), and Davis (1914) locks; the closed Sabin (1919) lock; the U.S. Power Plant; and the St. Mary's River Falls (rapids). A recently refurbished Canadian lock for recreational boats and Canadian power plants are on Ontario's side of the river. Plans have been proposed for a new lock to replace the Davis and Sabin Locks with a new larger lock. At present, only the Poe lock is able to handle ships as long as or longer than the *Walter J. McCarthy Jr.*

The lock area includes a grass and tree-lined park. The park, maintained by the U.S. Army Corps of Engineers, contains a visitors center with a theater showing a movie about the locks, historical photos and artifacts and a working model of a lock. The visitors center is staffed for questions and a board on the wall shows the names of the boats scheduled to lock through and the times they are expected.

TOP LEFT: An 1853 view of the locks at Sault Ste. Marie. (U.S. Army Corps of Engineers, Detroit District) TOP RIGHT: The busy Soo Locks, circa 1906. BOTTOM: The *Walter J. McCarthy Jr.* enters the Soo Locks after leaving Lake Superior. (U.S. Army Corps of Engineers, Detroit District)

this season to reduce draft, allowing them to make it through shallow areas. Smaller loads mean having to make more trips, thus lessening efficiency.

The Munuscong and Neebish channels through this portion of the St. Mary's River are so narrow passing Neebish Island that the bottom is visible just feet from the boat. So are the insides of homes and cottages along the shore. On this part of the trip, the *McCarthy* is joined close behind by another boat, the *Canadian Miner*, part of the Upper Lakes Group fleet of Seaway Bulk Carriers.

The *McCarthy* continues past several occupied osprey nests resting on navigational lights before moving into Lake Nicolet, a wide spot in the St. Mary's River. The channel narrows once again making a left turn at a ferry landing at the park at Mission Point and Island Number One, then it passes fishermen in front of the Edison Sault Electric Power plant and the Valley Camp Museum Ship. At 10:33 a.m., after getting clearance over the radio, the *McCarthy* shoehorns into the Poe lock at Sault Ste. Marie.

The *McCarthy's* 1,000-by-105-foot hull barely fits into the Poe lock. With only two and a half feet of space to spare on either side of the boat, it takes a clear mind and steady

ABOVE: The *McCarthy* approaches the Soo Locks on the St. Mary's River at Sault Ste. Marie, Michigan.

RIGHT: The *Oglebay Norton* enters the Soo Locks. The namesake of one of the oldest mining companies in the country, the 1,000-foot bulk carrier was launched at Sturgeon Bay, Wisconsin in 1978. (U.S. Army Corps of Engineers, Detroit District)

BOTTOM: The *David Z. Norton* enters the lock next to the *McCarthy*. The *Norton*, built at the American Ship-building Company in Lorain, Ohio, was launched in 1973.

hand to move the boat into the lock. With the assistance of bow thrusters and radioed information from crew stationed on board and from those dropped on shore, the boat creeps into position. The gates are lowered on either side of the boat and the operator closes the lock doors. A controlled flow of water enters the lock chamber and churns around the boat, slowly raising it. While the *McCarthy* rises in the Poe lock and the smaller *Canadian Miner* enters the MacArthur lock, a crowd climbs stairs to watch from high covered platforms.

In less than 20 minutes, the process is complete, and the *McCarthy* is on its way out of the locks, under the International Bridge (1962), passing the railroad bridge (1881) and the Compensating Works (1921) that controls

GREAT LAKES SHIPWRECK MUSEUM

The Great Lakes Shipwreck Museum is at the site of the former U.S. Coast Guard Station at Whitefish Point, Michigan. The lighthouse was built in 1861 and continues its service as a beacon on Lake Superior, marking the relatively calm waters of Whitefish Bay at the eastern end of the lake.

The museum includes a tour of the beautifully restored lighthouse keepers' quarters, artifacts from shipwrecks and other interpretive areas. Clearly the most poignant exhibit focuses on those who lost their lives aboard the *Edmund Fitzgerald*, a 729-foot ore carrier that sank tragically off Whitefish Point in a storm during November of 1975. Many around the world became interested in this story a year after the tragic sinking, when Canadian folksinger and songwriter Gordon Lightfoot's haunting ballad "The Wreck of The Edmund Fitzgerald" made its way to the No. 2 position on *Billboard* magazine's pop music chart. The boat rests on the floor of Lake Superior in 500 feet of water, 17 miles north-northwest of Whitefish Point. The bell from deck of the *Fitz* was recovered on July 4, 1995 and presented by the Province of Ontario to the crew members' families. It was polished and placed in the museum in November of 1995, 20 years after the ship went down as a tribute to the 29 men who lost their lives. A replica bell, inscribed with the names of each member of the crew, was placed on the wreck. The area in which the boat rests is regarded as an off-limits underwater graveyard.

TOP: The Great Lakes Shipwreck Museum at Whitefish Point, Michigan is on the site of the oldest active lighthouse on Lake Superior. (Chris Winters)
BOTTOM: The *Edmund Fitzgerald* was launched in 1958 at the Great Lakes Engineering shipyard at River Rouge, Michigan. The boat and crew of 29 were lost in a storm on Lake Superior on November 10, 1975. (Bob Campbell) Photos courtesy Great Lakes Shipwreck Historical Society.

STANNARD ROCK LIGHT

(NOAA)

The stone Stannard Rock Light was built on the reef in 1882 and was a difficult place psychologically for its keepers, including one keeper who threatened to swim for shore and another who had to be taken to shore in a straitjacket.

In 1961, when the light was being automated, an explosion destroyed the machine room attached to the structure and one of the three seamen on duty was killed.

the amount of water running out of Lake Superior into the St. Mary's River. As the river widens, the gigantic Algoma Steel plant is visible on the Canadian side. The *Canadian Miner* follows the *McCarthy* into Whitefish Bay and veers off to the right on a more northerly course.

Three hours later, the *McCarthy's* course curves left around Whitefish Point, making its way into the main part of Lake Superior. Through binoculars, a few people visiting the Great Lakes Shipwreck Museum can be seen walking on the desolate beach. The beach is a mix of white sand and beautifully colored rocks brought to this place from far away in Canada by ancient glaciers and made smooth by the action of wind, sand, water and ice.

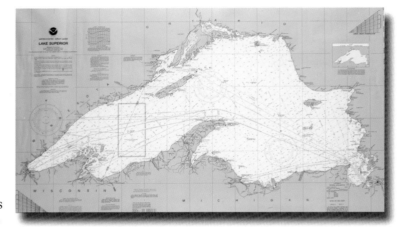

It takes 28 hours for the *McCarthy* to travel from the Soo to Duluth. For a few hours, between the Pictured Rocks National Lakeshore and Manitou Island off the Keweenaw Peninsula, the boat is completely out of sight of land. About 50 miles offshore from Marquette, Michigan and 15 miles from the *McCarthy*, Stannard Rock Light, a lonely sentinel, can be seen on the left. Third Mate Chris McKenzie tells of his visits to the light when he was in the Coast Guard.

Several miles north of the tip of the Keweenaw Peninsula, the boat changes course again, making a heading that takes the boat 120 miles down the lake to a point north of the Apostle Islands.

The northern location of the upper Great Lakes on the globe makes for long days in the summer and short days in a winter largely shrouded in darkness. On this, the 4th of July, after a fireworks show from distant Orchard Beach on the Keweenaw Peninsula, a hint of light after sunset is still visible after 11:00 p.m. EDT.

On the morning of July 5th, the *McCarthy* continues its journey down the western end of Lake Superior with the Apostle Islands National Lakeshore and the forests of northern Wisconsin on the left and the treed hills and cliffs along the Minnesota shore to the right. For the final 80 miles toDuluth, the distant small towns along Minnesota's Route 61 punctuate the sparsely populated shoreline. One by one, towns and landmarks come into view: Grand Marais, the plants at Taconite Harbor and Silver Bay, the famous Split Rock Lighthouse, and Two Harbors. Off the bow, framed by a steep ridge, Duluth slowly comes

RIGHT: A nautical chart of Lake Superior. (NOAA)

DULUTH'S CANAL PARK

Canal Park in Duluth is a well-developed tourist area and is a boat watcher's dream. Hotels, restaurants, shops, museums, an aquarium and a floating ore-boat museum, the 610-foot *William A. Irvin*, all attract thousands every year to the Duluth waterfront. The historic Duluth Aerial Lift Bridge, built in 1904 as a cable bridge for a gondola and redesigned in 1929 as a horizontal lift bridge, is the district's centerpiece. The city of 86,918 sits on rock bluffs up to 800 feet above the lake. Lake Superior's ancestor glacial lake was Lake Duluth, and the city is built on the glacial lake's escarpment. It is visually striking from the water or from the bluff.

TOP: A nighttime view of Duluth, Canal Park and radio/television towers perched atop the hill behind the city. MIDDLE: The Aerial Lift Bridge at Duluth. BOTTOM: A view to the south of Canal Park, the Aerial Lift Bridge, Minnesota Point and Superior, Wisconsin in the distance. The western end of Lake Superior is to the left, while the six-mile-long sandbar protects Duluth's harbor (right).

into view. Captain Smyth is pleased to keep the *McCarthy* ahead of the *Canadian Transport*, a 730-foot Upper Lakes Group boat. This boat, picking up a load of coal for the power plant on Lake Erie at Nanticoke, Ontario, has its sights set on the same dock space at Superior,

Wisconsin. If the Canadian boat made Superior first, it would mean the *McCarthy* would have to anchor in the lake, waiting for eight to ten hours for the *Canadian Transport* to load before heading to the dock. This time, luck is on Smyth's side; the *Canadian Transport* must drop anchor and wait.

As the *McCarthy* approaches Duluth, it makes its way past the *Ziemia Zamojska* from Szczecin, Poland, a "salty" anchored offshore, waiting to head to dock to load grain for the international market. A few minutes later, the boat aims between the parallel jetties leading into Duluth Harbor. Here, hundreds of people line up along both of the breakwaters, cheering, waving and taking photographs of the boat as it passes the Canal Park area. The *McCarthy* continues to churn water as it moves under the historic Duluth Aerial Lift Bridge, raised 138 feet above the water to provide safe clearance.

Captain Smyth turns the *McCarthy* left into the harbor, after passing under the bridge that links both sides of the sliced natural sandbar, creating the 24-mile-long Duluth-Superior

harbor. The next challenge is to maneuver the *McCarthy* around a working dredge removing sand and silt from the harbor, turn the boat on a dime and back it up a half-mile. The backing takes the boat under the Blatnick Bridge, carrying I-535 across the St. Louis River, which flows into the Duluth harbor basin. The boat continues in reverse to the dock of Midwest Energy, where the coal will be loaded. The Midwest Energy complex is vast and includes a railyard where trains make their way around the huge piles of coal. Powerful streams of water spray these massive piles of coal mechanically. The water is thrown hundreds of feet through the air, keeping coal dust down and reducing the chance of fire. Even a small spark could ignite a fire that could burn for days or weeks before it could be extinguished. The *McCarthy's* Chris McKenzie tells of a boat needing to get permission from authorities to dump a load of burning coal offshore into Lake Superior. Such occurrences are extremely rare and unlikely today with increased safety measures.

Once the *McCarthy* is tied up at Midwest Energy's coal dock, some crewmembers depart from the boat. McKenzie takes the opportunity to visit his home in Superior. Second Cook Ahmed Nasser rushes home to visit his wife and large family. Porter Debbie Kushman makes a stop at the payphone on the dock. Chief Engineer Al Desmond and one of his engineers, a burly and bearded man nicknamed "Bear," depart for their vacations. Their replacements come on board carrying duffel bags. Others head down the service road to a parking lot where their cars are waiting. Some take cabs to town to run errands.

Meanwhile, on board, those assigned to the loading process move the unloading boom out of the way and remove hatch covers with the boat's gantry crane. On the dock, a worker

TOP: Trains bring low-sulfur coal to the Midwest Energy facility at Superior, Wisconsin. The coal is loaded onto the *Walter J. McCarthy Jr.* and other lakeboats for transport to other Great Lakes ports.

BOTTOM: A nighttime loading of coal at Midwest Energy. The *McCarthy's* hatch covers are open. The holds are ready to be filled with coal from the boom that is in place over the boat.

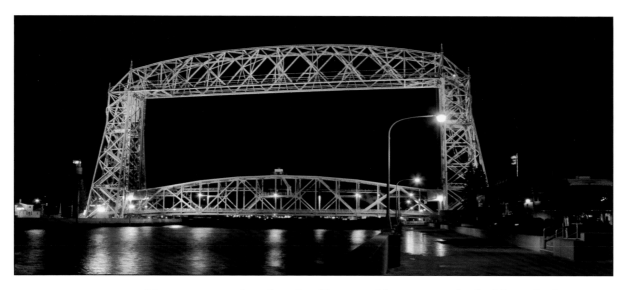

uses a remote control box to move the giant loading machinery over the hold on the boat to be loaded first. This machinery is moved to direct the flow of coal in a predetermined order into each of the cargo holds.

Crew operating ballast pumps work in sync with the loading process, pushing water out of the tanks. As the load increases, the ballast tanks are carefully drained from the boat or into other tanks to keep the *McCarthy* trim in the water. Loading takes eight hours and is a precision process of filling the cargo holds in a predetermined order. After midnight on July 6th, the *McCarthy* is loaded. With the crew that had gone ashore back on board, the boat slowly moves away from the dock. The *Canadian Transport* is already next to the *McCarthy*, having waited the day anchored offshore in Lake Superior. As the *McCarthy* makes its way quietly out of the harbor with 68,000 tons of coal, most of Duluth sleeps, save for the few hearty souls standing along the jetties at Canal Park watching the boat slip under the Aerial Lift Bridge and into the blackness of Lake Superior. From the deck of the *McCarthy*, Duluth's skyline sparkles, crowned by the flashing red lights of the numerous TV and FM radio towers lining the ridge overlooking the city. It is easy to see why the strand of lights from Duluth to Superior, circling the end of the lake, is called "The Necklace."

After two and a half days retracing steps across Lake Superior, the Soo Locks, St. Mary's River and Lake Huron, the *McCarthy* enters the St. Clair River. Throughout the night, 1st Mate Bill Stirton and 2nd Mate Al Flood have been in contact with Detroit Edison. It seems that wet weather has again slowed the unloading equipment at the St. Clair plant. This will mean delays as the Interlake Steamship Company's 1,013-foot *Paul R. Tregurtha* will still be at the dock when the *McCarthy* arrives.

The *McCarthy* continues on course into the St. Clair River as day breaks over the Blue Water Bridges and the lighted refineries of Sarnia. A short time later, the boat passes the Edison power plant and the unloading *Tregurtha*, heading to a slightly wider spot in the St. Clair River, where it makes a complete turn. At this point, the *McCarthy* moves to a point just downstream from the plant, dropping anchor. After waiting for nearly three hours, the *Tregurtha* is finally empty.

On the morning of July 9th, the *Walter J. McCarthy Jr.* hoists its anchor, pulls up to the St. Clair dock and begins to unload coal. Another of the more than 40 trips a season is complete, but in just 12 hours, the *McCarthy* will embark on another journey up great rivers and across huge lakes to Duluth-Superior. The cycle of *Life Aboard a Lakeboat* continues.

ABOVE: All is quiet during the wee hours of the morning before Duluth's Aerial Lift Bridge opens for departure of the *Walter J. McCarthy Jr.*

Epilogue

Lake Erie was the last of the Great Lakes to be discovered by Europeans, but it now supports a population of 13 million living within just a few miles of its shores. Lake Erie is a resource for industry, municipal water and recreation and food. More than a resource, though, it is the lifeblood of the region.

TOP LEFT: Lake Erie is well known for catches of walleye. (Rodger Klindt, N.Y. State Department of Environmental Conservation)

TOP RIGHT: Unloading the day's catch at Kingsville, Ontario.

BOTTOM: The fishing fleet at Port Dover, Ontario.

PAGE 266: Buffalo's water intake crib was built in 1908. The wind turbines began generating electricity in 2007 on the former site of a Lackawanna, New York steel mill.

PAGE 267, CLOCKWISE: A Port Clinton commercial fisherman mends a net. Fishing for steelhead at Elk Creek near Girard, Pennsylvania. The lighthouse at Marblehead, Ohio. The skyline of Detroit, Michigan.

Commercial Fishing

Lake Erie continues to provide food. The commercial fishing industry on Lake Erie began in the 1820s and grew until peaking in the 1880s. After a brief decline, catches increased when better fishing equipment was invented. Over the years a number of species have been caught including bass, walleye, crappie, catfish, lake herring, blue pike, yellow perch, sturgeon and whitefish. Pollution and overfishing led to another decline, and the heyday of commercial fishing ended by the 1950s.

Commercial fishing remains successful on the Canadian side of the lake. A limited commercial fishing industry operates in the United States, landing catches of whitefish, smelt, perch and other fish.

Sport Fishing and Boating

Lake Erie produces more fish for human consumption than the other four Great Lakes combined. The western portion of Lake Erie is heralded as "Walleye Capital of the World." Several hundred marinas line the shore of Lake Erie, more than 100,000 boats call the lake home and millions use Lake Erie's beaches every year.

Lake Erie at Work

Lake Erie is the backbone of Canada and the industrialized Northeastern U.S. Most automobiles in North America are built near Lake Erie, and the region continues to produce steel and countless other products.

Large shipping ports continue to operate on Lake Erie. Buffalo, Erie, Conneaut, Ashtabula, Fairport Harbor, Cleveland, Lorain, Huron, Sandusky, Toledo and Detroit continue as destinations for large lakeboats on the U.S. side of the lake. Windsor, Nanticoke and Port Colborne continue to handle transshipping on the Canadian side of Lake Erie.

Agriculture along Lake Erie's shores continues to be a major part of the economy of the region as well. Varieties of fruits, vegetables and grains are grown here, and wineries are plentiful in the region.

TOP LEFT: An aerial view of the Port of Toledo docks at the mouth of the Maumee River at Toledo, Ohio. (Toledo-Lucas County Port Authority)

TOP RIGHT: The grape harvest near Lake Erie's shoreline in northeastern Ohio.

MIDDLE: The NRG power plant at Dunkirk, New York.

Pollution

Lake Erie has been used and in many cases abused for more than 300 years. During the past 100 years, discharges of toxic wastes have sped up the process of eutrophication, the aging process of a body of water.

Before settlers arrived along its shores, Lake Erie had great populations of whitefish, pike, smallmouth bass, sturgeon and walleye. Waterfowl was plentiful and marshes lined much of the shore of Lake Erie, especially at the western end in Ohio and Michigan. These wetlands filtered water entering the lake, trapping sediments.

As the area was settled, dams were built on many of the rivers and streams leading to the lake, preventing fish from migrating upstream to spawn. Later, industrial and human wastes were dumped into the lake, forests were logged and marshes were drained. Farming practices left soil unprotected from washing into the lake.

By the early- to mid-20th century, Lake Erie was taking on a different look as larger mills and factories were built. Raw sewage was dumped into the lake along with millions of gallons of untreated industrial wastes. The Cuyahoga River caught fire several times before its famous fire in 1969. By the 1970s, conditions were at their worst and Lake Erie was declared "dead."

The fishing industry was virtually destroyed and recreational use was spotty. Piles of dead rotting fish along Erie's beaches were a common sight, and blooms of algae were abundant. The dead lake was actually alive with too many nutrients, causing the increased algae growth. When the algae mats died and decomposed, the oxygen was depleted, killing the fish.

In 1972, both Canada and the United States signed the Great Lakes Water Quality Act, establishing clean water guidelines. The reduction of phosphate levels was a key initiative in improving water quality. Other improvements, including new ways of farming, have reduced levels of nutrients entering the lake from animal waste and fertilizers. The Water Quality Act of 1987 further regulated the discharge of toxic chemicals and compounds into the lake.

Despite these improvements, Lake Erie continues to suffer from past problems, which remain from a time prior to legislation that prevented the dumping of toxic wastes into the lake. Toxic sediments in the lake and tributaries are a sobering reminder of years of abuse. Sediments in some areas contain high levels of polychlorinated biphenyls (PCBs), dioxin and mercury. The disturbance of these contaminated sediments, even for remediation, is a very dangerous proposition.

Overall, the quality of Lake Erie's water continues to improve, but there is still much work to be done.

TOP: The silhouette of steel mills at Detroit, Michigan.

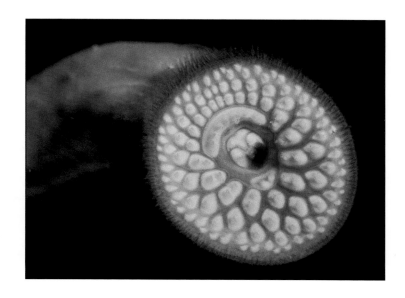

Invasive Species

Great Lakes shipping has introduced several non-native species to Lake Erie. In some cases, their presence has caused significant problems.

In the early 1920s, the sea lamprey, an eel-like fish native to the Atlantic Ocean, entered the Great Lakes through the Welland Canal. Lamprey, with disc-shaped mouths filled with sharp teeth, attach to fish and feed by sucking the body fluids and tissue out of the host. This predator caused the decline of whitefish and lake trout. Since the late 1950s, lamprey control programs have greatly reduced this problem.

Zebra mussels, native to the Caspian Sea region of Asia, were brought to the Great Lakes in ballast water from a ship sometime around 1988. The ballast water came from a freshwater European port and was released into Lake St. Clair, near Detroit where the mussel was first sighted. Zebra mussels now thrive in all of the Great Lakes and other connected waterways in the United States and Canada. The mussels create problems when they attach themselves to fishing nets and clog water intakes and pipes. Their sharp edges are a nuisance to swimmers and fishermen. Their presence costs municipal water companies, power plants and industry millions of dollars per year to control them. The zebra mussel has made Lake Erie's waters clearer by actually filtering it. This has been positive for swimmers, fisherman and boaters as well as for divers who enjoy exploring the numerous shipwrecks on the lake's bottom.

On the other hand, a half-inch-long, shrimp-like crustacean called diporeia has been virtually wiped out in parts of the lake. Diporeia are a crucial food for whitefish and for smaller forage fish such as smelt, alewives and chubs that are food for trout and salmon. Another invasive species, the New Zealand mud snail, now also inhabits Lake Erie.

Even non-native species have enemies. In the case of the zebra mussel, the enemy is another non-native species. The round goby and tubenose goby are bottom-dwelling fish that eat zebra mussels. Gobies were introduced into the Great Lakes in 1990, in the same manner as the zebra mussel, through contaminated ballast water released into Lake St. Clair. The goby also competes for spawning areas with native bottom-dwellers such as darters and logperch.

TOP LEFT: Zebra mussels. (Center for Great Lakes and Aquatic Sciences)

TOP RIGHT: Sea Lamprey. (Great Lakes Sea Grant Network Exotic Species Graphics Library)

BOTTOM LEFT: Sea lamprey attached to a lake trout. (U.S. Fish and Wildlife Service)

271

TOP LEFT: Breakwaters slow beach erosion on Presque Isle at Erie, Pennsylvania. (Ken Winters, U.S. Army Corps of Engineers, Buffalo District)

TOP RIGHT: A great blue heron at Kelleys Island, Ohio.

BOTTOM LEFT: The outflow of Lake Erie supports spawning grounds in the Niagara River. This king salmon was caught near Devil's Hole in the Niagara Gorge. (Courtesy: Charles "Chip" Mussen)

BOTTOM RIGHT: The Lake Erie shoreline at North Perry, Ohio.

Lake Erie as a Natural Resource

Those living along the Great Lakes' shores may take their waters for granted, but others around the world where fresh water is less plentiful covet this resource.

Some 55 billion gallons of water are already removed from the Great Lakes every day for irrigation, industry, power generation and municipal water supplies. Most of this water, about 52 billion gallons, remains in the Great Lakes basin through evaporation, seeping into the ground or being returned after it has been used and treated.

Today, proposals to fill great ships with water for sale to other countries are being made. At this time, the International Joint Commission has not allowed water to be taken from the lakes on this large scale. The Commission's position is that, despite the great amount of water in Lake Erie and the other Great Lakes, only 1 percent is replenished yearly through rain and melting snow. That does not leave much water to spare, so at this point, the lakes' water will not be sold to foreign countries.

The Future of Lake Erie

Lake Erie is young in geological terms. It continues to evolve through time, and the lake as we know it today will become a thing of the past. It is believed that Niagara Falls will continue to migrate upstream, eventually to the point where Lake Erie's waters enter the Niagara River. When this happens, Erie's water level will be lowered and a great river will once again flow through the Lake Erie basin, occupying the place where the lake was located. This is not the first time a great river has run through this basin. A river existed here well before Lake Erie came to be.

Don't mourn the loss of the lake, because Lake Erie will be with us for thousands of years in the future. Lake Erie is rich in history and will continue to shape the lives of those who live near its shores.

From the sights of lakeboats to views of great cities, from the hum of industry to the crashing sounds of great waves upon its shores, from the scent of grapes to the aroma of tomatoes simmering into ketchup, from the flavor of fresh perch to the taste of a cool glass of water, from the feel of a summer swim to the face-chapping blast of winter snow, the lake's influence on the region is significant.

Lake Erie truly is a Great Lake.

ABOVE: The beach at Long Point, Ontario.

DEDICATION

For my wife Mary, children Meghan and John,
parents Henry "Hank" and Patricia Langmyer and
my sister Kathryn "Kit" Langmyer Henderson.

IN MEMORY OF...

Sara Van Sicklin Egan   **1910-2000**

My grandmother. Wife, mother, grandmother, great-grandmother, educator and historian. "Gram" gave me my first book about the Great Lakes when I was 10 years old. She was well versed in the history of the Indians of Western Pennsylvania. Thank you for teaching me so much about the region's history.

E. Donald Burlingame   **1917–2003**

My father-in-law. Husband, father, grandfather, engineer and man of "all things scientific." Thank you for your help with information for the book, your passion for history and your interest and encouragement.

Jeffrey R. Morgan   **1960-2000**

My friend. Husband, father, son, brother, public accounting partner and outdoorsman. Thanks for being my college roommate and confidant. Thanks for your humor, sharing common interests and catching and cooking the best Lake Erie perch dinner I've ever had.

John F. "Jack" Buck   **1924-2002**

My friend and colleague. Husband, father, grandfather, Purple Heart recipient, broadcaster, Hall-of-Famer and goodwill ambassador. In his early years, Jack worked aboard the *J.H. Sheadle* on Lake Erie. Thank you for your stories about life on Lake Erie.

Michael J. Roszman   **1944-1993**

My friend and a mentor. Husband, father, grandfather and broadcaster. "Roz" and I worked together and flew over Lake Erie's shoreline. We lost him when his traffic helicopter plunged into the Niagara River. Thank you for your guidance, wry sense of humor and for sharing your interests with me.

CONTRIBUTORS

Amy Clingensmith Mongiovi is the owner of Clingensmith Communications, a firm specializing in editing, writing and photography. She began her career in journalism at a daily newspaper in Pennsylvania. Later, Mongiovi moved into public relations and to roles in higher education.

Garry McMichael is owner of Digital Imaging and Design, a firm specializing in graphic design and commercial photography. Garry spends his spare time traveling the back roads of the Missouri and Arkansas Ozarks, capturing its beauty with his camera, pastels and oils.

BIBLIOGRAPHY

Aiken, John; Wilhelms, John; Brunger, Eric; Aiken, Richard. *Outpost of Empires.* Frank E. Richards, Phoenix, NY, 1961.

Albert, George Dallas. *The Frontier Forts of Pennsylvania: Volume II (Western).* Commonwealth of Pennsylvania, Harrisburg, PA, 1916.

Altoff, Gerard T. *Oliver Hazard Perry and the Battle of Lake Erie.* The Perry Group, Put-in-Bay, OH, 1999.

Andrist, Ralph K. *The Erie Canal.* American Heritage, New York, 1964.

Ayers, R. Wayne. *Ohio's Lake Erie Vacationland.* Arcadia Publishing, Dover, NH, 2000.

Barrett, Harry B. *Lore & Legends of Long Point.* Patterson's Creek Press, Canada, 2000.

Barry, James P. *Ships of the Great Lakes.* Thunder Bay Press, Holt, MI, 1973.

Bates, Samuel P. *History of Erie County, Pennsylvania.* Warner, Beers & Co., Chicago, 1884.

Berton, Pierre. *Niagara: A History of the Falls.* Kodansha International, New York-Tokyo-London, 1997.

Berton, Pierre. *The Great Lakes.* Stoddart Publishing Company, Ltd., Toronto, 1996.

The Book of Ohio. C. S. Van Tassel, Publisher, 1903.

Borsvold, David. *Ashtabula.* The Ashtabula Great Lakes Marine and Coast Guard Memorial Museum. Arcadia Publishing Company, Dover, NH, 2003.

Borsvold, David. *Railroading in Conneaut.* Arcadia Publishing Company, Dover, NH, 2003.

Braider, Donald. *Rivers of America: The Niagara.* Holt, Rinehart and Winston, New York, 1972.

Brown, Richard C. and Watson, Bob. *Buffalo: Lake City in Niagara Land.* Windsor Publications, Woodland Hills, CA, 1982.

Buffalo Architecture: A Guide. The MIT Press, Cambridge, MA, 1981.

Butler, Margaret Manor. *A Pictorial History of the Western Reserve.* The World Publishing Company, Cleveland, OH, 1963.

Carpenter, Scott. *Lake Erie Journal: Guide to the Official Lake Erie Circle Tour.* Big River Press, Milford, OH, 2001.

Chard, Leslie F. *Out of the Wilderness.* The City of Dunkirk, Dunkirk, NY, 1971.

Down by the Bay: A History of Long Point and Port Rowan. Boston Mills Press, Erin, ON, 2000.

Dumych, Daniel M. *Niagara Falls.* Arcadia Publishing Company, Dover, NH, 1996.

Dumych, Daniel M. *Niagara Falls Volume II.* Arcadia Publishing Company, Dover, NH, 1998.

Ellis, William D. *Rivers of America: The Cuyahoga.* Holt, Rinehart and Winston, New York, 1966.

Erie: A Guide to the City and County. WPA. The William Penn Association of Philadelphia, Philadelphia, **1938.**

Erie County Pennsylvania: Erie Yesterday. Arcadia Publishing Company, Dover, NH, 1997.

Fairport Harbor. Fairport Harbor Historical Society. Arcadia Publishing Company, Dover, NH, 2003.

Grant, John and Jones, Ray. *Legendary Lighthouses.* The Globe Pequot Press. Old Saybrook, CT, 1998.

Gromosiak, Paul. *Daring Niagara: 50 Death-Defying Stunts at the Falls.* Western New York Wares, Buffalo, NY, 1998.

Gromosiak, Paul. *Nature's Niagara: A Walk on the Wild Side.* Western New York Wares, Buffalo, NY, 2000.

Gromosiak, Paul. *Niagara Falls Q & A: Answers to the 100 Most Common Questions About Niagara Falls.* Meyer Enterprises, Buffalo, NY, 1989.

Gromosiak, Paul. *Water Over the Falls: 101 of the Most Memorable Events at Niagara Falls.* Western New York Wares, Buffalo, NY, 1996.

Guerrein, Don. *A Concise History of Presque Isle.* Don Guerrein, Erie, PA, 2004.

Hamil, Fred Coyne. *Lake Erie Baron: The Story of Thomas Talbot.* Macmillan Company of Canada, Toronto, 1955.

Hansen, Michael C. *The History of Lake Erie.*

Hatcher, Harlan H. *Lake Erie.* The Bobbs-Merrill Company, Indianapolis, IN, 1945.

Hatcher, Harlan H. *The Great Lakes.* Oxford University Press, New York, 1944.

Hatcher, Harlan H. *The Western Reserve: The Story of New Connecticut in Ohio.* Bobbs-Merrill Company, Indianapolis, IN, 1949.

Hatcher, Harlan H. and Walter, Erich A. *A Pictorial History of the Great Lakes.* Bonanza Books, New York, 1963.

Hough, Jack L. *Geology of the Great Lakes.* University of Illinois Press, Urbana, IL 1958.

Jackson, John N., with John Burtniak and Gregory P. Stein. *The Mighty Niagara: One River – Two Frontiers.* Prometheus Books, Amherst, NY, 2003.

Judson, Clara Ingram. *St Lawrence Seaway.* Follett Publishing Company, Chicago, 1959.

Kriner, T.W. *In The Mad Water: Two Centuries of Adventure and Lunacy at Niagara Falls.* J & J Publishing, Buffalo, NY, 1999.

Kriner, T.W. *Journeys to the Brink of Doom.* J&J Publishing, Buffalo, NY, 1997.

Landon, Fred. *Lake Huron.* Bobbs-Merrill Company, Indianapolis, IN, 1944.

Larson, John W. Essayons: *A History of the Detroit District U.S. Army Corps of Engineers.* U.S. Army Corps of Engineers, Detroit, 1995.

Laurie, Margaret S. Lewiston: *Crown Jewel of the Niagara.* The Book Corner, Inc., Niagara Falls, NY, 2001

Leary, Thomas E. and Sholes, Elizabeth C. *Buffalo's Pan-American Exposition.* Arcadia Publishing, Dover, NH, 1998.

Leary, Thomas E. and Sholes, Elizabeth C. *Buffalo's Waterfront.* Arcadia Publishing, Dover, NH, 1997.

LeLievre, Roger. *Know Your Ships.* Marine Publishing Company, Sault Ste. Marie, MI, 2001.

The Lengthening of Niagara Falls. Buffalo, Niagara and Eastern Power Corporation. Printed by J.W. Clement Company, Buffalo, NY.

Lorain Ohio. The Black River Historical Society. Arcadia Publishing Company, Dover, NH, 1999.

Linhardt, Becky. *Kelleys Island: An Island For All Seasons.* Kelleys Cove, Inc., Kelleys Island, OH, 1995.

MacDonald, Cheryl. *A Summer Garden.* Port Dover Board of Trade, Port Dover, ON, 2001.

MacDonald, Cheryl. *Grand Heritage: The history of Dunnville, Canborough, Sherbrooke, Dunn, Moulton and South Cayuga.*

MacDonald, Cheryl. *Place Names of Haldimand-Norfolk.*

MacDonald, Cheryl. *Port Dover A Place in the Sun.* Port Dover Board of Trade, Port Dover, ON, 1998.

MacDonald, Robert J. and Frew, David *Home Port Lake Erie: Voices of Silent Images.* Erie County Historical Society Publications, Erie, PA, 1997.

Marchetti, Donna. *Around the Shores of Lake Erie.* Glovebox Guidebooks of America, Saginaw, MI, 1998.

Mason, Philip P. (Editor). *This is Detroit: 1701-2001.* Wayne State University Press, Detroit, MI, 2001.

McKinsey, Elizabeth. *Niagara Falls: Icon of the American Sublime.* Cambridge University Press, Cambridge, 1985.

Michigan: A Guide to the Wolverine State. WPA. Oxford University Press. New York, 1941.

Minnesota: A State Guide. WPA. Viking Press, New York, 1938.

Mollenkopf, Jim. *Lake Erie Sojourn.* Lake of the Cat Publishing, Toledo, 1998.

Morganstern, Martin and Gregg, Joan H. *Erie Canal.* Erie Canal Museum. Arcadia Publishing Company, Dover, NH, 2001.

Murphy, Dan. *The Erie Canal: The Ditch that Opened a Nation.* Western New York Wares, Buffalo, NY, 2001.

Nafus, Roland L. *Navy Island: Historic Treasure of the Niagara.* Old Fort Niagara Association, Youngstown, NY, 1998.

Nelson, Jeffrey R. *Erie, Pennsylvania.* Arcadia Publishing Company, Dover, NH, 1998.

New York: A Guide to the Empire State. WPA. Oxford University Press, New York, 1940.

Nute, Grace Lee. *Lake Superior.* Bobbs-Merrill Company, Indianapolis, 1944.

Ohio Guide, The. WPA. Oxford University Press, New York, 1940.

Pennsylvania: A Guide to the Keystone State. WPA. Oxford University Press, New York, 1940.

Percy, John W. *The Town of Tonawanda.* Arcadia Publishing Company, Dover, NH, 1997.

Plowden, David. *End of an Era: The Last of the Great Lakes Steamboats.* W.W. Norton & Company, New York, 1992.

Prothero, Frank. *The Good Years: A History of the Commercial Fishing Industry on Lake Erie.* Nan-Sea Publications, Port Stanley, ON, 1973.

Rose, Willam Ganson. *Cleveland: The Making of a City.* The World Publishing Company, Cleveland, OH, 1950.

Santella, Andrew. *Cornerstones of Freedom: The War of 1812.* Children's Press, New York, 2001.

Scharfenberg, Doris. *88 Great Vacations: Great Lakes.* Country Roads Press, Oaks, PA, 1996.

Seibel, George A. *Niagara-River of Fame.* Kiwanis Club, Niagara Falls, ON, 1986.

Seibel, George A. *Ontario's Niagara Parks 100 Years: A History.* Niagara Parks Commission, Niagara Falls, ON, 1985.

Shaw, Donald E. *Canals for a Nation: The Canal Era in the United States 1790-1860.* The University Press of Kentucky, Lexington, KY. 1990.

Smithsonian Guide to Historic America: The Great Lakes States. Stewart Tabori & Chang, New York, 1989.

Spear, A.W. *The Peace Bridge 1927-1977 and Reflections of the Past.* The Buffalo and Fort Erie Public Bridge Authority, Buffalo, NY, 1977.

Stewart, Darryl. *Point Pelee: Canada's Deep South.* Burns and MacEachern, Toronto, 1977.

Stone, Dave and Frew, David. *Waters of Repose: The Lake Erie Quadrangle.* Erie County Historical Society, Erie, PA, 1993.

Stonehouse, Frederick. *Great Lakes Crime: Murder, Mayhem, Booze & Broads.* Avery Color Studios, Inc., Gwinn, MI, 2004.

Styran, Roberta M. and Taylor, Robert R. *Mr. Merritt's Ditch.* Boston Mills Press, Erin, ON, 1992.

Switala, William J. *Underground Railroad in Pennsylvania.* Stackpole Books, Mechanicsburg, PA, 2001.

Tammemagi, Hans and Allyson. *Exploring Niagara.* Oakhill Publishing House, St. Catherines, ON, 1997.

Tielman, Timothy (Editor). *Buffalo's Waterfront: A Guidebook.* The Preservation Coalition of Erie County, Buffalo, NY, 1990.

Tesmer, Irving H. (Editor). *Colossal Cataract: The Geologic History of Niagara Falls.* State University of New York Press, Albany, NY, 1981.

Theobald, Ralph E. and Bingham, Robert W. *Niagara: Highway of Heroes.* Foster and Stewart Publishing, Buffalo, 1943.

Van Diver, Bradford B. *Roadside Geology of New York.* Mountain Press Company, Missoula, MT, 1985.

Van Tassel, David D. and Grabowski, John J. *The Encyclopedia of Cleveland History.* Indiana University Press, Bloomington & Indianapolis, IN, 1996.

Vogel, Michael and Redding, Paul F. *Maritime Buffalo.* Western New York Heritage Institute, Buffalo, NY, 1990.

Wachter, Georgann and Michael. *Erie Wrecks East: Second Edition.* Corporate Impact, Avon Lake, OH, 2003.

Way, Ronald L. *Ontario's Niagara Parks.* Niagara Parks Commission, Niagara Falls, ON, 1960.

Weissend, Patrick R. *The Life and Times of Joseph Ellicott.* Holland Land Purchase Historical Society, Batavia, NY, 2002.

Wellejus, Edward. *Erie: Chronicle of a Great Lakes City.* Windsor Publications, Woodland Hills, CA, 1980.

Whitten, Sally Sue. *Lake Erie Ports and Boats.* Arcadia Publishing Company, Dover, NH, 2001.

Wilder, Patrick. *Seaway Trail Guidebook to the War of 1812.* Seaway Trail, Inc., Oswego, NY 1887.

Wisconsin: A Guide to the Badger State. WPA. Duell, Sloan and Pearce, New York, 1941.

Woodford, Arthur M. *This is Detroit: 1701-2001.* Wayne State University Press, Detroit, 2001.

Young, Frank A. *Duluth's Ship Canal and Aerial Bridge.* Stewart-Taylor Company, Duluth, MN, 1977.

Zeisler, Karl. *A Brief History of Monroe.* Monroe Evening News, Monroe, MI, 1969.

ADDITIONAL SOURCES

AAA TourBook: Illinois Indiana Ohio. American Automobile Association, Heathrow, FL, 2004.

AAA TourBook: New Jersey Pennsylvania. American Automobile Association, Heathrow, FL, 2004.

AAA TourBook: Michigan Wisconsin. American Automobile Association, Heathrow, FL, 2004.

AAA TourBook: New York. American Automobile Association, Heathrow, FL, 2004.

AAA TourBook: Ontario. American Automobile Association, Heathrow, FL, 2004.

Associated Press

The Buffalo News

Christian Science Monitor

Cleveland Plain Dealer

Columbia Encyclopedia, Sixth Edition. Columbia University Press, New York, 2001.

Detroit Red Wings Media Guide, 2001-2002

The Detroit Free Press

The Detroit News

The Erie Times-News

Great Lakes Atlas, Environment Canada and U.S. Environmental Protection Agency, 1995.

Great Lakes Information Network (GLIN)

Great Lakes Seaway Review Magazine (various editions). Harbor House Publishers, Boyne City, MI

Knight Ridder Inc.

Michigan Atlas & Gazetteer. DeLorme Mapping Company, Freeport, ME, 1995.

Michigan Sea Grant

New York State Atlas & Gazetteer. DeLorme Mapping Company, Freeport, ME, 1987.

Niagara Falls (NY) Gazette

Ohio Atlas & Gazetteer. DeLorme Mapping Company, Freeport, ME, 1991.

Pennsylvania Atlas & Gazetteer. DeLorme Mapping Company, Freeport, ME, 1987.

Port Dover (ON) Maple Leaf newspaper

Toledo Blade

United Press International

Wisconsin Atlas & Gazetteer. DeLorme Mapping Company, Freeport, ME, 1998.

CREDITS

Every effort has been made to credit all sources correctly. The author and publisher will welcome any information that will allow them to correct any errors or omissions.

ACKNOWLEDGMENTS

The author wishes to acknowledge those who have helped either directly or indirectly in the preparation of this book: Thanks to Michelle Barczak, Michelle Papaj and Ken Winters of the Buffalo District of the U.S. Army Corps of Engineers for providing photographs and information on the ports of Lake Erie. Thanks also to Ted Bartolacci, Ginger Cinti, Roger LeLievre and Darryl Rice for the use of photos and historic postcards from their collections. My appreciation also goes to Patrick Welsh for his photographic consultation, Pat Hoppin for his hours of consulting, Glynn Young for editing, Susan Ennis for proofing, Rena Hasse for for her artistic concepts, Amy Clingensmith of Clingensmith Communications for her editing, proofing and marketing assistance and Garry McMichael for taking a trip around Lake Erie with me, his consultation, photographic work, photography lessons, design and layout work. Garry also was an incredible source of guidance and encouragement.

A debt of gratitude goes to the officers and crew of the *Walter J. McCarthy Jr.* including Captain Larry Smyth, Cathy Caderette, Debbie Kushman, Ahmed Nasser, Chris McKenzie and Bill Stirton, for sharing their lives aboard a lakeboat.

Sincere appreciation to Annita Andrick of the Erie County (PA) Historical Society, Barbara Bannan and Sean Ley of the Great Lakes Shipwreck Historical Society, Tom Bauerle, Lynette Berkey, Port Clinton's Mayor Tom Brown, Elizabeth Carnegie of the Ashtabula Great Lakes Marine and Coast Guard Memorial Museum, Tom Darro, Jimmy Davis, Frank Defino Jr. and the Tukaiz family, Mary S. Dibble, Heidi French and Mike Cummings of Heidi French and Associates, Bob and Anne Frisbie, Robert Griffing, Mark Guerra, Carol Hankner, Clint Hasse, C. Michael Hobart, Paul Kassay (Mr. Crystal Beach), Rick Kogan, Christine Korytnyk Dulaney of the Library of Congress, Lucian Greco and Paul Roger Ripa of the Peace Bridge Authority, Diana Hatfield of the North East (PA) Chamber of Commerce, Martha Long, Tom Lucia, Lori A. Morgan, Jack Murphy and Paul Pasquarello of the New York Power Authority, Marc Partin of the Wyandotte Museum, Jackie Paulus, John W. Percy, Dick Rakovan, Linda Reinumagi of the Niagara Falls Public Library Local History Department, Milt Rosenberg, Jerry and Cathy Seymour of Paramount Press, Ann Sindelar of the Western Reserve Historical Society Library, Paul Sponable of the New York State Thruway Authority, Krista Shotwell, Robert R. Spaulding, Susan Stiles, Joan Van Offeren, Norma Wallner, Peter Westaway, Dave Wobster, Joe Wojtonik and to Nicole Yacklon.

Thanks to Charles Brennan, and the late Jack Buck and E. Donald Burlingame for information and stories about Lake Erie. A heartfelt thanks to my grandmother, the late Sara Van Sicklin Egan, who helped fuel my interest in history. A debt of gratitude to my uncle, T. Robert Egan, who taught me about the water and put me to work on his lobster boat in Massachusetts. Also, my sister, Kathryn Langmyer Henderson, who took many of the photographs in this book. My appreciation goes to brother-in-law Dr. Stephen Henderson, niece Sarah Henderson, mother Patricia Langmyer and father Henry Langmyer for their assistance in so many ways; and to my wife Mary and children Meghan and John for understanding the importance of the time required to research and write this book. They willingly made their way around the lake with me on several occasions and often waited patiently while I worked on the book for "just a few more minutes."

I am grateful for the information and the assistance received from the following companies, institutions, museums, organizations and municipalities:

The Ambassador Bridge (Detroit International Bridge Company and Canadian Transit Company)
American Chemical Society
American Steamship Company
Amherstburg Chamber of Commerce
Amherstburg, Town of
Archaeological and Historic Sites Board, Department of Public Records and Archives of Ontario
Archaeological and Historic Sites Board, Ministry of Colleges and Universities
Archaeological and Historic Sites Board of Ontario
Archives of Ontario
Ashtabula, City of
Ashtabula County Convention and Visitors Bureau
Ashtabula Great Lakes Marine and Coast Guard Memorial Museum
Avon, City of
Avon Lake, City of
Avonhistory.org
Bacon Memorial District Library, Wyandotte Michigan
Bethlehem Steel Corporation
Black River Historical Society
Brock University
Brocton, Village of
Buffalo and Erie County Historical Society
Buffalonet.org
Buffalo Niagara Convention & Visitors Bureau Inc.
Canadian Club® Heritage Center
Case-Western Reserve University/Encyclopedia of Cleveland History
Cedar Point, Cedar Fair, L.P. (OH)
Center for Great Lakes and Aquatic Sciences
Chamber of Commerce of the Tonawandas
Chatham-Kent, Municipality of (Wheatley)
Chautauqua County Visitors Bureau
Chippawa, Village of, Citizens Committee
Cleveland State University Library/Great Lakes Industrial History Center
The Coaster Enthusiasts of Canada
Convention and Visitors Bureau of Greater Cleveland

Cuyahoga County Soldiers' and Sailors' Monument (Monument Trustees)
Delhi Tobacco Museum and Heritage Centre
Detroit Edison
Detroit Public Library
Detroit Regional Chamber
Diocese of Buffalo
Dossin Great Lakes Museum
Dunkirk (NY) Chamber of Commerce and Northern Chautauqua Chamber of Commerce
Elgin Community Development Corporation
Elgin.net
Environment Canada, Parks Service
Erie Canal Museum, Syracuse, NY
Erie (PA) Area Chamber of Commerce
Erie (PA) Area Convention & Visitors Bureau
Erie (PA) Maritime Museum
Erie County (PA) Historical Society
Erie Extension Canal Museum, Greenville, PA
Fairport Harbor Marine Museum
Fairport Harbor Village
Ford Motor Company
Fort Erie (ON), Economic Development Corporation of
Fort Erie Museums
Fort Malden National Historic Site
Fort Meigs State Memorial
François Baby House: Windsor's Community Museum
Fredonia, Village of
Friends of Rondeau Provincial Park
Geneva-on-the-Lake Visitors Bureau
Gibraltar, City of
Girard-Lake City (PA) Chamber of Commerce
Great Lakes Commission
Great Lakes Historical Society, Inland Seas Maritime Museum
Great Lakes Marine and Coast Guard Memorial Museum
Great Lakes Sea Grant Network
Great Lakes Shipwreck Historical Society
Great Lakes Shipwreck Museum
Greater Buffalo Convention & Visitors Bureau
Greater Toledo Convention & Visitors Bureau
Grosse Ile Historical Society, Grosse Ile, MI
Haldimand-Norfolk Economic Development
Haldimand-Norfolk, Tourism Association of
Heinz Canada
Henry Ford Museum & Greenfield Village
Historic Fort Erie
Historic Sites and Monuments Board of Canada
Historical Association of Lewiston, Inc.
Holland Purchase Historical Society/Holland Land Office Museum
Independence National Historical Park, Philadelphia
Isledegrande.com (Grand Island, NY)
Jack Miner Bird Sanctuary
Kingsville (ON), Town of
Kelleys Island (OH)
Kelleys Island Chamber of Commerce
Kelleys Island Historical Association
Lackawanna (NY) Steel Museum
Lake County Visitors Bureau
Lake Erie Islands State Park
The Lakeside Association
Leamington (ON), The Municipality of
The Library of Congress
The London & Middlesex Historical Society
London, City of
Long Point Region Conservation Authority
Lorain County Visitors Bureau
Lorain (OH) Public Library System
Lower Lakes Marine Historical Society Museum
Madison, Village of
Metropolitan Detroit Convention and Visitors Bureau
Michigan Historical Center, Michigan Department of State, Lansing, Michigan
Michigan Sea Grant Program
Monroe County (MI) Chamber of Commerce
Monroe County (MI) Convention & Tourism Bureau
Morton International, Inc.
Motown Historical Museum

National Grape Cooperative, Inc.
National Canal Museum
National Park Service, U.S. Department of the Interior
New York Power Authority
New York State Department of Environmental Conservation
The New York State Seaway Trail
National Archives of Canada
National Oceanic & Atmospheric Administration (NOAA)
New York State Department of Environmental Conservation
New York State Historical Society
New York State Thruway Authority
Niagara Falls (NY) Convention & Visitors Bureau
Niagara Falls (NY) Public Library, Local History Department
Niagara Falls (ON) Chamber of Commerce
Niagara Falls (ON), City of
Niagara Falls Thunder Alley-Rick Berketa, James Brown
Niagara Falls (ON) Tourism
Niagara-on-the-Lake Chamber of Commerce
Niagara Parks Commission
Norfolk County Public Library
Norfolk Historical Society
North American Black Historical Museum
North East (PA) Area Chamber of Commerce
North Perry Village
North Tonawanda, City of
Ohio Department of Natural Resources
Ohio Department of Transportation
The Ohio Historical Society
Ohio Sea Grant College Program
Ohio State Parks
The Ohio State University
The Ohio Turnpike Commission
Ontario Heritage Foundation, Ministry of Culture and Communications
Ontario Heritage Foundation, Ministry of Culture and Education
Ontario Ministry of Transportation
Ontario Power Generation
Ottawa County Historical Society
Ottawa County (OH) Visitors Bureau
Our Lady of Victory Institutions
Painesville, City of
The Park House, Amherstburg (ON)
Parks Canada
Patterson Library, Westfield (NY)
Peace Bridge Authority
Pennsylvania Canal Society
Pennsylvania, Commonwealth of, Department of Conservation & Natural Resources
Pennsylvania, Commonwealth of, Bureau of State Parks
Pennsylvania Department of Transportation (PENNDOT)
Pennsylvania Historical and Museum Commission
Pelee, Township of
Pelee Island, Public Relations
Pelee Island and Point Pelee in Sun Country, Lake Erie
Peninsula Chamber of Commerce
Perry's Victory and International Peace Memorial
Perry Village
Point Pelee National Park of Canada
Port Burwell Historic Lighthouse and Marine Museum
PortColborne.com (Port Colborne, ON)
Port Colborne, City of, Economic Development
Port Clinton Ohio, City of
Port Dover Board of Trade
Port Ryerse Historical and Environmental Association and the Ontario Heritage Foundation
Port Stanley Business Association
Port Stanley Terminal Rail, Inc.
Port Stanley (ON), Village of
Portland, Town of
Presque Isle State Park
Put-in-Bay Chamber of Commerce
Ripley, Town of
Rondeau Provincial Park
Saint Lawrence Seaway Development Corporation
St. Catharines Museum at Lock 3
St. Lawrence Seaway Management Corporation
Sandusky/Erie County (OH) Visitors Bureau

Silver Creek (NY), Village of
State of Michigan, Department of Environmental Quality
Statistics Canada
Tillsonburg District Chamber of Commerce
Toledo Area Chamber of Commerce
Toledo-Lucas County Library
Toledo-Lucas County Port Authority
Toronto Metropolitan Reference Library
TourErie.com
Trenton Historical Museum
Trenton, Michigan, City of
University of Western Ontario
U.S. Army Corps of Engineers, Buffalo District
U.S. Army Corps of Engineers, Detroit District
U.S. Brig Niagara
U.S. Census Bureau (www.census.gov)
U.S. Fish and Wildlife Service
U.S. Navy
Welch's
Welland Canals Foundation
Welland (ON) Public Library
Western Reserve Historical Society Library
Westfield/Barcelona Chamber of Commerce
Westfield Development Corporation
Westfield, NY, Village of
Willoughby Historical Society
Windsor, Essex County & Pelee Island Convention and Visitors Bureau
Windsor & District Chamber of Commerce
The Wyandot Nation of Kansas
The Wyandotte Museum, Wyandotte, Michigan
Youngstown, N Y, Village of

PHOTO CREDITS

Tom Langmyer: Dust Jacket (Buffalo Lighthouse), vi (Perry Monument), xii (all images), 1 (all images), 4 (above), 6 (above, right), 9, 10 (bottom), 11 (panorama), 13 (left), 14 (above), 16 (right), 21 (above), 27 (top left), 31 (above right), 36 (top), 41 (top), 44 (bottom), 47 (bottom), 48 (bottom), 60 (top, bottom), 63 (top left, bottom), 64 (above), 65 (top), 69 (bottom), 72 (top), 74 (panorama, bottom), 75 (middle, bottom), 76 (above), 80 (bottom), 84 (top right), 85 (top right), 89 (top left), 90 (bottom), 91 (top, middle left), 93, 96 (right), 97 (all images), 98 (bottom), 99 (top left), 100 (top right, bottom), 105, 106, (bottom), 110 (top), 113 (top left), 114 (bottom), 115 (top, bottom), 116 (top), 119 (top, bottom), 121 (above), 122 (top, bottom), 123 (all images), 128 (all images), 129 (bottom), 130 (top, bottom), 131 (top, bottom), 133 (bottom), 135 (bottom), 136 (bottom), 137 (top, bottom), 142 (top right), 143 (bottom), 144 (top, middle), 145 (bottom left), 147 (top), 151 (above), 152 (above panorama, middle, bottom), 153 (bottom), 154 (top), 157 (above), 160 (top, bottom), 161 (top, bottom right, bottom left), 164 (top, bottom), 165 (top), 166 (top right), 167 (top left, bottom), 168 (right), 169 (bottom), 170 (above), 171 (bottom), 172 (all images), 173 (all images), 174 (above), 179 (left), 181 (above), 182, 184 (top), 186 (all images), 190 (top, bottom), 191 (top), 192 (top), 193 (middle, bottom), 197 (bottom), 200 (top), 201 (bottom), 202 (above), 203 (bottom), 204 (top), 205 (top left, bottom), 206 (bottom), 207 (top, bottom), 208 (bottom), 209 (bottom), 210 (bottom), 212 (top left), 213 (top left), 214 (right, bottom), 216 (top, bottom), 217 (top, lower left), 218 (top right), 219 (bottom), 220 (bottom), 222 (top, bottom), 223 (top left, bottom), 224 (top left, bottom), 225 (bottom), 226 (top left), 232 (bottom), 233 (bottom), 236 (bottom), 237 (top), 240 (top), 241 (bottom right), 242 (top, bottom), 243 (top, bottom), 244 (above), 246 (top left), 247 (above), 251, 252 (right), 253 (above, bottom), 255 (bottom), 256 (above), 257 (top, bottom), 258 (right), 260 (above, bottom), 263 (all images), 264 (top), 265 (above), 266, 267 (top right), 268 (bottom), 269 (top right), 270 (top), 272 (top right, bottom), 273 (above), 274 (top)

Garry McMichael: Dust Jacket (Headlands Dunes State Park), 31 (bottom), 59, 159, 199 (top left), 208 (top), 238 (top), 267 (top left, middle, bottom), 268 (top right)

Kathryn Langmyer Henderson: Dust Jacket (photo of author), 65 (bottom), 91 (middle right, bottom), 96 (top, left), 184 (bottom), 185 (middle), 198 (bottom), 243 (middle), 255 (top left), 275 (Sara Egan)

U.S. Army Corps of Engineers, Detroit District: vi *(Walter J. McCarthy Jr.*/Detroit River)

Courtesy Henry and Patricia Langmyer: 274 (bottom left, bottom middle)

Courtesy Kathryn Langmyer Henderson: 274 (bottom right)

Courtesy Genevieve Burlingame: 275 (Donald Burlingame)

Courtesy Lori G. Morgan: 275 (Jeff Morgan)

Courtesy KMOX Radio: 275 (Jack Buck)

Courtesy Roszman Family: 275 (Mike Roszman)

Index

RAND McNALLY
OFFICIAL 1922
AUTO TRAILS MAP

DISTRICT NUMBER 4

EASTERN OHIO
WESTERN PENNSYLVANIA
S. E. MICHIGAN
NORTHERN WEST VIRGINIA

SOUTHERN ONTARIO
WESTERN NEW YORK
WESTERN MARYLAND

COPYRIGHT BY RAND McNALLY & COMPANY
MADE IN U.S.A.

NATIONAL TRAILS
OHIO STATE ROUTES
MICHIGAN TRUNK LINES
MAIN AUTO ROADS
RIVER OR STREAM
POPULATION FIGURES
MILEAGE SHOWN